A PEOPLE'S HERITAGE:
PATTERNS IN
UNITED STATES HISTORY

A PEOPLE'S HERITAGE: PATTERNS IN UNITED STATES HISTORY

Curtis B. Solberg
Santa Barbara City College

David W. Morris
Santa Barbara City College

JOHN WILEY & SONS, INC.
New York   London   Sydney   Toronto

Library of Congress Cataloging in Publication Data:

Solberg, Curtis B

  A people's heritage.

  Includes bibliographical references and index.
  1. United States — History. I. Morris, David,
1949–   joint author. II. Title.
E178.1.S67   973   74–34262
ISBN 0–471–81125–4

Printed in the United States of America

10 9 8 7 6 5 4 3 2 1

For Julie and Kristine

PREFACE

John F. Kennedy wrote that "American history is not something dead and over. It is always alive, always growing, always unfinished. . . . " This sense of continuity between the past, present, and future is of vital importance here. We believe that our national experience provides insights into present problems and their resolution in the future. In this spirit, we wrote this textbook.

In it, we trace certain patterns in American history that are essential to an understanding of our heritage. Some of these themes—such as United States foreign policy and political reform—are examined in traditional history textbooks. Other themes—like the historical roles of the racial minorities, the environmental crisis, and the impact of war on American life—are not usually included but are justified here because of their relevance to contemporary issues. Similarly, in Chapter 10, "The Spirit of '76," we examine contemporary America with reference to our common heritage and reappraise the nation's future on the eve of the bicentennial.

These broad themes cannot be discussed in detail in a single volume without sacrificing the sweeping sense of history's continuity. We have tried to avoid burying the contours of the American experience under mounds of historical data. However, we strike a balance, we hope, between the intellectual rigor necessary for a textbook and the academic backgrounds of beginning college students.

A *People's Heritage* is intended to meet a wide range of student interests. For the nonhistory major, it offers the essentials of the American experience in a relevant framework. For the history student who will pursue an in-depth study, it provides a firm foundation on which he can build by using the suggested readings that follow each chapter.

Although the book is intended for a one-semester survey course, it also can be used in the more traditional two-semester survey. It may be the student's sole reading assignment, or it may be a core text accompanied by supplementary readings. Furthermore, it can be adapted to varied approaches in the teaching of the American past. Although especial attention is given to the important themes in our nation's history, each chapter or theme is organized chronologically. By consulting the table of contents, the instructor can easily assign a reading that parallels his lectures.

We are grateful to Carl Beers and Wayne Anderson, our editors at Wiley, for their guidance and suggestions from the very inception of this book. We are also grateful to Ronald Bush; without him this book would not have been written. Robert Berlin and Ronald Seeley contributed to the research, and Martha Wadel gave us editorial assistance. Appreciation should be expressed to Elizabeth Merchant and Oscar Solberg, whose aid in reading proofs was invaluable. Finally, one of us (C.B.S.) is grateful to the members of the Board of Trustees at Santa Barbara City College for a sabbatical leave during 1973. This provided both of us with time for discussion and reflection about this book.

Curtis B. Solberg
David W. Morris

Santa Barbara, California

CONTENTS

Chapter One
The Quest for a New Society: An Emerging American Culture   **1**
    The Idea of America   2
    The Origins of the Quest   2
    Europe Comes of Age   3
    Varieties of the Mercantile Experience   6
    Why Did Europeans Come to America?   8
    Thwarted First Plantings   10
        Virginia   10
        New Netherlands   14
        Massachusetts Bay   14
        Georgia   16
    The Philosophy of the Unexpected   19
    America and the European Enlightenment   19
    Philadelphia: Laboratory of the Enlightenment   21
    An American Character Emerges   22
        A Challenge to Old Assumptions   22
        Equality and Optimism   23
        Mobility   24
        Practicality   24
    The Rise of the British Empire 1607–1763   27
    Unfinished Business   29

Chapter Two
"We, The People": The Development of an American Political System   **33**
    A Venerable Experiment   34
    The British Heritage   34
    Transplanted Englishmen   35
    Growth of Colonial Democracy   37
    The Empire Enforced   40
    Revolution   41
    First Government   44
    A National Constitution   45
    Hamilton, Jefferson, and Political Parties   48
    The Revolution of 1800   50
    Democratic Nationalism   51
    Jackson and the "Common Man"   54

"What is Man Born For . . . ?"   56
Sectionalism   60
The System Tested—Civil War   62

Chapter Three
The West in American Life   69
The Heritage of the West   70
First Americans   70
Colonizing the New World   71
An American West   73
Jefferson and the Agrarian Myth   75
"Trail of Tears"   76
Western Empire   78
Progress Follows the Frontier   81
The Wild, Wild West   84
"I Will Fight No More Forever"   85
"Our Brothers Who Were Sold"   87
Garden of the World   91
The Frontier Hypothesis   93

Chapter Four
**A Changing Scene: Social and Cultural Response
to the Industrial Revolution   97**
The Price of Power   98
Village America   98
The First Surge   100
Industrial Transformation   101
The Gospel of Wealth   103
Growth of the City—The Urban Frontier   105
Immigration "Salad Bowl"   109
Rural Reaction   111
Early Struggles of Labor   113
A Failure in Government   117
Strain on the Fabric of Society   119

Chapter Five
The People Versus the Interests: Reform in American Politics   125
A Definition of Reform   126
The People's Party   126
The Rise of Progressivism   129
Roosevelt, Wilson, and the "Success" of Progressivism   132

"Normalcy" and the Twenties   136
FDR Declares a "New Deal"   138
Legacy of the New Deal   142
A "New Frontier"   144
LBJ's "Great Society"   145
The "New Conservatives"   148

Chapter Six
The Exercise of Power: Foreign Policy of the United States   153
What Is America's World Role?   154
A New Nation's Diplomacy   154
Adopting Neutrality   156
Neutrality Tested   158
"Manifest Destiny"   161
A New World Power   164
Breaking with Tradition   166
The Failure of Neutrality   170
Cold War and Containment   173
The End of the Old Order?   177

Chapter Seven
The Impact of War on American Life   185
Americans and War   186
The Minuteman Mentality   186
Protest and Professionalism   189
Expansionism and the Military   192
America's First Total War   193
Conquest, Crusade, and Consequences   197
Growth of a Military-Industrial Complex   200
Perpetual War for Perpetual Peace   203
The Vietnam War   206

Chapter Eight
We Shall Overcome:
The Crusade for Human Rights in Modern America   213
" . . . with Liberty and Justice for All"?   214
European America's First Target: The Indian   215
The Black Man in a White Man's Country   219
The Mexican: A Stranger in His Own land   224
White America and the "Yellow Peril"   226
Past, Present, and Future   231

Early Stirrings Toward Equality   231
"I Have a Dream"   233
"Freedom Now!"   235
Black Nationalism in the Seventies:
A Farewell to Integration?   238
The Mexican-Americans   240
The American Indians: From Wounded Knee
to Wounded Knee   243
The New Feminism   247
Whose Problem?   253

Chapter Nine
Eco-Crisis: The Environmental Problem   257
What is at Stake?   258
Americans Against the Wilderness   258
Conquest Equals Progress: The Pioneer Mentality   260
The Beginnings of Appreciation   263
Protect Wilderness: A Preservationist Outlook   264
Wise Use of Resources: The Conservationist Impulse   267
Conservation and Preservation Clash   268
Environmental Engineering and the Ecological Perspective   271
American Environmental Problems   273
    Destruction of the Land   273
    Water Pollution   276
    Air Pollution   277
    Overpopulation and the Refuse of Affluence   278
The Energy Crisis: Target 1980?   279
"Spaceship Earth"   284

Chapter Ten
The Spirit of '76   289
Celebration?   290
History as Identity   290
The Technetronic Revolution   292
A New Economic Role?   294
Social Transition   295
The Price of Affluence   297
Retreat to the Past?   301
A Political Slump?   302
Capitalism—the Root of all Evil?   305
The Spirit of '76   306

Appendix 1
Declaration of Independence   311

Appendix 2
The Constitution of the United States of America   315

Index   337

A PEOPLE'S HERITAGE:
PATTERNS IN
UNITED STATES HISTORY

CHAPTER ONE

THE QUEST FOR A NEW SOCIETY: AN EMERGING AMERICAN CULTURE

1000 A.D.
Vikings land at Vinland.

1494
Pope Alexander VI divides the unsettled territories of the world between Spain and Portugal.

1607
First permanent English settlement in America at Jamestown, Virginia.

1629
Massachusetts Bay Colony founded by the Puritans.

1651
First in a series of acts of trade and navigation designed by Parliament to regulate British relations with the American colonies.

1763
End of the French and Indian War between England and France over control of North America.

THE IDEA OF AMERICA

Western man's quest for a "new" society can be seen centuries before the discovery and settlement of America. The early colonization of Massachusetts Bay was accompanied by the determination of the Puritans to establish a "City Upon a Hill." It was to be a perfect model of true Christian living that, by example, would reform the entire world. The expectation of many Europeans is reflected in their designation of the emerging trans-Atlantic community as the *New* World. In fact, one scholar refers to the United States as the "first New Nation."

In the postrevolutionary generation many Americans saw their new nation as a model for the world. Thomas Jefferson wrote that other peoples would come to regard America as "a signal for arousing men to burst the chains under which . . . ignorance and superstitions had persuaded them to bind themselves and to assume the blessings and security of self-government." The two centuries that have passed since Jefferson penned this statement have witnessed the United States' rise to global leadership. The millions of immigrants who streamed to America's shores during the nineteenth century gave evidence to the economic opportunity and political liberty they sought. In more modern times, as the newer nations of Asia and Africa have emerged, the United States continues to be a standard of national success throughout the world.

The emergence of this society is particularly interesting because of its unique pattern of development. Never before had a nation been created as the result of the movement of so many people from one part of the world to another. Moreover, its founders gradually realized that their grand blueprints for society were usually not adaptable to New World circumstances. Instead, American culture emerged in ways that were not anticipated and, in the process, forged the numerous traits that are part of the so-called American character. In order to understand the persistent interest in the idea of America, it is necessary to trace the sources of this quest for a new society whose basic contours had emerged by the time of the Revolution.

THE ORIGINS OF THE QUEST

For several thousand years man has dreamed of an Elysium, a more perfect place where he might live in harmony with his fellows and with God. This quest was pursued by the ancient Greeks, whose poet Homer speculated on the nature of a mythical Eden. Others also sang and wrote about this "other world" and, indeed, there is a marked similarity in the descriptions of the place found in the folklore of the

Irish, the tales of the Japanese, and the sagas of the Vikings. This literature, in spite of its tendency toward fantasy and the exotic, is important because it helped to stimulate the idea of an earthly paradise in the mind of Western man. But this other world seemed beyond man's grasp because of the fears and practical uncertainties involved in conquering the great seas and their monstrous inhabitants memorialized by old storytellers.

Recent evidence suggests, however, that as early as the year 1000 A.D. the Norsemen in their finely crafted Viking ships successfully crossed the Atlantic Ocean and became the first white inhabitants of the Western Hemisphere. Their settlement, called Vinland, located on the northern tip of Newfoundland, lasted for at least three years. The gradual failure of this early experiment in New World living was caused by a number of factors, including the climate, hostile Indians, and the lack of gunpowder.

EUROPE COMES OF AGE

The Norse seafarers who attempted the settlement of North America were casualties of history. Conditions were not yet ripe for the exploration and settlement that they sought to achieve. Indeed, for the next four or five hundred years, there is no record of further successful efforts by Europeans to conquer the "howling wilderness" of the New World. By the fifteenth and sixteenth centuries, the idea of ex-

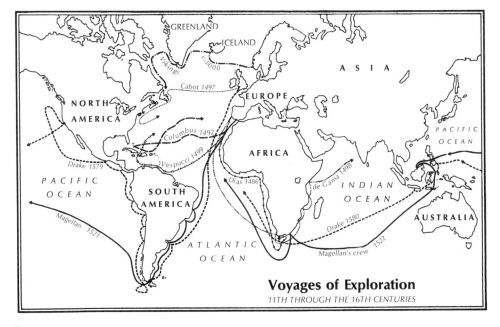

Voyages of Exploration
11TH THROUGH THE 16TH CENTURIES

pansion to the West had assumed a prominent place in European thought. There appeared an intellectual awakening that liberated man from the traditional religious and political authorities and encouraged him to exercise his curiosity to learn more about his universe and, therefore, about himself. Guided by observation and reason, this emphasis on individual will and achievement bred a restlessness and self-reliance that provided the necessary dynamism for the explorers, adventurers, and men of commerce of Europe's early modern period.

At the same time, progress in science and technology helped to facilitate the crossing of the ocean and the search for the fabled garden of Eden. By the fifteenth century more seaworthy ships were built capable of traversing the Atlantic, and more reliable naviga-

Intrepid Vikings crossed the Atlantic Ocean in their open boats and made settlements in North America five centuries before Columbus' discovery in 1492. Scholars continue to unearth evidence that other peoples were pre-Columbian, including the ancient Phoenicians, the Japanese, and possibly the Greeks and Romans.

tional instruments (like the compass) were refined. It had been possible to sail on the Mediterranean guided only by one's instinct and the North Star, but venturing into the fearsome Atlantic required a more exact science. These were also the years that witnessed the invention of the printing press and gunpowder, both essential to a people intent on learning the best avenues to expansion and conquest.

Commercial development also paved the way for Europe's widening horizons. After the twelfth century the simple farm economy based on local production and village self-sufficiency began to be replaced by an agricultural system made more sophisticated by the rise of trade and banking. Moreover, during the Christian Crusades of the twelfth and thirteenth centuries, knights from the castles of Europe brought home from the Near East exotic goods rarely enjoyed in the western world before—spices, silk, tapestries, precious stones, and new ideas in art and architecture. Henceforth, merchants began to establish trade links with the markets of the East to buy the luxury goods which the moneyed class in Europe demanded.

By the end of the fifteenth century, the Commercial Revolution had gone beyond European boundaries and the Near East. In an effort to circumvent the long and costly journey overland from the East and through the Mediterranean, Europeans began to talk of an all-water route to the Orient. Merchant-adventurers were interested not only in trade with the Indies, but they also desired to find new sources of gold and silver, as the Oriental trade had drained Europe's store of precious metals. Before the peoples of Europe could embark upon such expeditions involving expansion and trade, it was necessary for them to achieve some semblance of nationality. Only by consolidating their internal resources could nations begin to look outward. And it was in the fifteenth, sixteenth, and seventeenth centuries that the *nation-state* system of Western Europe developed. The new nation-state was characterized by (1) a strong monarch who, by his personal power and prestige, could draw the many diverse parts of his kingdom together, and thereby centralize his authority; (2) an economy that promoted national self-sufficiency; and (3) a minimum of any energy-consuming religious friction. As the European nations began to assume their modern shapes on the map, explorers and navigators like Columbus, Cabot, Da Gama, Magellan, and Drake were sent around the globe to seek glory and riches for their kings.

VARIETIES OF THE MERCANTILE EXPERIENCE

Although Columbus' encounter with America had been preceded by that of other voyagers (it is not generally known that he had visited the Norsemen of Iceland prior to his fateful voyage of 1492), the excitement generated by his discovery led to a much broader interest in trans-Atlantic exploration. Until the sixteenth century, the Mediterranean Sea had been the hub of western civilization, the nerve center that connected its various peoples. The state that controlled the Mediterranean usually dominated the political arena. After Columbus returned to the courts of Spain with the news of the

New World's wealth, control of the Atlantic and what lay beyond became a prerequisite for global power.

Meanwhile, other nations were dreaming of new riches. Spain's early adventure into this era of commercial competition was paralleled by Portugal which, by the early sixteenth century, had established a trading empire that extended from India through Indonesia. The fear of overlapping claims between the two Catholic countries was calmed by Pope Alexander in 1493 when Spain and Portugal were allowed to divide the non-Christian world between them. Consequently the discovery of America and the opening of the sea route to the Far East touched off a flurry of activity among the other nation-states, who rejected Spain and Portugal's exclusive claim to these newly discovered lands. For example, France and England sent out sailors and explorers during the sixteenth century, and the Netherlands developed a fairly large commercial empire in the Indies. But in general, it was not until the seventeenth century that the monarchs of these countries had adequately resolved their internal problems and consolidated enough national power to follow up successfully the discoveries made by their adventurers and begin their colonization efforts. These efforts signaled the real beginning of competition for empire in the New World.

Those nations participating in this overseas expansion formulated policies to regulate the trade and territories that they acquired. Although nation–states differed in their efforts at colonization, it is important to recognize that all of these nations sought the same objective: to utilize their overseas possessions to increase the wealth and power of the mother country. This aim provided the concept fundamental to the economic theory called *mercantilism.* Accordingly, colonies were important because they promoted the economic self-sufficiency of the mother country. Not only might they provide raw materials unavailable at home, but they also represented potential markets for the finished goods produced in the mother country. With the fear of overproduction plaguing seventeenth-century Europe, colonies were also deemed an excellent outlet for the surplus population of the Old World. Finally, mercantilist theory contained the idea of "contingent necessity"—that is, if one nation failed to take advantage of the opportunities of colonial expansion, another nation would, causing a relative decline in power and prestige of the reluctant nation.

Colonies were therefore crucial to a nation's power, and the race for empire in America that began with the Pope's partition of the world in 1493 continued for the next three centuries. Indeed, it was the

Spanish galleons returning to Spain filled with the riches from the mines of Mexico and South America that whetted the appetites of the other powers. The rivalry that ensued in seventeenth-century America was heightened by the efforts of the Dutch who colonized the region of the Hudson River Valley, the Swedes who settled on the Delaware River, the French whose North American empire grew rapidly after Louis XIV became king in 1658, and finally, the English, who were the last to enter the race for power through trade. Although a latecomer, England by 1763 demonstrated her superiority as an imperial power. What was England's colonial secret of success?

Although other powers had enjoyed a headstart in the development of their colonial empires, the English were able later to close that gap. While the Spanish and Portuguese were actively engaged in colonization during the sixteenth century, the English House of Tudor needed time to consolidate its political power before it could follow up the discoveries of John Cabot in 1497 and 1498. The rise of trading companies, founded yet not controlled by the king, contributed to the eventual success of England's colonial venture. Instead of a completely centralized colonial bureaucracy under the personal direction of the king, as was the case with France's king, Louis XIV, hundreds of independent trading companies enjoyed considerable freedom in establishing their capitalist enterprises around the world—in the Far East, in India, in Russia, and in America.

An additional advantage enjoyed by England was her status as an island. Freed of the cost of maintaining a large standing army, the English built a great navy that served both as an element of defense of her worldwide empire and as an important link in her commercial trade. Finally, unlike much of Europe where workers of the lowest class were required to serve their local rulers, there was no serfdom in England. Instead, a class of workers free from bondage to the soil existed, including resourceful and hardworking women. In contrast, the populations of New France and New Spain included few women from the Old World. English women were prepared for the rugged life across the Atlantic and, by serving as the basis of the family unit, they contributed to the rapid growth of society in English America. By the 1760s, the English colonial population outnumbered the French by 15 to 1.

WHY DID EUROPEANS COME TO AMERICA?

Economic forces at work in the Old World had created insecurity for many of its people. In England, for example, what had been feared as "over-population" was actually the dislocation of thousands of subsistence farmers who had been evicted from the soil by the enclosure acts. This parliamentary legislation allowed public lands to be enclosed in order to raise sheep for the high profits of the expanding textile industry. But the adverse effects of this economic transition were not limited to the poor farmer. Rising inflation during the sixteenth and seventeenth centuries touched the land-owning middle class or gentry. Living largely on fixed incomes, they found their economic security slipping. This provided the reason for many to emigrate to America.

Nor can religion be ignored as a factor leading to emigration. Although the legend that early America was populated by people seeking religious freedom in the New World may be exaggerated, it is nevertheless true that some migrants left their homeland because of the dangers they saw to their faith. In England, for example, some Puritans and other dissenters were antagonized by the Crown's unsympathetic posture toward them, and even suspected that King

Early in the seventeenth century Europeans were learning about America's abundance. This imaginary portrait depicts English knights hunting and fishing in Virginia in 1618. Graphic scenes like this one were important in promoting the European interest in America.

Charles I was secretly pro-Catholic. Thus, while persecution may not have been as overt as the legend suggests, religious reasons figured into the decision of some Englishmen to migrate to the New World. Another impelling motive for English migration to America was the desire for land. While other forces were important, such as frustrations at home, religion, and the quest for adventure, the greatest reason seems to be the desire to become an independent landowner.

By the early seventeenth century, the reports of the early explorers were coupled with an increasing mass of information about America from the first settlers. They and other propagandists promoted the New World as the perfect spot for European settlement. Poets, ballad writers, pamphleteers, and preachers touched on the same theme, praising the land for its fertility. According to such publicists, the bounty of the American paradise was endless.

Europe's seventeenth-century vision of America, therefore, seemed to be composed of three elements: romance (adventure), religion (Puritanism and other dissenting faiths), and riches (the promise of mercantilism). This Old World vision was not to be realized, however, because ultimately the hopes or theories of European thinkers and dreamers did not fit squarely with the realities of America's future. Ironically, in seeking one dream they found another.

THWARTED FIRST PLANTINGS

Early in the seventeenth century, when the first settlements were made in America, the concept of "American" was nonexistent. The settlers saw themselves as Europeans living abroad. Their efforts to duplicate their old way of life are evidenced by the names they chose for their new homes—*New* Sweden, *New* Netherland, *New* England, *New* Spain and so forth. These colonials believed that this "New" civilization would be a mirror reflecting its European parent. Their serious, detailed intentions can be seen in the initial efforts to establish many of the colonies, including Virginia, New Netherland, Massachusetts Bay, and Georgia.

VIRGINIA

In 1607 James I issued a charter to a trading company called the Virginia Company of London. Besides the hope of finding gold as the

The gentleman-adventurers who comprised the major part of the early labor force of Virginia were reluctant to dirty their hands in manual labor. Not until the Virginia Company of London began importing indentured servants did the colony enjoy prosperity.

Spanish had done, this group of private investors was authorized to establish a profitable trade in fish and furs. This plan was followed for the first two years after three ships carrying 144 men landed on the James River to establish the colony of Virginia. During this period more than 300 persons were sent to Jamestown. An examination of this labor force reveals the expectations of the company. Gentlemen outnumbered laborers by four to three. Also, there was a curious assortment of craftsmen, including jewelers, goldsmiths, tailors, blacksmiths, and a perfumer. There was a glaring absence of occupations necessary to establish a settled agricultural community.

Officials of the Virginia Company of London soon learned, however, that quick riches were not to be found. Starvation, disease, and mutiny threatened the company's operation from the outset. Before 1607 was over, only 38 men were still alive at Jamestown. The company slowly realized that there would be no quick returns from the search for precious metals or the development of trade in fish and furs. If there were to be any profits, they would have to come from agricultural pursuits.

This change in the company's objective posed problems. A shift to a farming economy required not only a larger supply of manpower, but also a qualitatively different one. Now that the lure of gold was an empty hope, workers were needed who could support themselves from the soil and return profits to the company's investors. The enterprise received its first stroke of luck in 1612 when experiments with the tobacco leaf showed great success. In order to motivate large numbers of persons to come to Virginia and exchange the relative comforts of life in England for the hazardous conditions in America, the company began the *headright* system in 1618. Fifty acres of land were offered to anyone willing to come to Virginia as an employee of the company. An individual could collect a headright for himself and also for every member of his family and any servants he brought over. Responding to the offer of free land, almost 5000 Englishmen came to Virginia during the next six years.

The company discovered that the reforms designed to solve its problems led to a new dilemma. Many of the planters who responded to the offer of free land began to complain of friction with their company employer. In an effort to avoid such discontent, in 1619 the company permitted the establishment of the House of Burgesses, the first democratic legislative assembly in English America. The company hoped that its program might be more widely accepted if it had the added approval of representatives of the planters. (See Chapter 2,

Women were scarce in the early history of the colonies. No one realized their value better than the gentleman colonists who paid 120 pounds of tobacco each for their prospective brides. Not only did the arrival of women contribute to the stability of the colonies, but they also made life more amenable.

pp. 36 for details.) Finally, in an effort to improve the morale of the colonists, the company in 1620 began to ship women to Virginia to be auctioned off as wives of the planters.

The company was digging its own grave. In a sense its reforms succeeded too well. Virginia's population was booming by 1624. The simple employer-employee relationship that was implicit in the company's original plan disappeared, and gradually the employee developed new roles that competed with his loyalty to the company. Now the settler was a landowner, a husband and family man, and perhaps a legislator serving the citizens of his district. Many planters decided to cease exporting their tobacco through the company organization and to operate independently. In short, the transition of Virginia from a simple business enterprise to a complex society was occurring rapidly. The King finally acted in 1624 by withdrawing the charter of the company and making Virginia a royal English colony, with an appointed governor and council to rule under instructions from the Crown. Although the colonists now found themselves directly under the King's rule, they were gratified to find that their legislature and local courts of law were not disturbed under the new royal edict.

NEW NETHERLAND

The Dutch were as active as the English in extending their commercial empire. As early as 1609, Henry Hudson's discovery of the river that now bears his name provided the Dutch Republic's claim to one of the finest areas in North America. In 1621 the Dutch West India Company, similar to the Virginia Company of London in its structure and absolute power, was created. In spite of the tradition of democratic self-government in the Dutch mother country, however, no popular representation was allowed in its New World colony. A governor and his council appointed by the Company had sole authority. To plant the permanent settlements needed to secure its claim to an area, the Company announced in 1629 that anyone who financed the colonization of 50 families of tenant-farmers would be granted a large tract of land. The grantee of each of these large estates was known as a *patroon*. This proprietor exercised enormous authority over his domain, including all political, economic, and judicial powers.

It was not likely that the Dutch colonial system would succeed in America. Serfdom and the small kingdoms it had supported for centuries in Europe were made possible by a scarcity of land. The desire to establish similar feudal domains in America was doomed to failure because of the vast availability of land. Great quantities of the patroons' best lands were not cultivated simply because they could not attract farmers to work under such an outmoded system. This, coupled with the lessening international prestige of the Dutch, spelled a period of decline for them, and in America their possessions were surrendered to the English in 1664.

MASSACHUSETTS BAY

The thwarted purpose of New Netherland's initial design was echoed by the efforts of the Puritans to establish in the New World a "City Upon a Hill" that would serve as a model of the true church for all Christendom. Having met no success in reforming or "purifying" the Church of England, the Puritans decided in 1629 to leave the mother country. But they left not to escape a "sinful and unclean world" like their Pilgrim cousins who founded the Plymouth Bay Colony a decade earlier. The founders of the Massachusetts Bay Colony recognized that they could not turn their backs on evil, but rather must confront the real world and cope with its imperfections. It is significant that they retained their membership in the Church of England after migrating to America.

In order to effect the reforms necessary to restore Christ's true church, they secured a charter from the King and set out to make their experiment in holy living a reality. In keeping with their emphasis on an individual's conscience, these Puritans advocated the Congregational form of church government. This doctrine emphasized the power of each individual parish to govern its own affairs and make its own decisions, without any interference from the civil authorities. To establish this exemplary society the Puritans looked to the Bible; by a thorough study of the scriptures one might understand God's will. They knew that their heavenly city could not be realized without a learned clergy to aid in the interpretation of holy writ. The New England town helped to facilitate this need. Not only did it permit the people to come together for the regular worship of God and instruction of their children, but it also provided the proving ground for the town meeting, with its underlying democratic ideal.

Very soon the Puritans encountered challenges to their community that threatened it to its very foundations. Only six years after the initial settlement, the Reverend Roger Williams criticized his fellow Puritans on various grounds, including the interference of the civil authorities with the affairs of his own congregation at Salem, and the illegal expropriation of land from the Indians. A year later a more serious threat appeared when Anne Hutchinson, a member in good standing of the Boston congregation, raised some controversial issues. She also questioned the authority of the civil magistrates in church matters. Rejecting the sole authority of the clergy to interpret Scripture, she claimed that she had received direct divine revelations. Already the Puritans were learning that the individualism implicit in the Congregational ideal was acceptable only to a certain point. The freedom of the individual had its bounds, they concluded, when it conflicted with society's need for order. Both Williams and Hutchinson were banished from the Bay Colony and both established colonies in exile in Rhode Island.

Dissent rose in other quarters as well. By the 1650s Baptists and Quakers began entering Massachusetts from neighboring colonies to spread their "false" doctrines among the Puritans. The authorities of the Bay Colony administered whippings, bodily mutilation, and even the death penalty to adherents of sects that dared to defile Massachusetts with their "ungodly"messages. These actions elicited from exiled Roger Williams of Rhode Island the admonition: "Yourselves [only] pretend liberty of conscience." The Puritans found their "divinely guided" government under increasing attack not only from dissenters in the colonies, but also from England, where religious toleration began to flourish under Charles II. Under these pressures the Puritans' hold on Massachusetts weakened, and the last dying gasp of their religious dogma was manifested in the fanatical witch-burning hysteria of the late seventeenth century. The excesses of the witch trials during the 1690s seriously discredited the old religious order.

Thus the Puritan dream of a perfect Christian society to serve as a beacon of light to the entire world began to crumble soon after the experiment was launched. Yet certain aspects of the Puritan legacy persisted, influencing the development of American culture to present times. The Puritan stress on a learned clergy led to the founding of Harvard College in 1636 and a public-supported grammar school system that has molded the course of educational excellence throughout American history. The seventeenth-century town meeting provided further impetus to the idea of responsible and democratic government. The strong emphasis the Puritans placed on work and the accumulation of wealth, with the suggestion that a Christian's labor was a part of his offering to God, contributed to the *Protestant work ethic;* to work hard is to please God. Nor is civil disobedience, which has assumed such prominence in modern life, a new doctrine. Rather, the determination to follow one's conscience at whatever cost is sharply illuminated by Roger Williams, Anne Hutchinson, and the Quaker martyrs. Finally, the Puritans' belief that they were God's Chosen People, destined to establish a "City Upon a Hill" has figured in the modern American mentality. It has been argued, for example, that the United States' involvement around the world in the twentieth century is a modern reflection of the Puritans' sense of mission, and is manifested by the belief in the suitability of democratic institutions for all people.

GEORGIA

As the Puritans reluctantly learned that their cherished dream would not be realized, the long rivalry between the English and Spaniards in the South created a desire in the Carolinas for a buffer colony on the Spanish border. Responding to this need for better frontier defense, a group of philanthropists in Parliament led by James Oglethorpe received a charter from King George II in 1732, authorizing them to establish a colony between the Altamaha and Savannah Rivers. The creation of Georgia went beyond the usual motives for settlement; although defense was a serious consideration, the colony was also designed to serve other purposes. Stirred by the plight of paupers in England imprisoned for failure to pay their debts, Oglethorpe and other idealists were inspired to establish a colony in the New World which might offer relief and opportunity to these people and to Protestant refugees from Europe as well. The charter from the King placed the government of Georgia in the hands of proprietors who were to serve as trustees for the colony.

The plan mapped out by these social architects in London was noteworthy for its detail. The colony was divided into areas that were perfect squares. In each quarter of the square was centered a smaller square designed as grazing land for cattle. The trustees envisioned the entire colony covered by such checkerboard villages. Furthermore, the charter restricted land grants (usually to 50 acres) and controlled the inheritance of land in an attempt to provide the colony with numerous farmers who might also serve as frontier defenders against their Spanish neighbors. Prohibitions against Negro slavery and rum reflected the idealism of the founders. The fantastic neatness of this scheme was equaled by the trustees' vision of Georgia's place in England's mercantile system. It was decided that silk would be the perfect staple from the colony, thus making unnecessary the costly silk imports from elsewhere in Europe and the East. On each 50-acre plot, therefore, the settler was required to plant 50 mulberry trees. Because this experiment in Georgia enjoyed public support—from both Parliamentary appropriations and the gifts of charitable individuals in England—there was no need for the settlers to pay taxes. Thus, a legislative assembly to levy taxes was deemed unnecessary. For years the colonists in Georgia were not allowed to practice self-government.

It is obvious that Oglethorpe and the trustees were trying to make Georgia fulfill a European dream. In their effort to make the colony the protector of the Carolina frontier, a refuge for the unfortunate and unemployed of London and Europe, and a producer of valuable semi-tropical silk, these men were projecting ideals which they assumed were the correct ones for Georgia.

The gratitude of the settlers, many of them arriving penniless and full of expectations, did not last for long. They soon learned that 50 acres of pine-barren Georgia was insufficient to support a family. The incentive for improving the land was removed by the trustees' inheritance policy, which prevented a man from leaving his land to his sons. In addition, the absence of self-government was certain to fuel the discontent of Georgians who saw Englishmen in neighboring colonies enjoying significant political liberties.

The trustees were fearful that any concessions to their original blueprint for Georgia would lead to the failure of the entire experiment. And yet as early as 1738 they permitted a series of modifications in their land policy, including a relaxation of the laws regarding the inheritance and sale of land, and the size of the land holdings. Soon the government officials were in full retreat; as the size of the land parcels increased, so did the need for black slave labor. Explaining that conditions in Georgia had changed, the trustees now acknowledged the need for a slave economy. The prohibition against liquor was also repealed. The silk scheme was the last to die. In 1742 nearly one-half the silkworms in Savannah died, proving that the climate of Georgia was not warm enough for the cultivation of mulberry trees. Furthermore, the production of silk required a highly skilled, cheap labor force—one that was not to be found in Georgia, where labor was scarce and therefore expensive.

The fortunes of Georgia's experiment had fallen badly, and in 1752 the trustees returned the charter to the Crown, before its 21 year term had expired. Statistics are unclear, but it is certain that many of the colonists had abandoned Georgia for the greater opportunities found in the Carolinas and other English provinces. Georgia was becoming a deserted colony, and by the time of the Revolution, it was the least prosperous and least populous of all of England's North American possessions.

Why had this noble experiment failed? The colonists who came to Georgia in quest of opportunity found a plan devised by the Old World imagination. Indeed, Benjamin Franklin's now-classic advice to potential European immigrants echoed the unsuitability of that plan. Instead of instant security as the lure to prospective Americans, Franklin praised the mobility and opportunity made possible by America's abundance. The flexibility and openness to the realities of the New World were absent during the trusteeship of Georgia. After 1752 the province became a royal colony, directly under the rule of the King and his appointed officials. This arrangement would continue until the Revolution.

THE PHILOSOPHY OF THE UNEXPECTED

In spite of their elaborate plans for colonization in America, those Europeans who tried to dictate the early contours of the colonies were insensitive to what one historian has called "the whisperings of the environment." In simple terms, America's physical abundance made European thinking obsolete. For example, the Old World's large population coupled with its restricted land mass meant that many European people could never imagine themselves as independent landlords. This was apparent in seventeenth-century England, where inflation and an increasing demand created land prices that only the well-to-do could afford.

It was an altogether different story in America. There the immigrant found an abundance of natural riches that was staggering. One European, speaking of the mystery of Virginia early in the eighteenth century, exclaimed: ". . . the length extends into the wilderness, which is not known to any one and the end is impossible to find." Other observers concluded that this grandeur was matched by the richness of the soil that they believed would never be exhausted. Livestock flourished in the English colonies, and a visitor from England was surprised by the absence of game laws that for centuries had imposed restrictions on hunting in his native land. Indeed, America's natural bounty was so great that a Polish tourist was shocked to find that in eighteenth-century New Jersey the most common method of gathering nuts was to first cut down the tree. It should be no surprise that the European mind, nourished on the principle of scarcity, should find it difficult to grasp the significance of America's abundance.

AMERICA AND THE EUROPEAN ENLIGHTENMENT

During the eighteenth century there arose a philosophical movement that provided the European with a new perspective on America. From the intellectual awakening and the rise of modern science in the fifteenth and sixteenth centuries came the Enlightenment of the eighteenth century. Rejecting the all-powerful God of the Old Testament who glorified Himself and damned sinners, the European intellectuals contributed to a new philosophy called rationalism. Experience had shown these thinkers that through reason and observation man might gain a clearer understanding of his universe. This point of view contained a profound confidence in man and his capabilities. It suggested that through careful observation, he might construct more perfect social and political systems (see Chapter 2 for the political aspect of the Enlightenment). Belief in progress became a cornerstone to Enlightenment thought. The French philosopher Condorcet believed that there was no limit to the potential advance of man's knowledge; indeed, the application of reason would enable man to achieve perfection.

Enlightenment ideas made the New World once again the focal point of the European mind. For centuries it had been America's physical environment that had made such an impact on the Old World. But by the late seventeenth century, a new society was rising on the eastern coast of North America that upset traditional European thought as much as the discovery by Christopher Columbus had 200 years earlier. The full impact of this new society would not be felt until it resulted in the American Revolution itself, but its outlines became increasingly clear to expectant Europeans during the eighteenth century. Actually, knowledge of America in Europe had never been very substantial, but as lines of communication developed certain general impressions of economic opportunity and social progress in the colonies began to emerge. In the European mind the image of American abundance was gradually replaced by America as the "new social ideal."

Influenced by the principles of the Enlightenment and intent upon exploring new avenues for improving society, Europeans exhibited great interest in the nature of the culture that was taking root in America. By the middle of the eighteenth century, the number of social critics and observers who crossed the Atlantic to gain their own first-hand impressions could be counted by the hundreds. Many of these European visitors exaggerated and engaged in fantasy in their reports, but even those who found American society repugnant or crude agreed that it differed from its European parent by offering more to the common man.

One of America's attractions was its social structure. Although most of the colonies had developed some degree of class stratification by the mid-eighteenth century, society as a whole did not harden into the exact patterns found in England or Europe. The easy availability of land provided the key to the free flow of American society; nor was the ownership of land restricted to people of wealth. A Frenchman noted: "Landed property is so easily acquired that every workman who can use his hands may be looked upon as a person who will soon become a man of property." Social position was determined by land and its very abundance no doubt discouraged class rigidity. Indeed, it was not uncommon for indentured servants who sold their labor for a period of from three to seven years in exchange for trans-Atlantic passage to be granted a piece of land upon completion of their term of service. Because of America's bounty, contemporary observers concluded that progress was a reality in the English provinces.

Europeans learned that America's abundance made the social structure more equalitarian than in Europe. The rank and status of European society were largely absent in the colonies. One European observed: "The rich stay in Europe, it is only the middling and poor that emigrate." This "leveling principle" not only created a social structure that was more fluid, but it led to other characteristics that commanded the attention (and sometimes respect) of America's European audience. For example, the scarcity of labor encouraged a relatively high standard of living in America. A French aristocrat-tourist noted: "There is not a family even in the most miserable hut in the midst of the woods, who does not eat meat twice a day at least, and drink tea and coffee; . . . the proverbial wish of 'having a chicken in every pot' is more than accomplished in America." Other foreign travelers admitted that there was less poverty in England's colonies than in Old World society. Crime in general seemed far less rampant than in Europe, and because of the opportunities available an Englishman remarked that there were "but few idle drones in the hive."

PHILADELPHIA: LABORATORY OF THE ENLIGHTENMENT

Americans seemed to be a busy people. Nowhere was this more apparent than in the rapid rise of urban communities in the colonies. Philadelphia, founded in 1682, commanded the special admiration of her European visitors. Not only was the City of Brotherly Love regarded as the loveliest city in America, but even European cities paled in comparison. The capital of Pennsylvania provided "evidence" that the ideals of eighteenth-century intellectuals could be realized. The utilitarian idea of the betterment of society was of direct concern to these people who were interested in America. Not only did Philadelphia boast of wide streets laid out at right angles (and flanked by sidewalks), street lamps, and water pumps at frequent intervals, but a sewer system brought an unprecedented modern air to the city. The citizenry was offered clean and modern facilities in the hospital (accommodations were even provided for "lunaticks") and free medicine was distributed to the poor. There was an enlightened prison system, a university, two academies, and a library founded by Benjamin Franklin in 1742. Printing became a lucrative business in Philadelphia, and the birth of the American

Philosophical Society in 1744 signaled the city's rise to prominence among the intellectuals of the trans-Atlantic community.

What astounded Europeans most of all was the deliberate planning that accompanied Philadelphia's growth. The transition from country to city was occurring at explosive speed, and by the time of the Revolution the most significant social and humanitarian achievements had been made in Pennsylvania. Although the Enlightenment embraced both sides of the Atlantic, it was at Philadelphia more than anywhere else that practice kept pace with theory.

AN AMERICAN CHARACTER EMERGES

Progress was self-evident to the citizen of Philadelphia and his provincial cousins elsewhere in the colonies. Even if most Americans were not familiar with the Enlightenment philosophy itself, their common sense told them that the wilderness was giving way to civilization. And as the profile of American society emerged, so did the so-called American character.

A CHALLENGE TO OLD ASSUMPTIONS

During the early years of colonization Old World social patterns were transplanted to the New World—as the initial efforts in Virginia, New Netherland, and Georgia suggest. The colonies were seen as a projection of Europe across the Atlantic. These settlers who came assumed that they would retain their old habits, manners, and customs indefinitely. Although the rigors of life in the American wilderness demanded some adjustments to New World conditions, it was believed that these adjustments would be temporary. Sooner or later, colonial society would become the mirror image of European culture.

The changes that these transplanted Europeans underwent were usually subtle ones, and sometimes scarcely noticeable. Moreover, the adjustments proved to be less temporary than had been expected. As second and third-generation colonials were born in America without any first-hand experience in traditional English society, the image of the old social patterns became less familiar. Time was blurring the blueprint.

By the eighteenth century, the arrival of thousands of non-English immigrants contributed even more to the breakdown of a plan that was basically English in origin. Migrants from the European continent were made welcome in most of the English colonies and mingled readily with descendants of the first settlers. After 1685 French Protestants called Huguenots appeared in Virginia and the Carolinas,

Pennsylvania, New York, and New England (like the Revere family). In the mixed population of New York, the commerce-minded Dutch asked few questions about a settler's religion or ethnic background. As early as 1646 eighteen languages could be heard along the Hudson River. Besides the Dutch, New York's diverse population included Frenchmen, Danes, Norwegians, Swedes, English, Scotch, Irish, Germans, Poles, Bohemians, Portuguese, Italians, and Jews. By the end of the seventeenth century, Pennsylvania had also become a pluralistic colony in language, culture, and religion. In 1700 the population of England's North American possessions numbered 250,000 persons. By the 1760s it had soared to almost two million. German migration alone during the first seven decades of the eighteenth century equaled the total population in 1700. The rate of this growth and the cultural diversity that occurred during the eighteenth century helped the Americans to realize the irrelevance of European social models.

Because time made the original designs of colonization less relevant to the real situation in America, men began gradually to realize that they must develop a society that was in tune with the New World environment. Unknowingly, the colonials were seeking a new identity.

EQUALITY AND OPTIMISM

The sense of identity that emerged was closely related to the American social system. Not only was the socioeconomic structure more fluid, but there was less distance between the classes. In fact, from the beginning the colonial social profile differed from the mother country's. By eliminating the well-born and those of extreme poverty from migration to America, the role of the middle and lower classes who crossed the Atlantic was magnified. From this relatively narrow range of social groups, a distinctly American social structure evolved. America's population was of the "middling sort." Perhaps this is what a French observer meant when he noted that "the rich and poor are not so far removed from each other as they are in Europe."

If there was an aristocracy in America, it was a working aristocracy whose ranks were more open than its European counterpart. One foreigner visiting in eighteenth-century Virginia was surprised to witness the representatives to the House of Burgesses take their seats, coming straight from the tobacco fields still dressed in their work clothes and muddied boots. Another tourist noted: "For here the poor man who is industrious finds opportunities enough for gain, and there is no excuse for the slothful." Whereas in Europe "equality" meant that all men should enjoy roughly the same position or power, in America the emphasis was on "equality of opportunity." Ambition and talent, in other words, were the most important criteria (other than "color") for entrance into America's affluent society. Those who were willing to exert themselves and industriously apply their talents would succeed. One European tourist concluded that America was "the best country in the world for poor men." Such opportunities encouraged an optimistic spirit and the belief that by the sweat of his brow, an American might enjoy a better life than had been possible in the Old World.

MOBILITY

The way to wealth often required that the American not settle down too soon. During the colonial period settlers were constantly on the move westward where land was cheaper and, it was hoped, opportunity more available. Not only did farms change owners frequently, but also a move to a place several hundred miles away did not seem to bother the colonist in the least. The European tradition that fostered strong ties between man and his land was conspicuously absent in the colonies. Americans seemed to be a people without roots whose vision was focused firmly in the future rather than nostalgically on the past. A French traveler, commenting on this characteristic of mobility, noted: "Americans, indifferent in love and friendship, cling to nothing, attach themselves to nothing. . . . Four times running they will break land for a new home, abandoning without a thought the house in which they were born. . . ."Indeed, the American would "part with his house, his carriage, his horse, his dog—anything at all," if only he was "offered a tempting price."

PRACTICALITY

To the extent that colonial American culture had crystallized, it reflected a practical character in the arts and sciences, learning and religion.

The theatre and music were sadly undernourished in the colonies, nor had the other fine arts and literature matured significantly. Originality in architectural design was also still in its infancy. One critic noted, for example, that there were 30 church buildings in Philadelphia, yet "costly and artistic decoration is not to be found in them." European observers who crossed the Atlantic during the eighteenth century agreed that the Americans were a practical people who had not yet developed a need for the "frills" that adorned Old World societies.

From a European perspective, the education system in England's colonies commanded no more respect than the arts. Institutions of higher learning were particularly vulnerable to criticism. Even Harvard College, founded as early as 1636, was the subject of skepticism by Europeans who saw the school primarily as an institution for clerical studies. Although the elementary schools in some colonies enjoyed some respectability, in other provinces they were virtually nonexistent.

Certain factors help to explain the low status of the arts and education in the society of young America. Simply because America was so young, she had not yet had the opportunity to develop her cultural institutions. One could find in the colonies no palaces or castles, nor any painters in the tradition of Leonardo or Michaelangelo. To establish a cultural tradition required more time than young America had yet experienced. It was also difficult for the arts to flourish because the practical American took advantage of the easy abundance promised by the farming life or the trades. Consequently, little of the artistic genius that existed had yet surfaced. This practical or pragmatic turn of mind was observed by a German visitor: "America has produced as yet no sculptors or engravers. But stone-cutters find a pretty good market." Finally, Americans seemed to stress values other than the traditional aesthetic ones. Profits from commerce consumed the interest of the urban class whose support was essential to the arts, while the vast majority of Americans who lived in rural areas had little inclination and even less opportunity to pursue the accomplishments of highly civilized life.

The role of learning in America was also the result of conditions unique to the New World. Intellect for its own sake was considered irrelevant in the colonies. Some observers noted, for example, that Virginians wished to learn only what was necessary, and in the shortest and best method. If the formal aspects of learning were of minimal importance, perhaps it was because there was merit in America's school of nature. A young British soldier wrote home to his sister in 1756 that there was "as much to be acquired in the Woods of America" as in the English schools. Although "learning" in the European sense was less developed in America, Americans were possessed of good sense and were avid readers. Politics was one topic on the lips of ordinary citizens, encouraged by considerable freedom of the press, and the liberty of discussion exercised in the taverns and other public gathering places. This practical approach is understandable because in America politics had a real, practical application. The education of girls also revealed this utilitarian bent. In colonial soci-

According to one admirer, Benjamin Franklin "tamed both lightning and the French court." A man of great versatility, the author of *Poor Richard's Almanac* embodied the American success story, rising from lowly origins to that of an international celebrity as a politician, scientist, and as a philosopher commenting on the American character.

ety sewing was considered one of the more important skills they should learn, far more useful to them than a knowledge of science or literature. Even in the "better" homes of the colonial period the difficulty in engaging houseservants dictated that the young women be trained as housekeepers themselves.

In contrast to the arts and learning, the sciences were in a more advanced and healthier state. Even in this field, however, it was the applied or practical sciences that were most firmly established. A number of eminent American scientists became pioneers in their fields, including the international celebrity from Philadelphia, Benjamin Franklin. Franklin was regarded by the trans-Atlantic intellectuals as the perfect example of the practical scientist, and certainly his stove, bifocals, and shaving cream were designed to be useful to humanity. Similarly, a German scientist called the lightning rod "that beneficent discovery of the great Franklin."

The thread of practicality seen interwoven in the arts, sciences, and learning was also noticeable in American religious life. During the colonial period, most settlers were preoccupied with the task of clearing the land. In addition, the distances between places and the subsequent isolation of the people tended to make the regular worship of God difficult for many of the colonials. Despite the many European sects that came as cultural baggage to the New World, religious doctrine in colonial society dwindled in importance by the late eighteenth century. And yet, if theological ardor tended to cool in the American environment, the church became quite useful as a social and moral institution. Instead of the frequent violence and bloodshed that had characterized the European religious scene of the previous century, the American church served as a school in Christian morals and ethics, and created occasions for neighbors to meet each other on a fairly regular basis. Americans definitely regarded themselves as a religious people. People who did not attend in order to hear the preaching came to join in the socials. Religion in general was considered a "good thing." Except for the religious fervor of seventeenth-century Puritanism in New England and a spirited religious revival in the 1730s and 1740s called the Great Awakening, churches in the colonies had abandoned their Old World emphasis on theology. Instead of stressing doctrinal matters, colonial religion assumed a more practical role by exhorting moral behavior and providing a social meeting place. This practical character of religion was echoed also by the political roles assumed by many church leaders. Not only was the right to vote and hold office in New England during most of the colonial period restricted to members of the established church, but the people who made the basic decisions regarding local government in colonial Virginia did so from their positions as officers in the church governing boards of each congregation.

THE RISE OF THE BRITISH EMPIRE 1607–1763

During the encounter between European immigrants and the American environment that was developing into a new culture, the British Empire was also taking shape. As late as 1650, however, there was no overall blueprint for the regulation of England's colonies. London's first New World settlements were born a half-century earlier, and were making desperate efforts to survive in the American wilderness against overwhelming odds. A uniform policy for the colonies was a difficult task because of their considerable diversity in governmental structure, purpose (economic, religious, social), economic development, and ethnic composition.

The year 1651 marks the beginning of a new relationship between the mother country and the colonies. The first Navigation Act was issued by Parliament in that year, defining the colonies' commercial and industrial roles within the Empire. New agencies were created to enforce the new imperial decrees. Royal officials were sent to the colonies as a further assurance that the colonials would observe the mercantile restrictions. Central to this imperial design was the mercantilists' belief that the colonies were to remain in an inferior position to the mother country. No provision was made for them to grow eventually into a relationship of equality with the government in London. Instead, England would remain at the center and the colonies would continue as dependencies. By the early eighteenth century this basic arrangement had been established and would continue largely unchanged until after 1763.

Was it reasonable to expect this parent–child relationship to endure indefinitely? Actually, for most of the colonial period the effects of the British Acts of Trade and Navigation were minimal because as much as 90 percent of the colonial economy was based not upon commerce and trade directly, but upon agriculture. Thus, the immediate impact of the trade laws was felt only by a limited number of the total colonial population. Not until American farmers surpassed their own needs in production did they begin to confront the commercial regulations of the Empire. Indeed, contemporary scholars would generally agree that the benefits of empire membership were greater than the disadvantages. For most of the colonial period there was little hostility expressed toward the mother country and in fact the colonials prospered under the rule of Parliament. Nor was later legislation, like the Hat Act of 1732 and the Iron Act of 1750, oppressive. Although such Parliamentary decrees were designed to protect English producers of these goods from colonial competition, America's negligible industrial development during the eighteenth century minimized the adverse effect of that legislation on the colonies.

Colonial prosperity was reinforced in part by the permissive aspects of British mercantilism. For various reasons, including foreign wars and internal strife, there was never a whole-hearted effort by London officials to enforce the mercantile policy in America. The Molasses Act of 1733 failed because Prime Minister Robert Walpole realized that efforts to enforce the law might arouse the ire of the Americans and result in even more serious problems for the Empire than the colonials' illegal trade with the French and Spanish islands in the Caribbean. Thus, involved in war on the European continent and wary of antagonizing the colonials too much, the British government practiced a policy known as "salutary neglect" whereby the colonies were allowed considerable freedom in their economic and political development.

Finally, relations between London and the colonies seemed healthy because much of the American gentry class emerging by the end of the seventeenth century was beginning to imitate consciously the ways of their English counterparts. The Virginians of Chesapeake society, for example, were active participants in the Church of England, and attempted to pattern their life-style after the model provided by the traditional English country gentleman. The desire to imitate the values of the mother country was interpreted as another stabilizing force to preserve the British imperial system.

Despite that apparent stability, changes were occurring in America. As long as policymakers remained flexible and were attuned to the shifting realities of colonial life, they had a chance of maintaining their hold over their American domain. Too often, however, such factors as the distance across the Atlantic, the totally inadequate communication system to bridge that geographical gap, and the mercantile mentality prevented a clear understanding of those realities. Moreover, the isolation of the provinces during the seventeenth century had allowed strong ties to exist between London and the individual colonies. But as civilization in the New World wilderness matured, that relationship was altered. The eighteenth century witnessed the development of a transportation and communication system that encouraged stronger intercolonial ties. This increased the colonists' self-sufficiency and self-awareness, causing a corresponding decline in their dependence on London. They were more American than they knew.

UNFINISHED BUSINESS

The turning point in the relations between the English colonies and the British government came in 1763. After 80 years of intermittent warfare in America, a defeated France surrendered her American possessions in Canada to the English. Great Britain had won the contest for global supremacy. After many years of "salutary neglect," the English government now turned her full attention to her colonies, hopeful that the Americans would share in the costs as well as the benefits derived from the elimination of the French threat in North America.

Parliament's decision to levy taxes on colonial Englishmen, beginning with the Sugar Act (1764) and the Stamp Act (1765), provoked an angry response from the Americans accompanied by the realization of just how far they had diverged from the norms of the mother country. For a long time they had been slowly maturing, although neither they nor the authorities in London had perceived this coming of age. Although many of the colonists had tried to imitate English society prior to 1763, they now recognized that a unique culture had sprung out of their own native soil. That uniqueness was best described by the celebrated French aristocrat, Jean de Crévecoeur, who migrated to America in 1765. In a series of essays penned in 1783, de Crévecoeur posed the question "What then is the American, this new man?":

. . . whence came all these people? they are a mixture of English, Scotch, Irish, French, Dutch, Germans, and Swedes. From this promiscuous breed, that race now called Americans have arisen. . . . In this great American asylum, the poor of Europe have by some means met together, . . . to what purpose should they ask one another what countrymen they are? Alas, two thirds of them had no country. Can a wretch who wanders about, who works and starves, whose life is a continual scene of sore affliction or pinching penury; can that man call England or any other kingdom his country? . . . No! Urged by a variety of motives, here they came. Every thing has tended to regenerate them; new laws, a new mode of living, a new social system; here they are become men. . . . Here the rewards of his industry follow with equal steps the progress of his labour; his labour is founded on the basis of nature, self-interest; can it want a stronger allurement? . . . The American is a new man, who acts upon new principles; he must therefore entertain new ideas, and form new opinions. From involuntary idleness, servile dependence, penury, and useless labour, he has passed to toils of a very different nature, rewarded by ample subsistence. This is an American. . . .

It was clear that a new society had been born in the New World wilderness. It only remained that this new sense of American identity be translated into political terms; and that is the story of the American Revolution. Finally, because of the Revolution, America would continue to occupy an important place in the European mind.

SUGGESTIONS FOR ADDITIONAL READING

Farley Mowat, *West Viking*, (1965). A fascinating reconstruction of ancient Norse explorations in North America.

J. H. Parry, *The Age of Reconnaissance*, (1963). The story of European geographical exploration, trade, and settlement outside the bounds of Europe in the fifteenth, sixteenth, and seventeenth centuries.

Edmund S. Morgan, *The Puritan Dilemma: The Story of John Winthrop,* (1958). An examination of the founding of Massachusetts Bay and the conflict between freedom and authority.

Daniel Boorstin, *The Americans: The Colonial Experience,* (1959). A study of the evolution of an American civilization from its European beginnings.

Clarence Ver Steeg, *The Formative Years 1607–1763,* (1964). An explanation of the forces that converted transplanted Englishmen into provincial Americans.

Benjamin Franklin, *Autobiography.* A provocative, inside view of colonial America by the most famous American of his era.

CHAPTER TWO

"WE, THE PEOPLE"
THE DEVELOPMENT OF
AN AMERICAN POLITICAL
SYSTEM

1619
House of Burgesses established in Virginia: first democratic legislature in North America.

1763
End of the French and Indian wars between England and France over control of North America.

1774
Battles of Lexington and Concord: first shots of the American Revolution.

1776
Declaration of Independence.

1777
Articles of Confederation drafted: the first constitution of the United States government.

1789
The Constitution adopted to replace the Articles of Confederation.

1800
Election of Thomas Jefferson, marking the emergence of the two-party system.

1828
Election of Andrew Jackson, signaling the growing spirit of democracy in the American political system.

1854
Kansas-Nebraska Act fails to cool North–South tensions.

1861
Confederates fire on Fort Sumter, beginning the Civil War.

A VENERABLE EXPERIMENT

When American farmers at Lexington and Concord met British soldiers and began the Revolutionary War, they did indeed fire "the shots heard 'round the world." For the American colonists were the first to wage a successful struggle for independence against an imperial power in modern history. Their example encouraged many of the leaders of the French Revolution and, later, the founders of Latin American independence. The Constitution established by the original 13 states in 1789 was destined to be as influential as the Revolution of 1776. It has been copied, modified, and adopted by more nations than any other governmental form, including the British parliamentary system.

The reason that the American political system enjoys this honor is not because it is a utopian solution to the problem of government, but simply because it works well. America's brand of democracy has survived wide disagreements among its members, a civil war, several devastating economic depressions, and foreign conflicts, while still managing to guarantee its citizens a relatively high level of civil liberties. Under this system the United States has grown and prospered. But the "Founding Fathers" only created the framework of government—later politicians continued to build on this framework as conditions changed and new issues arose. Institutions like the two-party system developed and new ideas like government-sponsored public works evolved until, by the time of the war with Mexico, the political system appeared to be complete and secure.

Yet this system would be severely strained by the controversy over slavery that finally ended in the Civil War. In Abraham Lincoln's words, the war was a test of whether America "or any nation so conceived and so dedicated, can long endure." In one sense the system itself failed when guns were taken up to settle a political issue. But just as the nation "endured" the war, so did America's political system.

THE BRITISH HERITAGE

Many of the colonists' ideas about government came from the parliamentary system in England. Even though that island nation was a monarchy, the royal authority wielded by its king was not absolute. He was required to share power with Parliament, a legislative body made up of nobles (House of Lords) and elected commoners (House of

Commons). Only Parliament could raise taxes for the Crown, so the king had to pay attention to its views or risk losing money to run his government. As a result of this type of limited government, Englishmen felt secure against tyranny.

They were also accustomed to living in a society that was less rigid than most of those found in continental Europe. Early kings of England had sought support from the landed commoners (gentry) and merchants against the hostile nobles, making the gentry influential in politics. Compared to the societies of France and Spain, class lines were much more fluid. Middle-class farmers could become wealthy landowners, and prosperous landowners and merchants could aspire to become nobles, frequently through marriage. Englishmen were proud of the fact that England was ruled as much by law as by a king. The Common Law (court and royal decisions that evolved into basic definitions of justice) was supreme in the land. In theory, at least, it guaranteed even poor people recourse to the courts of justice.

Most important, the everyday workings of government at the local level were managed by the gentry. Within the Common Law they could handle affairs largely on their own. Though not genuine representatives of the people, their interests were similar enough to make them fair legislators. In Parliament they received training in political leadership that enabled them to maintain wide freedom of action in dealing with the king. Struggling to increase their power and influence in government, they realized the importance of political liberty and jealously guarded their rights.

All of these traditions—limited government, the principle of representation, the supremacy of law, local self-government, recourse to the courts, and the political power of landowners and merchants-traveled across the Atlantic to the New World with the colonists as political baggage. These settlers regarded themselves simply as transplanted Englishmen.

TRANSPLANTED ENGLISHMEN

Not long after their arrival in America the colonists realized the necessity for forming some kind of government. Problems occurred as the settlements struggled to cope with unforeseen difficulties that required a formal decision-making process to resolve them. Guidance from England, except in broad generalities, was impossible because of the time required for a ship to cross the Atlantic. Besides, England was too caught up in her own political and religious problems to give her colonies firm instructions or govern them as closely as Spain did her empire.

The Virginia Company, which had been chartered by the king to colonize part of North America for the Crown, was having its own troubles. Regimented and forced to work for seven years as company laborers, the settlers had no personal incentive to make the colony more than a limited success. (See Chapter 1, pp. 10–13 for details.) At the outset, a governor and his council chosen by the Company ruled Virginia. In 1619, however, the governor suggested that they "might have a hande in the governinge of themselves." Virginians would be allowed to form a House of Burgesses in free elections, and to act with the governor and his council in making laws. America's first representative legislature was created mostly in the hope that giving the colonists some political participation would, together with offering land grants, stimulate them to raise Virginia's profits. For more than 20 years the House of Burgesses convened in dubious legality until 1639, when the King of England authorized its annual meetings. Americans had taken their first step in securing home rule.

In New England events took a different turn from the beginning. Before the Pilgrims had left Holland in 1619 to form a religious colony in America, they secured a promise from England's king that he would not "molest" them in their new land. While still at sea they drew up the Mayflower Compact, agreeing to "combine ourselves together into a civil Body Politick" to make "just and equal Laws . . . for the general Good of the Colony." After establishing the Plymouth Bay Colony, they created a government with an elected governor and assistants.

The Puritans who established themselves at Massachusetts Bay in 1629 north of Plymouth were not so democratically minded. They had set out to build a model religious community based on the Bible and God's will, a "City Upon a Hill," for their English brethren to emulate. Originally eight Puritan "freemen" or leaders, claimed all political power for themselves as "God's elite" and, in consultation with the clergy, ruled the settlement. But soon the other members of the Puritan church's congregation demanded "freeman" status and a voice in their government. They were granted the authority to form a General Court, whose delegates would be elected from every town in the colony, and the power to elect Magistrates (several men who acted as supreme justices in the General Court). But the Magistrates still retained the ultimate power of vetoing General Court measures and deciding matters of law. In Governor John Winthrop's view, the Magistrates were "gods upon earth" and were to act as God's "vice-regents" in keeping the community within His will. Puritan government was therefore a mixed democracy.

In fact, both the government that arose in New England and the one that ruled Virginia were mixed democracies with elements of representative and aristocratic rule combined. Even colonies that were established after these first settlements had this mixed type of government with varying degrees of democracy. First Virginia, then New York and New Jersey became royal colonies and had their governors appointed by the Crown. Brief experiments in feudal systems, where a "lord" would manage huge estates tended by tenant "peasants," failed in Maryland and the Carolinas and these colonies eventually adopted governor–assembly political systems. Some colonies were more democratically minded than others—Rhode Island and Connecticut elected their governors as well as their assemblies.

But whatever the initial system, by 1700 all the American colonies except Georgia were operating under a governor–assembly form of government. By creating this type of political system the colonists were actually copying in modified form the government they had left behind in England—self-rule by gentry at the local level under the Parliament-King system. And like the parent Parliament, colonial assemblies quickly set about acquiring more political influence and power.

GROWTH OF COLONIAL DEMOCRACY

The most important factor that aided the assemblies in their quest for power was the easy availability of land. As in England, land or property was the requirement for voting in the American colonies. But in England land was scarce and voters few, while in America it was there for the taking. Consequently, the number of people directly involved in the political process in the colonies was actually greater. Though there were religious qualifications for voting in many of the colonies, few who met the property qualifications were denied suffrage unless they belonged to a particularly "notorious" sect. In colonial Massachusetts of the 1770s, for example, it has been estimated that as many as 80 percent of the province's adult white males were voters. The assemblies spoke for this large constituency, something that colonial governors could hardly ignore.

Originally, the appointed governors possessed broad powers. They could call the assembly to meet or adjourn it at any time, veto any legislation passed by the representative bodies, appoint and dismiss colonial officers, command the militia, and make grants of land. In Crown colonies, the governor was responsible to Parliament and to the King and had to send colonial legislation to England for final approval. Even in the self-governing colonies of Rhode Island and Connecticut where the governors were elected, they had most of the powers of appointed governors.

But governors had to depend upon the assembly for money to operate their colonies. Early in their existence, these representative bodies had demanded the exclusive power to tax, based upon the historic right of Parliament. Virginia's House of Burgesses did not allow the governor to "lay any taxes upon the colony, theire land or commodities, otherwise than by the authoritie of the Grand Assembly." Massachusetts' assembly felt that it was not "safe" to pay taxes levied by the governor "for fear of bringing themselves and posterity into bondage." Before 1700 all of the colonial assemblies had won the exclusive power to tax. With this power, they gradually gained further political influence and authority in colonial government. The English Parliament refused to pass laws urged by the colonial governors to make the assemblies more subservient for fear that such laws would be used as precedents to limit Parliament's own authority. Thus, American assemblies gradually grew in power until by the 1750s they could pass laws for their respective colonies, avoiding governors' vetoes and even on occasion direct orders from the King.

Colonial government was slowly transcending its English origins and evolving along independent lines. By undermining the governor's authority, the assemblies were weakening England's hold on her colonies, since it was through the royal governors and their appointed officials that Parliament and the Crown tried to rule. Colonists had taken the English privilege of local rule and made it into a right, overriding in many cases parliamentary "interference" in American affairs as if their assemblies were sovereign little parliaments within colonial territory. With its wider voting base, government in the colonies was far more democratic than its English counterpart, and the representative assembly came to be regarded as the legitimate lawmaking body in the colonies. Complained one Englishman, "The New England Governments are all formed on Republican Principles and those principles are zealously inculcated in the Minds of their Youth in opposition to the Principles of the Constitution of Great Britain." Another royal official wrote back to London arguing that "the authority of the Crown is not sufficiently supported

By the time that Patrick Henry gave his famous "Give me liberty or give me death" speech before the Virginia assembly on March 23, 1775, most of the colonial legislatures had wrested power from local crown-appointed officials. The firebrand from Virginia was not alone. As Parliament became more dictatorial, colonial resistance grew.

against . . . a republican spirit in the people, whose extreme jealousy of any power not immediately derived from themselves" produced suspicion against royal authority.

THE EMPIRE ENFORCED

The British had encouraged this growing spirit and practice of local rule by their policy of "salutary neglect" toward their American colonies. This policy was born out of necessity. England had allowed private corporations and wealthy families wide latitude in settling North America for the Crown because the English government had neither the money nor the military power to colonize on its own. Even after most of the American colonies had been settled, the King was obliged to let them rule themselves within a general framework of restrictions and obligations that were loosely enforced. Only after England had dealt with its own religious and political problems could Parliament and the Crown turn to organizing the nation's growing empire. Gradually, Great Britain brought eight of the 13 American colonies under its direct control and enacted a series of commercial laws designed to tie colonies and mother country closer together economically. But divisions of opinion in English politics and the lack of an imperial bureaucracy to oversee the system, combined with a growing colonial tendency to resist controls, prevented it from being implemented.

This salutary neglect came to an end with the French and Indian War of 1754–1763. At the beginning of this war, London was careful not to arouse American hostility by directly taxing and drafting the colonists. Instead, the King called upon the assemblies to provide quotas of supplies and soldiers, even footing the bill for most military expenses the colonies incurred. After the conflict was over the British government was faced with a staggering debt. Since England had fought for her empire, it seemed only fair to government decision-makers that the empire share part of the war debts and yield more benefits to the mother country. In this frame of mind, Parliament passed laws to eliminate illegal trade between the colonies and the foreign West Indies, and applied new duties and taxes to the colonies to raise revenue. Troops were to be stationed in the provinces to keep order and prevent Indian troubles, naval vessels would patrol the coasts to catch smugglers, and more efficient tax-collecting methods would be instituted. Great Britain was determined to centralize control of her empire and run it at a greater profit.

Most of this imperial program was not new—its principles and even some of its specific measures had been embodied in the old series of commercial laws that were issued beginning in 1651. But the difference was that the new laws were being strictly enforced; salutary neglect was over. For the colonists, who had been used to running their own affairs under the old, lax system, the change in policy was jarring. Economically, the new system intensified a recession brought on at the war's end by taking more money out of the colonies. It also struck the profitable smuggling trade (not considered "criminal" in America) of many merchants and imposed new taxes on planters already burdened with debts. Politically, it meant that the colonists' cherished "right" of local rule through representative assemblies was being replaced by centralized control from England. In the decade after 1763 commercial laws embodying taxation were enacted by a Parliament in which Americans had no representative and no elected voice to speak for their interests. This was directly contrary to what the colonists regarded as their "rights as Englishmen," and they were determined to resist any encroachments upon those rights.

REVOLUTION

Opposition movements sprang up throughout the colonies against the new imperial system. Even those who did not participate in the general uproar and who felt bound by Parliament's measures resented the British attitude. "It piques my pride," wrote one such colonist on a visit to England, "to hear us called 'our colonies, our plantations,' in such terms and with such airs as if our property and persons were absolutely theirs. . . ." Americans who joined the outcry against the new taxes were more than "piqued." In Virginia, representative Patrick Henry labeled King George III a tyrant, and pamphlets approved by the House of Burgesses declared that anyone supporting Parliament's right to tax Virginians "shall be deemed an Enemy to this his Majesty's Colony." The royal governor of Massachusetts had his home burned to the ground. Delegates from nine colonies sent a letter to the King maintaining that since Americans were not represented in Parliament "no Taxes ever have been, or can be Constitutionally imposed upon them, but by their respective Legislatures." New England merchants even organized a group of their fellows in 1765 and convinced them not to import any manufactured goods from England.

Faced with this widespread resistance and pressure from British merchants stifled by nonimportation, Parliament repealed most of the tax laws, including the controversial Stamp Act of 1765 which had required colonists to buy special stamps for all newspapers and legal documents. However, it refuted the colonists' "no taxation without representation" argument by affirming its "full power . . . to bind the colonies . . . in all cases whatsoever." Desperate for revenue but hoping to pacify the colonies, a new administration won passage of a new series of acts in 1767 that taxed colonial imports—an indirect tax hopefully less objectionable to the Americans.

That hope was ill-founded. Once again the colonies exploded in anger and resistance. Mobs assaulted British troops in New York. In Boston, citizen–soldier antagonism exploded into violence and several civilians were shot in a brawl later labeled the "Boston Massacre" by revolutionary propagandists. England directed the governors of Massachusetts, Virginia, and New York to dissolve their colonial assemblies that were refusing to cooperate with parliamentary orders. Actually, the meager amount of money collected under the taxes was not worth the trouble. For the second time, in 1770, Parliament repealed its own measures. Yet another British ministry tried to solve the problem, settling in 1773 on a single tax on tea, designed to help an ailing English shipping company and uphold the "supremacy of Parliament" over the colonies.

The American temper, which had been quiet during the three-year lull between repeal of the old taxes and passage of the tea tax, flared up almost overnight. New York and Philadelphia sent the tea shipments back to Britain as soon as they arrived. Charleston locked it up in a warehouse. In Boston, where the governor appeared determined to force the tax's acceptance, patriots disguised as Indians boarded the ships and dumped the tea into Boston harbor. The "Boston Tea Party" evoked "great Wrath" in Britain and resulted in the passage of the Intolerable Acts in 1774. Boston harbor was closed by naval blockade, army troops were sent and housed in private buildings, town meetings were banned, and British General Horatio Gates was given practically unlimited authority.

This move against Boston was seen throughout the colonies as striking at "the liberty of all Americans." Revolutionary tracts written at this time indicate that many colonists felt that there was a conspiracy afoot in England to deprive them of their accustomed liberties and even their rights as Englishmen. The treatment of Boston, a city under martial law, and the act of stripping Massachusetts

When Boston radicals, influenced by the rhetoric of Sam Adams, boarded three British ships in the town harbor, and dumped more than 300 chests of tea overboard, England's reaction was one of outrage. Parliament responded with the Intolerable Acts, which precipitated the Revolution. It is ironic that these men of principle found it convenient to disguise themselves as Indians in their illegal act.

of her representative institutions seemed to indicate a "plot," though today it is apparent that none existed. Since all the colonies had in some manner defied parliamentary authority, many provincials feared that they might share Boston's fate. Every colony except Georgia sent delegates to a Continental Congress that gathered in Philadelphia on September 5, 1774 to decide on a common position and present a united front to Great Britain. Revolution still seemed too extreme—George Washington was satisfied that independence was not "desired by any thinking man in all North America." The delegates finally agreed not to import goods from England nor export any materials and called upon local underground committees to expose violators as "enemies of American liberty." A letter was sent off to King George III and the congress adjourned, deciding to meet again in May, 1775. But before that letter ever reached London, the King had determined that "Blows must decide." On April 19, 1775, British troops out of Boston on a mission to destroy illegal caches of gunpowder ran into some local "Minutemen" who had been secretly training to fight just such a move. At Lexington someone fired a shot, and after an exchange of gunfire eight Americans were dead. The War for Independence had begun.

The final break between Great Britain and her American colonies came mainly because the Americans were not interested in the British goal of creating a more efficient empire, particularly at the cost of their democratically based representative form of "home rule." Politically, socially, and economically, Americans had outgrown the subordinate position England attempted to force upon them after years of local self-rule. Americans no longer saw their interests as identical with English concerns and, rather than submit to outside measures, they determined to fight to preserve their rights.

FIRST GOVERNMENT

Though the armed clashes at Lexington and Concord meant war, Americans were reluctant to finalize the break with England. Delegates of the Continental Congress met again in May and asked the King for redress of American grievances. They protested that only in "defence of the freedom that is our birthright . . . against violence actually offered" had Americans resorted to arms. But the King labeled the "rebels" as "desperate Traitors" and announced Britain's determination to suppress the American "rebellion." The struggle wore on and the costs in lives and property mounted. It divided Americans themselves into opposing camps of Loyalist and Patriot, the former retaining their allegiance to the Crown. England's use of the Loyalists, Indians, slaves, and German mercenaries against her former countrymen angered the patriots and deepened the split. With no British concessions forthcoming, the Continental Congress took hesitant steps toward independence and sought French aid. Thomas Paine's pamphlet *Common Sense* helped to convince many Americans that a complete separation from the mother country was the only solution. Finally, the Congress decided to make the break and issued a Declaration of Independence on July 4, 1776, resolving that "these United Colonies are, and, of right, ought to be free and independent states." Ironically, much of the rationale for independence came from John Locke, an English political philosopher writing to justify England's rebellion against her own King nearly a century earlier. In the Glorious Revolution of 1689, Locke had argued that when government is no longer responsive to the people, they have the right to overthrow it and establish a new one that would be more responsive to their needs. This idea became popular during the eighteenth-century Enlightenment, and offered a convenient justification for Thomas Jefferson when he wrote the Declaration of Independence to explain America's rebellion.

The newly "free and independent states" now had to form governments to take the place of those they had as colonies. Essentially, the states retained the same governmental structure—a two-house legislature and a governor to act as executive. Only now the upper house was elected instead of appointed by the governor, and the governor himself was carefully circumscribed in his powers and either chosen by the legislature or directly elected. Every state drew up a constitution and a bill of rights that confirmed the principles of democratic government and representative institutions. Qualifications for voting and holding office were essentially the same as in the colonial period, with such low property-holding requirements that nearly every white male over 21 could vote and most were eligible to hold office. Most important, the constitutions formed a supreme law that no single branch of the government could alter as Parliament continually did in England.

Formation of a loose national government followed along these same lines—close adherence to colonial forms with an eye to preventing any one governmental organ from abusing its power. More than a year after proclaiming American independence in 1776, the Continental Congress finished drafting a plan called the Articles of Confederation. Basically, the Articles legally established the temporary system under which the Americans had been fighting for a year. Congress was empowered to wage war, conduct foreign relations, and raise and borrow money. For troops and taxes it had to depend on the states, which retained the powers of regulating trade and levying taxes. There was no president except the presiding officer of Congress—executive powers were divided between the states and the Congress itself. Under this government the American states won French aid, solved the frustrating problem of financing the war, and fought it to a successful conclusion. Shortly after the struggle ended, Congress managed to convince the states to yield their western lands to the national government, and several laws were enacted to promote western settlement and bring the territories into the Union as new states.

A NATIONAL CONSTITUTION

Weaknesses in the Articles of Confederation soon became apparent to many, however. The American states were united only in name; in practice, each preferred to act largely without regard for the consequences to neighboring states or the national government. Without the power to tax or to regulate interstate commerce, Congress had difficulty trying to repay money it had borrowed during the Revolution and difficulty attempting to negotiate new commercial treaties with other nations. The economy had slumped into a postwar depression because of a lack of hard currency and the fiscal policies of various states. Congress was also unable to counter Spanish attempts to weaken American settlements in the old Southwest. Neither could the government force the British out of forts along the Great Lakes area that were supposed to have been turned over to the United States after the Revolution. Knowing that Congress could not depend upon the states for support, these foreign nations simply ignored America's diplomatic representatives. One frustrated delegate complained that the national government was "responsible for everything, and able to do nothing."

Two groups of Americans sought to alter this predicament by giving the government more power. One group was composed largely of merchants, businessmen, a few planters, and other large landholders who were discouraged by the economic slump and by the barriers to interstate trade created by conflicting state policies. These men also deplored Congress's inability to negotiate new commercial treaties to offset the loss of trading privileges held when America was part of the British Empire. The other group consisted of Revolutionary leaders in politics and war, men who had worked for the creation of a truly national government during the War for Independence. These nationalists were alarmed at the indecisive way in which Congress had reacted to a rebellion by debt-ridden farmers under Daniel Shays in 1786 and at the complete lack of respect America commanded abroad. One of them remarked that there was "something. . . contemptible in the prospect of a number of petty states, with only the appearance of union . . . weak and insignificant in the eyes of other nations." These two groups had many members in common, and late in 1786 they began to work for revision of the Articles to strengthen the national government.

After several false starts, a convention was called to meet in Philadelphia in May of 1787 with the purpose of "revising" the Articles of Confederation. Delegates from all the states but Rhode Island attended. The representatives were nearly all nationalists; a majority had college degrees (uncommon in the eighteenth century), and it is safe to say that no abler or more intelligent body of Americans has ever been gathered together under one roof. It quickly became apparent that the Articles were doomed. No one even submitted a proposal for retaining the current structure of government, the prime consideration being that it would be impossible to gain the unanimous approval of all states required by the Articles for any amendments. The convention then turned to the task of constructing a completely new constitution, one that would embody a more powerful and centralized national government within a representative framework. Though most members were acquainted with political theory, they chose to concentrate on precedent. "Experience must be our only guide," warned one delegate, "Reason may mislead us." Debates, discussions, and arguments followed as the delegates sought to protect the interests of their states and reconcile their ideas on the forms and powers the new government should assume.

The final result was a Constitution that was a "compact of compromises." Its outstanding feature was balance: balance between state and federal power, between the three branches of the national government itself, and between "mobocracy" and aristocracy. The new federal government would have the power to bind the states in matters of taxation, regulation of commerce, treaties, and war, but the individual states retained significant powers of their own. Within the national government the legislative (Congress), executive (office of President), and judicial (Supreme Court) branches were given different powers and responsibilities that both helped prevent any one from becoming dominant and required cooperation. Delegates who were fearful of "too much democracy" were satisfied with the indirect election of Senators (by state legislatures) and the President (by an electoral college). Others wary of a government too far removed from "the people" contented themselves with the direct election of Representatives and the device of impeachment.

Few of the delegates were entirely happy with their creation, and several refused to endorse the document because it was not exactly what they thought it should be. On many points—the exact powers of the Presidency, the precise line between federal and state authority—the Constitution was vague. This would be the cause of furious constitutional debates in the future, but it would also give the document a flexibility needed to meet changing conditions later generations would face. On one detail the Constitution was crystal clear—it was the "supreme law" of the land and derived its authority directly from "We, the People of the United States." Most of the Philadelphia delegates did sign the completed document. Perhaps their feelings were best summed up by Benjamin Franklin: "Thus I consent . . . because I expect no better, and because I am not sure that it is not the best."

Now the nationalists launched an aggressive campaign to convince the nation to adopt this new Constitution. Widening their support by trying to bring in all Americans who were in some way dissatisfied with government under the Articles, they concentrated on the state conventions that had to ratify the Constitution. They adopted the name "Federalists," since "nationalists" frightened many Americans concerned with states rights. "Antifederalists" opposed ratifying the Constitution, fearing that it gave too much power to the central government and would threaten individual liberties. The Federalists countered the latter argument by promising to enact a bill of rights that would protect the people's traditional liberties. Three of them—Alexander Hamilton, John Jay, and James Madison—wrote "The Federalist Papers," arguing in the nation's newspapers that the Constitution provided exactly the right balance of authority and freedom that Americans needed. Though frequently in a majority when state conventions met, the antifederalists lost ground through poor organization and negative arguments, and the Federalists emerged as the victors. By 1789, all of the states had approved the Constitution except Rhode Island (which joined in 1790). The United States had a new national government.

HAMILTON, JEFFERSON, AND POLITICAL PARTIES

The Federalists had no problem securing the Presidency for their candidate George Washington. He was nearly everyone's choice. Washington was not a brilliant or daringly original man, but as General of the Armies during the Revolution his patience, impeccable character, and patriotic determination to build a strong America had made him the country's most admired and best known figure. He was well aware as he took office that his administration was the "first of everything," and that its actions would "serve to establish a Precedent" for the conduct of future administrations.

Washington also knew that above all else the new government had to establish its authority and stability by dealing firmly with the problems that Congress under the Articles had been unable to solve. Encouragingly, both the House of Representatives and the Senate were firmly in Federalist control, and the President had many men skilled in political affairs within his administration. However, differences soon arose not only with the antifederalists but even within the Federalists' own ranks.

The first clashes came over Alexander Hamilton's economic program for the nation. Hamilton had been Washington's aide during the Revolution and now headed the Treasury Department. He thought that the authority and stability of the central government, as well as the economic prosperity and international standing of the United States as a whole, depended upon placing financial matters firmly in the hands of the federal government. His "Report on Public Credit" proposed that the central government assume all state and national debts, create a national bank, and pass new taxes. Not only would Hamilton's proposal establish American credit abroad by paying off the foreign debt incurred during the Revolution, but it would also attract the support of moneyed men for the government by creating a stabilized economy favorable to their self-interest. Since this program required the use of powers that the Constitution only implied, Hamilton and his following tended to interpret that document broadly.

Secretary of State Thomas Jefferson and Congressman James Madison disagreed. They saw that Hamilton's program was slanted toward merchants and businessmen at the expense of farmers. Madison fought government assumption of debts because it would favor the northern states (which still owed large sums) over the southern states (which had largely paid theirs). Jefferson entered the fray over the bank issue. He observed that the Constitution gave Congress no power to create a national bank, and warned that to "take a single step beyond the boundaries . . . specially drawn around the powers of Congress is to take possession of a boundless field of power, no longer susceptible of any definition." Around Madison and Jefferson gathered a group of antifederalists and former Federalists determined to oppose Hamilton's policies.

Gradually, these interests began to coalesce into two political parties. Hamilton and the Federalists (chiefly northern merchants, businessmen, and wealthier tradesmen) worked to promote their commercial interests and to augment the power of the national government. The followers of Madison and Jefferson, calling themselves "Republicans," were generally planters, small farmers, or craftsmen. They felt that the Federalists discriminated against agrarian interests, and feared that the trend toward a more powerful central government with aristocratic overtones threatened individual liberties and the very principle of democratic government.

Neither Republicans nor Federalists particularly liked the idea of political parties. Federalists in particular feared the growth of "factions" as enemies of national unity, and Washington branded party spirit as the "worst enemy" of popular government. Jefferson once remarked that "If I could not go to Heaven but with a party, I would not go there at all." Increasingly, however, the Federalists regarded themselves as the champions of order and national unity, seeing the Republicans as conspirators against the government. The Republicans in turn felt obliged to oppose what they considered discrimination against agrarian interests and threats to democratic government. They regarded themselves as a loyal opposition. By 1792, party spirit was strong and Republicans and Federalists had already begun to organize along national lines.

THE REVOLUTION OF 1800

As a new group just formed, the Republicans had a good deal more organizing to do than the already well-established Federalists. Madison began rallying a Congressional opposition and joined Jefferson in creating a pro-Republican press. But Washington's popularity was so great that the Republicans did not oppose his reelection in 1792. Jefferson finally decided to quit Washington's administration as the President's attitudes hardened and became more identified with the Federalists. Party lines continued to stiffen over a new issue—foreign policy.

When the French Revolution began in 1789 it was hailed throughout the United States as a triumph of republicanism over monarchy. But when the revolt in France took a radical and violent turn, many Federalists were horrified. War broke out between Great Britain and France and threatened to involve the United States as well. Both Hamilton and Jefferson counseled Washington to declare neutrality despite America's treaty of alliance with France dating back to the American Revolution. Jefferson and the Republicans, however, generally admired France and wanted American policy to remain friendly to Paris. Hamilton and the Federalists, who considered the British government a model of strength and order, were determined to stay on good terms with England at any cost. They sent John Jay to London to work out Anglo-American problems that were straining relations between the two nations. Jay returned with a treaty that essentially capitulated to the British position and aroused furious opposition from the Republicans and much of the country. Jay's treaty was barely approved.

This was an issue that the Republicans could bring before the voters. With Washington retiring, they felt Federalist candidate John Adams was vulnerable. The election of 1796 was close, but Adams just managed to edge out Jefferson for the Presidency. Once in office Adams was faced with a foreign policy crisis. France regarded the Jay

Treaty as a violation of America's earlier treaty with her and began seizing United States vessels that traded in the British West Indies. A peace commission sent by Adams to Paris was greeted with demands for bribes and treated with near contempt. When these French actions were made known to the nation, a public uproar followed that catapulted President Adams and the Federalists to new heights of popularity and eclipsed the Republicans. From 1797 to 1800, an undeclared war raged on the high seas between France and the United States.

Many Federalists took this opportunity to call for legislation that would muzzle their Republican opponents, whom they considered "a great body of domestic traitors." In 1798, the Federalist-dominated Congress passed the Alien and Sedition Acts that provided for strict control and supervision of "enemy" aliens, and a fine and imprisonment for anyone who published "false, scandalous, and malicious writing" against the federal government. Under this law four out of five of the editors of leading Republican papers were convicted. Alexander Hamilton, still a power in Federalist circles, won authority to head a large army that he hoped to use against Republican critics. But the Republicans refused to be intimidated. Madison and Jefferson authored the Kentucky and Virginia Resolutions that maintained that the national government had assumed "undelegated powers" and therefore the states had a "duty" to prevent the government from exercising those powers in its territory.

Each party strongly believed that it had to win the elections of 1800 to "save the country" from the other. But the Federalists had weakened themselves by dividing over President Adams' decision to end the undeclared war. They were also unpopular because of the Alien and Sedition Acts and the high taxes necessary to support a larger army and navy. Jefferson took advantage of this by promising to repeal the repressive acts, limit the power of the national government, and reduce its operating expenses. The Republicans swept the election, but Presidential candidate Jefferson and Vice-presidential candidate Aaron Burr received the same number of electoral votes. In such cases, election laws required that Congress decide who would be the next President. There the Federalists tried desperately to block Jefferson's victory by throwing their support to Burr. Only when several Federalists abstained for fear that a perpetual deadlock would cripple the country did Jefferson finally win.

The new Republican President referred to his party's victory as the "Revolution of 1800." Although the changes it brought about were not quite revolutionary, important ones did occur. Most significant, political parties and the principle of loyal opposition became established facts of the American political scene. A Republican victory through the electoral process in a bitterly fought election had been accepted, and this meant that changes in the nation's course would be decided at the ballot box. The election also marked the beginning of a long decline into oblivion for the Federalist party, whose aristocratic image proved an insurmountable handicap. Political power had shifted from the Northeast to the South and West, where the Republicans were strongest. As the Republicans were more agrarian and democratically minded, their rise to power meant the ascendency of agricultural interests and a more democratic course for the national government.

DEMOCRATIC NATIONALISM

President Thomas Jefferson lost no time in charting such a course. He proposed a "wise and frugal government," and set about lowering taxes and reducing the national debt. Wishing to leave men free to "regulate their own pursuits," his administration generally tried to minimize the regulatory functions of the national government. Yet Jefferson also favored the "encouragement of agriculture and commerce as its handmaid." The Republicans aided the westward movement by making it easier for settlers to claim land on the frontier and by sponsoring the explorations of Zebulon Pike and Lewis and Clark. Jefferson's administration also bought the Louisiana Territory from the French in 1803, despite constitutional scruples over its authority to do so. This purchase doubled the national domain and secured for American commerce a Mississippi outlet, the trading port of New Orleans.

The Republican government also faced a dangerous dilemma. The factor that contributed most to American prosperity seemed at the same time to threaten the United States with war. After a short peace, Great Britain and France had gone to war again in 1803. At first, the increased demand for neutral vessels to carry goods normally shipped by the belligerents brought a meteoric rise in American commerce on the high seas. As the European conflict intensified, however, both Britain and France began to resent the Americans, who were growing rich by trading with both sides. They began seizing United States ships and cargoes in violation of American neutral rights, and Britain even forced some American seamen to serve in its navy. Jefferson and later Madison used all their power to boycott

Americans were proud that they had been able to withstand the onslaught of the greatest military power in the world. The feeling that they had actually won a victory over England in 1815 united the Americans in a new sense of nationalism.

trade with the belligerents, hoping to get them to respect United States rights. But despite coercive efforts that dwarfed those of the Alien and Sedition acts, the measures failed. America finally went to war with Britain in 1812 when France offered to make concessions that London refused to match.

Though America came close to losing the War of 1812, Americans were proud of having stood up to the world's greatest power. A new sense of nationalism swept the country, dooming the Federalist party, which had opposed the war. The Republicans emerged from the conflict to win an overwhelming victory in the elections of 1816—so overwhelming that for the next eight years they were virtually unopposed. In the new spirit of nationalism, they increased efforts to settle the West, develop natural resources, and become economically independent of Great Britain. The national bank was re-created, tariffs or taxes were imposed on imports in order to protect American industry, and internal improvements (roads, canals) were encouraged by the government. In a few cases, such as the National Highway and harbor improvements, the government even sponsored such efforts. With his victory in 1816, President Monroe conducted a national goodwill tour that helped unite the country and inaugurate what one newspaper called the "era of good feelings."

Although Monroe was reelected in 1820, the "good feelings" were fast disappearing. A financial crisis and economic depression caused by overspeculation in Western lands were increasing voter dissatisfaction. Sectionalism had become more apparent over the issues of slavery and regional power in Congress during the debate over Missouri's entry into the Union in 1820. The Republicans were also on the verge of a split. Many party members were tired of the "Virginia Dynasty" that had ruled the nation for more than 20 years, and the party organization could no longer command the allegiance of other ambitious leaders determined to win the Presidency for themselves and their following by appealing directly to the people.

JACKSON AND THE "COMMON MAN"

This splintering of the political parties surfaced in the election of 1824. Four candidates, all with their own groups of supporters, ran for President. No one was able to win a majority of the electoral votes and the decision went to the House of Representatives. Andrew Jackson, whose victory at the Battle of New Orleans had made him a national hero, expected victory since he had won the most popular and electoral votes. But another candidate, Henry Clay, threw his support to Jackson's rival, John Quincy Adams, and Adams was chosen President. When Adams selected Clay to be his Secretary of State, Jackson and his followers accused the two of making a "corrupt bargain" and withdrew their support from the new President's administration. Adams found every move he made, even his forward-looking program of internal developments, blocked or frustrated. Referring to this program, Adams lamented that "the system of internal improvements by national energies . . . The great object of my life . . . has failed."

He was also about to lose the Presidency to his archenemy, Andrew Jackson. Ever since his defeat in 1824, Jackson had been building support for a new effort in 1828. His standing as an heroic national figure helped him greatly, especially since almost all of the states now allowed the people to vote directly for Presidential electors (for an explanation of the electoral system, see Article II Section I of the Constitution). He was identified with the aspirations of the common people, symbolizing the nationalistic, western, democratic mood of the nation. The new Democratic party formed around Jackson, attracting newspaper and political support. The election itself was one of the dirtiest in American history—Adams being accused of gross corruption and Jackson of murder and immorality. More voters than ever before turned out at the polls, their new interest in politics encouraged by the Democratic party's emphasis on making Jackson's election a result of the "will of the People."

To gain the support of voters in the early nineteenth century—sometimes called the Age of the Common Man—the new Democratic party led the way in campaign techniques that identified the candidate as "one of the people."

Jackson triumphed, and after the Inauguration many "common men" followed him all the way to the White House to have a free-spirited party on the lawn. The victory destroyed the Republican party's hold on the country, restoring the nation to a competitive two-party system grounded in popular support. It also meant that parties would go to greater and greater lengths to win that support through strong state organizations and careful cultivation of the voter. The Democrats themselves were eventually "out-democrated" by the Whigs, who instituted the national nominating convention and a circus-carnival atmosphere to American politics—mass meetings, parades and songs, party badges, and an even stronger emphasis on the candidate being a "man of the people." Jackson and his supporters had so successfully characterized the election as a battle between the masses and the special interests that many people saw Jackson's election as *their* victory.

The new President immediately set about "reforming" the government. He replaced old civil servants with fellow Democrats, considering that he had a mandate from the people to do so. His administration launched an attack upon the United States Bank, which the Democrats considered an aristocratic institution designed for the benefit of a few wealthy financiers. Throughout his two terms, Jackson attempted to offer "equal protection and equal benefits" to the masses and won the favor of small capitalists by passing a tariff that protected them from foreign competition and gave them a free hand from governmental regulation. The emphasis was on free and fair competition—excluding the Indians, whom the Jackson administration forced west of the Mississippi. But reform was not merely the concern of the White House. All across the country there were religious crusaders, humanists, militant prohibitionists, educators, and seekers after utopia proclaiming the need to transform American society into a model of perfection for the rest of the world.

"WHAT IS MAN BORN FOR . . . ?"

This reforming impulse that swept the United States from the 1820s to the outbreak of the Civil War had its sources deep in Americans' own assumptions about their country and themselves. Aware that America was on trial in the eyes of the older European states, the vast majority of citizens were vitally interested that their democratic system of government should prove itself an unmatched success. Such concern created a strong patriotism that, as one foreign observer noted, "wearies even those who are disposed to respect it." Yet the growing prosperity of the young nation astounded even visiting celebrities like English novelist Charles Dickens, who marveled that "there is no other country on earth which in so short a time has accomplished so much."

Americans were proud of their achievements, but growth and change stimulated expectations that rose more rapidly than actual

Outdoor camp revivals were emotional affairs. One observer noted that people would writhe in "spiritual agony" and cry for forgiveness. He also commented that "if heaven is to be taken by storm," these revival preachers were the ideal leaders for the assault.

accomplishments. Men and women alike, intent on closing the gap between what was and what could be, raised the cry of reform. In so doing they ardently believed they were hurrying progress and establishing the United States as a social ideal for other peoples to copy.

Implicit in their humanitarian philosophy and reform efforts were the twin beliefs that man was worth bettering and that society could be bettered. These beliefs were largely due to the religious reawakening that swept the nation in the early nineteenth century. Americans had always viewed themselves as a religious people, and even foreigners had observed that morality was considered the very basis of "good" society. Revivalist preachers like Charles Finney spoke of man's worth, the power of individual action, and of a golden age that was within the grasp of Christian believers. Congregations were exhorted to do "good works" and entered the ferment for reform optimistically convinced that society was perfectible.

Outside the Christian churches were others who sparked the reform impulse. Ralph Waldo Emerson was a church "dropout," but his philosophy of Transcendentalism insisted on the human potential for good and the necessity for mental and moral independence. "Whoso would be a man," Emerson wrote, "must be a nonconformist." Individuals had a power "new in nature," he insisted, and that power was virtually boundless. Fellow Transcendentalist Henry David Thoreau was Emerson's nonconformist personified. Thoreau had no confidence in the economy ("Trade curses everything it touches") or in the government (which, he remarked, "never of itself furthered any enterprise but by the alacrity with which it got out of its way"). He emphasized instead the person's responsibility to be true to himself and his own conscience. Both Emerson and Thoreau acted as society's critics, rebelling against its materialism and conformism, and became two of the "counterculture's" earliest members.

Many social activists of the period formed themselves into local or even nationwide organizations to attain their goals. One such group was the American Peace Society, formed in 1828 to campaign against personal and international violence. Despite much effort the membership remained small and its influence was further reduced over the issue of whether it was moral to fight defensive wars. The National Temperance Union, on the other hand, drew thousands of supporters in its crusade against "demon rum" in the 1840s. At the time drinking was very widespread and records indicate that it was not uncommon for a man to consume a half-gallon of whiskey a night. Union leaders linked liquor to robbery, child-beating, pauperism, and a host of other ills. At the crusade's height a smattering of Northern states passed a prohibition law, but most states stubbornly refused to "go dry." Perhaps the most successful of the reform movements was the drive for expanded public education. Believing that democracy would be better served by educated voters, the movement adopted the motto "In a republic, ignorance is a crime." Private academies and grass-roots "self-improvement societies" sprang up as public enthusiasm grew. By 1850 the idea of tax-supported elementary schools was accepted throughout the United States and 10 years later the nation had the lowest illiteracy rate in the world.

Other humanitarians concentrated on improving the conditions of society's outcasts—criminals, the poor, the aged, and the handicapped or mentally ill. Most of these efforts were sparked by individuals who had directly confronted the conditions of these unfortunates and had been shocked into action. One example would be the experience of Dorothea Dix, who was transformed from a mild-

Dorothea Dix visited asylums like this one in Blockley's Almshouse, in Philadelphia. Her determination to publicize these crowded and inhumane conditions contributed to the marginal reforms that were made before the Civil War.

mannered Sunday-school teacher into a militant advocate of better treatment for the mentally ill by a visit to a South Carolina "reformatory." Her work resulted in considerable changes for the better in the care of the mentally and emotionally disturbed. Many similar campaigns were waged on behalf of other outcasts, whose conditions were significantly improved.

Although women were quite active in all aspects of the reform movement and enjoyed more respect and greater freedom in the United States than in any other country in the world, they were still legal inferiors and bound by convention to a certain "place" in society. A few states even allowed husbands to beat their wives "with a reasonable instrument." Activists Elizabeth Stanton and Lucretia Mott and other women reformers angry about discrimination against them convened a Women's Rights Convention in New York in 1848. They rose in speaking platforms across the nation, insisting that all men *and* women were created equal and demanding the right to vote. Although they did not win their point at the time, they did achieve the right to enter a few advanced schools on an equal basis, to control their own property in some Western states, and to enter formerly closed professions.

Out on the western frontier and in the more sparsely settled areas of the country experiments in communal living were taking place. These "counterculturists" were convinced that the best way to reform society was to establish "pilot" communities—small models carefully designed to be successful examples of the "good life." Explained one communitarian, "If we can, with a knowledge of true social principles, organize one community rightly, we can, by organizing others like it . . . establish a true social and political order." Over a hundred of these experiments were begun before the Civil War, all seeking to solve various social problems. At Nashoba, Tennessee, a small band of reformers sought to devise a system whereby slaves could earn their freedom while working on the plantation. This attempt to gradually end the institution of slavery failed when the liberal lifestyle of Nashoba became known and hostile social pressure forced the reformers to quit. Another experiment at New Harmony, Indiana was even more ambitious. The designers hoped to create an ideal social environment that would prevent crime, poverty, and nearly every other contemporary evil. But after several years New Harmony collapsed from internal conflicts and lack of money.

Even as the reformers and communitarians moved to perfect American society, another force was beginning to tear the country in two. President Jackson's harrowing confrontation with South Carolina over a state's right to nullify (declare void) a federal law indicated that sectionalism was coming to the fore in American politics.

SECTIONALISM

This tendency of American politics to arrange itself along geographic lines was present early in the country's history. It arose chiefly out of regional differences in economics. The South, being dominated by the planter class, sought cheap imports to supply its need for manufactured or processed goods and protection for the slave labor system that was the backbone of its economy. The West, consisting mainly of small farmers, desired open markets for its crops and low taxes that would not eat away their meager profits. The North, largely controlled by the merchant classes, wanted a high protective tariff against competitive foreign goods and taxes which would support a national government strong enough to maintain a good climate for investment and growth. These areas had overlapping interests and frequently combined to gain their goals. Southern and Western representatives, with the common agrarian interest in expansion to gain more land, allied to vote for war in 1812 in the hopes of conquering Canada and the Floridas. They were also eager supporters of President Jackson's policy of Indian removal.

These sectional alliances came and went, depending upon the issue. The North was frequently able to get Western support for tariffs by promising that some of the funds would go for internal improvements in transportation or communication, and by appealing to the West's heady nationalism. Certain combinations proved to be turning points in the nation's political history. When the eastern seaboard states split over Hamiltonian policies that favored Northeastern merchants and financiers, Southerners were able to elicit the help of Western states to win the election of 1800 and oust the Federalists. Jackson's own triumph in 1828 was due as much to the Democrats' ability to unite both the South and the West behind him as it was to the Eastern workers' support.

Southerners quickly became disillusioned with President Jackson when he made it clear that they could not expect reduction of the currently high tariffs. South Carolina decided that its own rights and interests were being ignored, and invoked the doctrine of nullification by attempting to prohibit enforcement of the tariff law within its sovereign boundaries. This "states rights" doctrine, developed by Senator John C. Calhoun, had its roots in the Kentucky and Virginia Resolutions written by Jefferson and Madison to combat the repressive Alien and Sedition Acts. States rights advocates contended that the Constitution was really a compact of sovereign states, any one of which could declare null and void a law passed by Congress that it considered to be unconstitutional. As a last resort, it could even secede from the Union altogether. Jackson's position on this theory was unknown until he rose at a formal dinner and stared Calhoun straight in the eye, offering the toast "Our Federal Union, it must be preserved!" Finding herself alone and threatened by an invasion of federal troops, South Carolina backed down. After this incident, Calhoun concentrated on building a sense of southern solidarity so that, if another trial came, the whole region could act together more effectively against federal power.

That trial was coming, and it centered upon the very basis of Southern society and economy—slavery. Slavery had been an irritating issue in American politics since Thomas Jefferson in the Declaration of Independence tried to blame its introduction into America on George III. The framers of the Constitution had made a special provision for slaves, counting them as three-fifths of a person for the purposes of representation and taxation. The "peculiar institution" of slavery had been on the decline until 1793 when the cotton gin made the mass cultivation of cotton immensely profitable. Now, more than ever before, the cheap labor supplied by black slaves seemed necessary. Faced with slavery's apparent economic advantages and the unwillingness of most Southerners to tolerate a large free black population at home, antislavery movements in the South made little headway.

In the North societies dedicated to freeing the blacks had more success. By the 1830s they were exerting considerable influence upon politics. The northern abolitionists considered slavery a moral blot on the nation—a violation of both the Declaration of Independence's "all men are created equal" and Christian ethics. Even in the North, however, abolitionism never became a mass movement. Prejudice, the fear of wage-earners that free blacks might take over their jobs, and the desire of many Northerners to remain on good terms with their southern neighbors made the antislavery forces a vocal minority subject to scathing denunciation and even physical attack. But they were heard. As abolitionists like William Lloyd Garrison stepped up their charges that the institution of slavery violated Christian ethics, many Southerners began to represent slavery in a positive light. They rationalized that, by supporting an educated, cultivated society, slavery was a positive good.

By the 1840s sectional differences were transcending the sphere of economics and entering the field of morality. The issue of abolitionism now overshadowed other reform crusades until it seemed the only reform issue. Other causes were dwarfed into insignificance and the "evil of bondage" monopolized attention. While it had been difficult enough to compromise and make adjustments for these differences within American politics when the issue was economic, it became even more difficult when the problem was couched in moral terms. Sectionalism, complicated by the slavery question, was threatening to make the American political system unworkable.

THE SYSTEM TESTED—CIVIL WAR

The acquisition of the Southwest in 1848 as a result of the Mexican War brought the issue of slavery to a head. As agrarian areas that needed new lands, the South and West had been the moving forces (aided in part by Northeastern merchants interested in Oregon and California as bases for Pacific commerce) behind the spirit of expansionism and "manifest destiny" that had swept the nation into war. Now the status of these western lands had to be determined. The southern slave interests wanted to extend the institution into the territories and open up vast lands for cotton cultivation. But western farming interests wished to make the area available to small farming settlers, hoping to exclude slaves both for moral reasons and because they feared planters would take most of the land. Southerners opposed this, realizing that if they did not gain at least half of the new states as slave states they would lose their equal voice in the Senate and be at the mercy of interests that were at best indifferent to them.

As the arm of government responsible for the territories, Congress tried various compromises. In 1850 California entered the Union as a free state, and a more stringent law requiring all escaped slaves to be returned to their owners was passed. The Democrats, with most of their support in the South and West, labored to hold their party together by approving the Compromise of 1850. But no one was satisfied. The Midwest, now closely tied to the Northeast by a system of canals and railroads that allowed a profitable exchange of produce and manufactured goods, increasingly identified its interests as northern. Abolitionists were finding a growing audience, and their cause received a great boost from Harriet Beecher Stowe's novel *Uncle Tom's Cabin*, an emotionally appealing attack on slavery that became immensely popular. In this atmosphere, laws requiring that fugitive slaves be returned to their owners seemed outrageously immoral and were subjected to widespread contempt. Many states even passed "Personal Liberty Laws" directly contrary to the federal ordinance.

An increasingly isolated minority, Southerners saw their society and institutions under continuing attack. They were incensed by the "criminal" resistance of the North against returning slaves they regarded as property rightfully theirs. These slaveholders fearfully recalled black uprisings like the one in Virginia led by Nat Turner in 1831 that slaughtered 60 whites, and they were angry at abolitionist propaganda that seemed to encourage slave unrest.

Growing hate and suspicion between the two sections made settling the question of slavery in the territories more difficult. In an attempt to solve the problem and hold his disintegrating party together, Democrat Stephen Douglas proposed that the new states decide for themselves whether to admit slaves or not. His proposal was tried in Kansas and Nebraska after 1854. But "freesoilers" and slaveholders rushed into the area trying to gain a majority for themselves and control the decision, resulting in a bloody conflict that killed the compromise. Tensions ran so high in Congress itself that one southern congressman, claiming an abolitionist senator had in-

Emotions ran high in the Senate debates in May 1856 over the extension of slavery into Kansas. Southern Congressman Preston Brooks took abolitionist Senator Charles Sumner's incendiary two-day speech on the subject personally, and responded by beating Sumner into unconsciousness before his colleagues on the Senate floor. The fact that Brooks was made a hero in the South and Sumner a martyr in the North revealed the widening gap between the two sections.

sulted a member of his family, beat the offending senator into unconsciousness.

In the North a new political party appeared in 1854 that based its platform on the principle that slavery should not be allowed to expand into the territories. Calling themselves "Republicans," they failed to win the election of 1856 that put a prosouthern Democrat in the White House. With the Congressional elections of 1858, these Republicans were gaining in strength. By catering to northern economic desires for a high tariff, internal improvements, and a homesteading act, the new party became more popular in the North while being deemed the embodiment of folly and evil in the South.

Differences between the two sections were now so great that it would only take a spark to set off an explosion of anger and resentment that would break the nation in two. John Brown's raid on Harper's Ferry in October of 1859, an attempt by an antislavery fanatic and his followers to establish a republic for blacks in western Virginia, convinced most Southerners that the welfare of their section was not safe in the Union. As the Presidential election of 1860 approached, Democrats convening in Charleston, South Carolina split over formation of a party platform. Southern Demo-

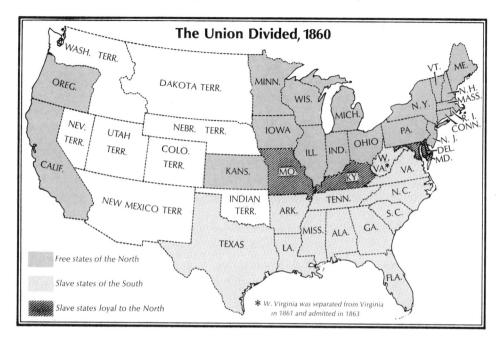

The North's large population and economic strength gave it a decisive edge over the Southern Confederacy in the protracted war that ensued. Because California and Oregon made no significant contribution to the war effort, they are not included in the accompanying graph.

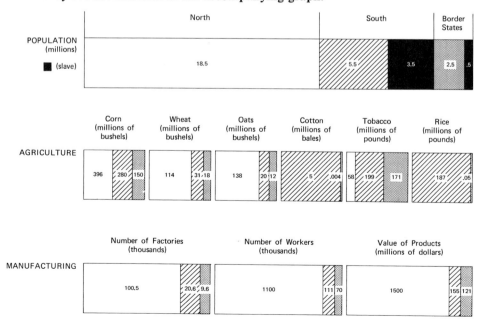

crats broke away from their party to nominate their own candidate. Elated, the Republicans chose Abraham Lincoln as their standard-bearer (chiefly because he came from the Northwest and was not so prominent that he had many enemies) and identified themselves with northern economic interests and the increasingly popular stand of forbidding slavery in the territories. Although he did not win a majority of the popular vote, Lincoln carried all the Northern states and won enough electoral votes to be elected President.

Southerners were positive that the Republican victory meant that they would only meet further hostility and that their interests would be ignored if they remained in the Union. Well-organized, persuasive secessionists loudly called on their states to leave the Union. And they convinced most Southerners. South Carolina was the first to sever its ties with the national government, followed by six other southern states. They met and formed a new nation, the Confederate States of America. The Confederates proceeded to take over all federal offices and military posts in the South. In Washington, congressional compromises floundered on the question of extending slavery into the territories. Determined to uphold federal authority, President Lincoln sent supplies to beleaguered Fort Sumter in Charleston harbor. Rather than allow them through and have the fort remain in control of the harbor, the Confederates forced the fort to surrender after bombarding it for two days. The Civil War had begun.

In one sense, the American political system had failed. The decision at the ballot box had been opposed by nearly half of the country, and the Union itself was split. Political disagreements had exceeded the bounds of peaceful compromise, taken on highly emotional overtones, and ended in violence. The system's apparent failure would be costly—more Americans would die in the war than in all the wars America had fought before or would fight afterwards. But the advocates of Union finally won, restoring the old political system and the United States itself. In doing so they put to rest the idea of secession (though not states rights) and vastly increased the power of the federal government over individuals (military draft and martial law that suspended some rights) and over its general role in the economic and political affairs of the nation.

SUGGESTIONS FOR ADDITIONAL READING

George Dangerfield, *The Awakening of American Nationalism*, (1965). An examination of the people, ideas, and forces that contributed to the growth of national unity up to the 1830s.

Morton Borden, *Parties and Politics in the New Republic, 1789–1815*, (1967). A chronicle of the emerging American political system from its birth in 1789 through its first critical tests and the War of 1812.

John William Ward, *Andrew Jackson: Symbol for an Age*, (1955). A portrait of Jackson as the symbol of the "common man" in an increasingly democratic age.

Clifford S. Griffin, *The Ferment of Reform, 1830–1860*, (1967). An account of the many humanitarian causes and utopian plans that filled this period.

Bruce Catton, *The Coming Fury*, (1961). A study of how shortsighted, angry politicians made crucial decisions without realizing the real consequence—Civil War.

David Donald, *Lincoln Reconsidered*, (1956). A reexamination of some of the myths and misconceptions that surround the people and events of the Civil War.

CHAPTER THREE
THE WEST
IN AMERICAN LIFE

1763
Pontiac's Indian rebellion against British domination.

1785–87
Northwest ordinances encourage American westward expansion.

1803
President Jefferson's Louisiana Purchase doubles the national domain.

1838
Removal of Indians from the Southeast along the "Trail of Tears."

1848
Treaty of Guadalupe-Hidalgo: the Southwest ceded to the United States after Mexican–American War.

1849
California Gold Rush sparks a renewed interest in westward migration.

1862
Homestead Act opens millions of acres of government land to public settlement.

1890
End of the Plains wars; Indians sent to reservations.

1893
Frederick Jackson Turner's "Frontier Hypothesis" explains the impact of the frontier experience upon the development of the American character and institutions.

THE HERITAGE OF THE WEST

No segment of American history is as popular today as the winning of the West. The saga of the frontier is the theme of countless books and novels. Cavalry and Indians are still battling for television audiences. Even Japan and Italy have copied the "western" movie. If America has a folk hero it is the cowboy, and time has not dimmed the popularity of country-western music, rodeos, or ranch life in many areas of the nation.

But America's western heritage is more than movies and rodeos. The West's natural resources are the foundation upon which this nation has built the most prosperous economy in the world. Conquest of the West also meant the destruction of the Indian's way of life, and to a lesser degree, the Mexican's. These peoples still have difficulty adapting to a new life in Anglo-American society. Despite this mixed legacy, many historians feel that America's western experience has had a profound effect upon the country's institutions and national character. Individualism, a tendency to be always on the move, to identify growth with progress, to lean toward informality and egalitarianism, and to develop democratic government have been partially attributed to the influence of a western frontier. So has the national inclination for violence.

How did the frontier encourage these traits? How did Americans view the West as their society was being carved out of the wilderness?

FIRST AMERICANS

For several thousand years before a European set foot in the New World, Indians had lived here long enough to make well-worn paths. In North America alone there were almost 200 major tribes, each with its own set of customs and manners. Most of the tribes occupying the Atlantic coast were relatively small. Further inland, close to Lakes Ontario and Erie, was the famous Iroquois Confederacy, the Five Nations whose system of tribal cooperation so impressed Benjamin Franklin that he copied it in planning for a federation of the thirteen colonies. Not only was each tribe obliged to come to the aid of the others in time of war, but land controlled by any member tribe was open to all. To the south was a loose Indian confederation led by the Creeks, known as the Five Civilized Tribes because of their agricultural pursuits. Like the Iroquois, their member tribes cooperated in war and commerce. Other single tribes like the Shawnee, Sauk, and Fox also roamed the country west of the Alleghenies.

Across the Mississippi, Indian life was different. There it was based on the horse and the bison. The Sioux, Cheyenne, Pawnee, Comanche, Kiowa, and Arapaho were tribes with mobile cultures. Tepee villages were set up and then moved again with the flow of the seasons and the buffalo. Nearly every necessity used by these Plains Indians was taken from this great shaggy animal that roamed the area in huge herds. Horses introduced by Spaniards enabled the Indians to follow the buffalo.

Far older by centuries than their cousins of the Plains, the Pueblo Indian tribes of the Southwest were also vastly different. They lived in a town-oriented culture, in apartmentlike dwellings of adobe often situated on nearly inaccessible cliffs. Developing irrigation methods, the Pueblos lived on subsistence farming and hunting in the arid Southwest. Apparently war had not touched most of these tribes in several thousand years, nor were they troubled by class divisions. Their neighbors to the northwest, the Californian Indians, pursued a more primitive way of life and were still living in a Stone Age culture as late as the California Gold Rush. Nez Perces and Shoshoni led quiet lives in the valleys of Oregon and Idaho. Finally, there were the Eskimo people in Alaska, whose placid, family-centered culture was sustained mainly by fish and whale blubber.

These peoples were the first Americans. The coming of the European was to prove a more disastrous event than all the Indian wars combined, for it would destroy the Indian's way of life.

COLONIZING THE NEW WORLD

Why did they come? After 1500 the monarchs of the newly united nations of Europe began to search for ways to increase their power and wealth (see Chapter 1, pp. 6–8 for a discussion of mercantilism and the nation–state system). Spanish conquistadors conquered the immensely wealthy empires of the Aztecs and the Incas, and Spain grew rich off the profits of her New World territories. Other countries tried to follow Spain's road to success, seeing the New World as a source of economic opportunity for the Old.

Many of the English colonists saw it in the same light. They came to the New World hoping to better their economic and social status, something that was nearly impossible in the rigid societies from which they came. Others made the dangerous journey across the Atlantic fleeing religious persecution, seeking a "promised land" where they would be free to worship and establish a new religious order. So came Puritans, Quakers, French Huguenots, Baptists, and many other sects. With them came soldiers of fortune, mercenaries seeking riches and adventure. Not a few were forced to come over —debtors and criminals were frequently given the choice of jail or immigration to the New World; the colony of Georgia was filled with them. For all of these people, North America's Atlantic seaboard was the West, a land of opportunity.

And they came laden with "gifts." Besides the wild horses whose ancestors were brought over by the Spaniards, Europeans gave the Indians the gun, liquor, and epidemic disease. Indeed, according to a recent study, North America's population of 10 million Indians at the time of the New World's discovery was reduced by millions as a result of contagious diseases imported by the white men. Fields and villages abandoned by plague-struck Indians provided Puritan settlers with land that had already been cleared. Liquor became practically addictive to many Indians, making them dependent upon unscrupulous white traders at the same time it ruined their health. Still, the Indians were generally dealt with in a friendly (if not always honest) manner. For they had control of the land, they knew how to raise New World crops important to the colonists, and they offered a profitable trade to the white men. As long as the settlements were small and the colonists few in number, peace with the Indians was precariously maintained.

But as the colonies expanded, the Indians resisted this encroachment of their tribal territories. When they became more of a hindrance to colonial expansion than a help to the settlements' existence, they were wiped out under the pretext of "retaliation" for some offense. In these wars the colonists were frequently aided by other Indians whose tribes were rivals. In this manner, the Native American helped bring about his own destruction. These conflicts usually proved short and brutal. A governor of Plymouth observed during the burning of an Indian town in New England, "It was a fearful sight to see them frying in the fire . . . and horrible was the stink and stench thereof. But the victory seemed a sweet sacrifice and they gave praise thereof to God. . . ."

The eastern areas were soon cleared of Indians and wilderness, both being driven west to the fringes of colonial settlement. The gradual infusion of white culture was destined, however, to destroy the Indian's way of life. Recent evidence suggests, for example, that the goods offered by seventeenth-century Dutch and English traders soon resulted in the depletion of some furbearing animals. In 1633 alone, the Dutch purchased some 30,000 beaver and otter skins, exhausting Iroquois hunting lands in upper New York. The virtual extermination of these species of animals contributed to the heightened rivalry of the tribes, and was a major factor in much of the seventeenth-century forest warfare.

The ecological imbalance provoked by this wholesale slaughter was accompanied by a growing dependence upon the white man for such goods as food, clothing, tools, and weapons to support the Indian's livelihood. Thus, by the 1760s, although the Indians were no longer able to exist without these subsidies, the British embarked on a new restrictive policy regarding Indian gifts. Having evicted the French from North America in 1763, the British, in an effort to economize, declared that henceforth the Indians must fend for themselves. No longer could they expect "presents" from the English. The result was a well-organized uprising led by Chief Pontiac. Fueled by economic desperation, and compounded by certain religious overtones, Pontiac's Rebellion in 1763 became almost a religious crusade against the white man's culture. But that rebellion was futile as England now controlled the North American continent. There was no longer any room for the decisive political role played by the Indians for more than a century in the contests between England and France in the New World.

The victorious English were determined to consolidate their gains made at the expense of the French and the Indians. In order to prevent costly Indian wars in the future and to reserve land speculation and fur-trading opportunities for the English crown, the Proclamation Line of 1763 was issued, forbidding the colonists from expanding westward.

AN AMERICAN WEST

This law angered the colonists. Frontier settlers believed it provided security for the Indian at their expense, and land speculators and fur traders resented the government monopoly on western lands. Colonists had begun to think of the Frontier as *their* West, just as they were beginning to feel more like Americans with their own interests than like European colonists.

The Revolutionary War between the American rebels and the British, both sides complemented by their Indian allies, made the frontier a battleground once again. After peace was concluded in 1783, the Indians watched as settlers poured into the Northwest.

Neither the heavy forests, the Appalachian Mountains, a lack of good roads and transport, nor Indian hostility could stop them. They generally came in four waves: hunters and trappers who came west to make money in the fur trade and live off the land; pioneers who squatted on the land and barely made a living, usually moving on after a few years; farmers who cleared the land to settle permanently; and merchants and townsmen who set up services and supplies for the growing settlement, connecting it with more established towns further east. These migrations were not forced. People were not fleeing from persecution or starvation. They simply saw an opportunity for adventure and for bettering their economic or social conditions by moving west, where everything seemed more wide open.

Faced with this migration, the United States government began to develop a western policy. Part of that policy was established in the Northwest ordinances of 1785 and 1787, which provided a system of land survey and sale while enabling the new territories to become states in the Union when they reached a certain population level. The West was to be incorporated into the rest of the nation. Another part of that policy dealt with the Indians. Here the frontierman's unwavering desire to remove the Indians was becoming the aim of the government. By a policy of enforced treaties, frequently concluded by Indian chiefs without authority to sign anything, the United States began driving the Native American out of the way of white migration and onto land beyond the foreseeable reach of settlement. When many of the Indians resisted, some joining with the Spaniards in the South or the British in the North against American expansion, armies were sent against them. Tecumseh, a Shawnee, made an effort to unite all the Indians east of the Mississippi in a common war against the United States. "He is," wrote the territorial governor of Indiana, "one of those uncommon geniuses which spring up occasionally to produce revolutions and overthrow the established order of things. . . ." That same governor led a military force against some of Tecumseh's followers who, instead of waiting for him, launched a premature attack and were defeated. Tecumseh's aura of invincibility was shattered, and his Indian alliance fell apart. The five "Civilized" tribes concluded treaties that allowed them to keep their lands in the Southeast, and most of the Indians of the Northwest were driven off beyond the Mississippi. America's Northwest territory was secure.

Still, the frontier settlers were not entirely happy with the western policy of their government in Washington. They felt it had moved too slowly against the Indians, that its policy of hard currency and taxes discriminated against them by making it difficult to obtain loans for buying land and maintaining a farm, and that it was simply too far away and preoccupied with "eastern problems" to do them much good. Westerners were developing interests of their own. Nevertheless, the pioneer's "pacification" of America's territories was fast making him a legend in his own time.

JEFFERSON AND THE AGRARIAN MYTH

"Some few towns excepted," wrote one American, "we are all tillers of the earth, from Nova Scotia to West Florida." For Thomas Jefferson and other agrarian idealists, this was as much a political statement as a social or economic one. Jefferson saw the farmer as the cornerstone of the American Republic. "The small landholders," he wrote, "are the most precious part of a state." He felt that by producing their own goods and by constant contact with nature and nature's God, they would have the economic self-sufficiency and moral character needed to wisely support a republic. The large western territory would allow the farmer plenty of room for expansion, preserving America's agricultural society and thereby insuring that the United States would maintain its republican form of government. Jefferson considered it his duty as President to foster agriculture, enlarge the West, and remove any obstacles to agrarian expansion.

Following this conviction, Jefferson devoted much of his time to western problems. When the French takeover of New Orleans and the Louisiana territory threatened to close the West's commercial lifeline down the Mississippi, the President negotiated with Napoleon to buy the city. The French emperor, whose European entanglements prevented him from taking proper advantage of the area, decided to sell the whole territory. Jefferson quickly accepted the bargain in 1803, despite personal scruples about his constitutional power to do so. The nation's area had been doubled, and Jefferson congratulated his countrymen on their possession of "a chosen country, with room enough for our descendants to the thousandth and thousandth generation."

To explore this country the President sent out Meriwether Lewis and William Clark. Beginning in 1803 they went up the Missouri, across the Rocky Mountains, and down the Columbia recording their observations of the land and its Indian inhabitants. Zebulon Pike was also sent out on two expeditions, one up the Mississippi to its source and another into the Southwest. The information gained proved useful to future pioneers and settlers. Jefferson's administration also reduced the price of western land, made it easier to obtain, allotted part of it for schools, and encouraged the building of roads.

As it grew economically stronger and became more densely populated, the West's influence in national affairs increased. Western representatives in Congress led other war enthusiasts in the series of events leading to the War of 1812. They maintained that only war would end the Indian menace by allowing the invasion of Canada to destroy British support of the hostile tribes. Congressman Henry Clay of Kentucky was also worried about the state of the western economy, whose depression many of his constituents felt was due to British maritime practices. When war finally came, brought about in part by the War Hawks in their desire to wipe out the Indians and conquer Canada, many Americans considered victory to be "a mere matter of marching." They were confident that the "embattled farmer" of the Revolution and the frontiersman would easily defeat the British and Indians. To such an extent had the agrarian myth grown that the farmer–frontiersman was considered invincible in war as well as the main support of the republic in peace. General Jackson's unexpected victory at New Orleans, where his motley force of "sturdy yeomen" defeated British regulars, appeared to justify this belief. The "common man," a farmer–frontiersman, was the nation's symbol of superiority.

"TRAIL OF TEARS"

General Andrew Jackson rode to victory in the Presidential elections of 1828 as the "Hero of New Orleans" and the "champion of the common man." His success was indicative of the nation's pride and confidence in the western farmer–frontiersman, of which he was the symbol. That confidence was also reflected in the liberalized voting laws passed in most states before 1828 that gave the vote to the small landholding "common man." On Inauguration Day, mobs followed their hero Jackson to the White House and proceeded to invade that sanctuary, muddy boots and all. Observed one lady spectator, "Ladies and gentlemen only had been expected. . . . But it was the People's day, the People's President, and the People would rule."

"The People" expected certain things from the new President. They had largely ignored former President Adams' program for internal improvements because they were suspicious of the centralized gov-

ernmental power it would require. Continued waves of western settlers and free-wheeling entrepreneurs that made up Jackson's democratic constituency simply wanted a "free hand" and as little interference from Washington as possible. The President could little afford
to alienate them.

In 1828 the Five Civilized Tribes of the Creek, Cherokee, Chickasaw,
Choctaw, and Seminole had firm treaties with the United States government guaranteeing them possession of their traditional lands. But
the states of Mississippi, Alabama, and Georgia were increasingly
eager to take these lands and open them for white settlement and
speculation. Following the discovery of gold in Cherokee territory,
Georgia began to pass laws that defied those federal treaties and
court orders. This legislation also destroyed the Indians' system of
government modeled after that of the United States, and deprived
them of their lands. The Cherokees, along with other Indian tribes
being subjected to the same sort of illegal actions, sent delegations to
Washington to protest. Secretary of War Eaton admitted that the
federal government was simply unable to support its own treaties.
Enforcement would have required United States troops, an action
that would have made Jackson instantly unpopular in the West. The
President had already made up his mind to compel the "civilized"
tribes to give up their lands and move west of the Mississippi into
new reservations, where Jackson promised them they could stay "as
long as grass grows or water runs."

Most of the Indians were simply unable to resist combined state
and federal pressure to move. Settlers used liquor, fraud, and violence to drive off these Native Americans. First the Creeks, then the
Chickasaw and Choctaw ceded their lands and were moved in mass
migrations devastated by hunger, disease, and exposure. A few young
army officers did their best to take care of the Indians entrusted to
them, but they were very few. On two occasions the Cherokees took
their case to the Supreme Court. Finally, the Court ruled in the Indians' favor and Chief Justice John Marshall wrote a hot denunciation of state and federal actions. But Jackson refused to implement
his decision. The President had the last word—"John Marshall has
made his decision," he remarked acidly, "now let him enforce it." By
1838 the Army began the removal of the Cherokees from their land in
Georgia. Along the "Trail of Tears" that led west, nearly one-fourth of
the tribe perished. Even Indians who had cooperated in the removal
of their brethren found themselves and their families ousted, victims
of broken promises. Florida Seminoles fought the government from

"We were drove off like wolves, and our people's feet were bleeding with long marches" wrote one Creek Indian who followed the "Trail of Tears." Another chief commented sadly that white Americans eager to force the tribes off their ancestral lands "cannot appreciate the feelings of a man that loves his country."

the Everglades for 10 years and cost Washington 1500 American troops and 20 million dollars to remove. Finally, all but a few were swept aside by the American encroachment on the frontier.

WESTERN EMPIRE

By the late 1830s this westward march of Americans was beginning to be regarded as a natural, inevitable course of action. Even before the Revolution, writers had remarked that the succession of powerful civilizations seemed to move from east to west—"Westward the course of empire takes its way." Benjamin Franklin had seen America as the seat of a new world power, and Thomas Jefferson believed that the entire continent would be peopled from the "original nest" of east coast states. Enough time had passed since the winning of American independence to bolster the conviction in the 1830s that America's experiment in democracy was the wave of the future. The West was the key to this expanding American empire, for it would provide the raw resources of power and room enough for a growing populace. As conqueror of the West, the farmer–frontiersman was not only the main supporter of democratic government and cherished republican institutions but also the enthusiastic agent of American expansionism. Heady with exuberance at the picture of a nation on the move, convinced that the farmer–frontiersman was invincible, Americans began speaking of a "manifest destiny to occupy and to possess the whole of the Continent which Providence has given us."

"Manifest destiny" was an emotionally charged call to "subdue the continent . . . to establish a new order [democracy and republican institutions] in human affairs . . . to cause a stagnant people to be reborn [referring to the Mexicans] . . . and to shed a new and resplendent glory upon mankind. . . ." This combination of agrarian expansionism, missionary idealism, and plain arrogant nationalism was fast becoming a powerful force in national affairs. It was also

In this artist's rendering, the spirit of Manifest Destiny (here garbed in the form of a goddess) guides the American people in their conquest of the continent. Under her protective presence, white settlers boldly take possession of the land, unmindful that the Indians regarded this move as an intrusion of their domain. From the artist's perspective, the Indians seem to offer little resistance, simply retreating along with the buffalo.

molding the shape of the westward movement, making it a matter of right and an indicator of national progress.

Neither geographical nor national barriers could slow that movement with the force of "manifest destiny" behind it. For years the Great Plains, that wide expanse of grassland stretching from the prairies west of the Mississippi to the foot of the Rocky Mountains, had been regarded as the "Great American Desert." Suffering great extremes of temperature, roamed by warrior tribes like the Sioux and Cheyenne, the area was considered a barrier to further expansion by many Americans. But as early as the 1820s "mountain men," trappers and hunters working for fur traders in the West, crossed the "desert" to comb the forests of the Pacific Northwest for beaver. Others penetrated the Mexican deserts of the Southwest to tie St. Louis, Missouri and Santa Fe, New Mexico together by trade. In the 1820s trails were blazed through the Rockies and the Sierra Nevada, opening the West Coast to adventurous American pioneers.

When settlers poured into Texas in the 1820s and California in the 1840s they did not find an empty land occupied only by Indians. This entire area belonged to Mexico, which had revolted against Spain and established its independence in 1821. Mexican people had lived on the land for many years. But they were few, and at first Mexican leaders felt that American immigration would help settle the area and benefit the Mexican economy. Americans like Steve Austin and Sam Houston were encouraged to bring settlers into Texas. Soon the new immigrants outnumbered the original Mexican inhabitants. The two groups did not get along well; the Americans, coming from a Protestant culture, disliked the Mexican's Roman Catholic religion, and could not understand the Mexicans' apparent indifference to the work ethic. Furthermore, they interpreted Mexican antipathy toward their institution of slavery as hostility. When Mexico tried to curb the settler's growing dominance of Texas by reasserting its authority, the "Texans" proclaimed their independence in 1836 and defeated a Mexican army sent to put down their rebellion. Nine years later the United States annexed Texas, much to Mexico's anger.

California was a different story, although here too Mexico's control was slipping. Mexican political influence in the province was so weak that an American naval captain observed: "I found a total absence of all government in California." The landed Mexican grandees, with their huge estates, were more concerned with their own affairs than with the area's government. But the American settlers were neither powerful nor numerous enough to repeat the Texas independence-annexation pattern, nor could Washington buy the province from Mexico, whose government and people were already outraged by United States annexation of Texas in 1845.

"Manifest destiny," however, would not be denied. Midwesterners had populated Oregon territory in the 1840s and wrung most of it from the British with threats to fight for the "whole of Oregon." A diplomatic compromise was reached and expansion had won another victory. Urged on by settlers' claims of California's richness and merchants' reports of the province's importance to trade, expansionists were finally able to lure the United States into war with hostile Mexico.

The conflict with Mexico was the result of "manifest destiny" sentiment and the expansionist tendencies inherent in the westward movement. It also marked the height of American expansion, as it brought California and the entire Southwest into the Union as new territories with the defeat of Mexico in 1848. "This occupation of territory by the people," proclaimed one newspaper, "is the great movement of the age."

Ironically, this opening of the West for settlement was creating as many problems as opportunities. A crisis was approaching over the issue of slavery. The Old Southwest east of the Mississippi had adopted this "peculiar institution" from Virginia and the Carolinas to produce the high-profit crop of cotton. The Old Northwest, settled by immigrants from New England, New York, and Pennsylvania, had continued to farm the same diversified crops cultivated in those states. By the 1830s the agrarian myth had split in two. The North still saw the independent frontiersman-farmer as the myth's hero and the Republic's strength. The South, on the other hand, idealized the plantation worked by slaves and preferred to support a new aristocracy. As new territory opened in the West, each section struggled to extend its ideal until finally the nation was plunged into a Civil War in 1861.

PROGRESS FOLLOWS THE FRONTIER

Even before the Civil War, changes were taking place in the "Old West" between the Appalachians and the Mississippi. Small farmers whose land barely supported their own families were being replaced by large commercial farmers who grew crops for sale on the national market. To these agriculturalists anxious for open markets, the building of roads and canals to speed their produce to buyers in the cities

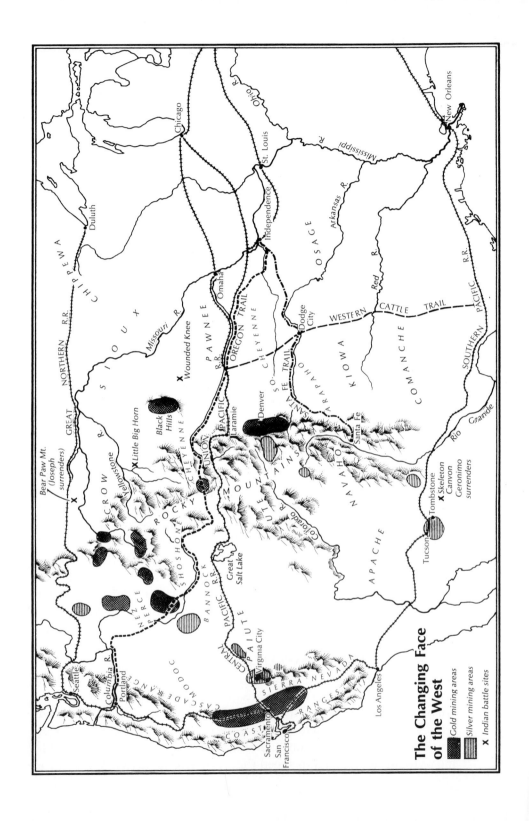

The Changing Face of the West

Gold mining areas
Silver mining areas
X Indian battle sites

New Orleans

Mississippi R.

Ohio R.

Chicago

St. Louis

Duluth

Independence

Arkansas R.

CHIPPEWA

OSAGE

Red R.

Omaha

SIOUX

PAWNEE

Missouri R.

Wounded Knee X

OREGON TRAIL

CHEYENNE

Dodge City

WESTERN CATTLE TRAIL

KIOWA

COMANCHE

SOUTHERN PACIFIC R.R.

GREAT NORTHERN R.R.

Bear Paw Mt.
(Joseph surrenders)

X

Black Hills

X Little Big Horn

Yellowstone

CROW

ROCKY

CHEYENNE

UNION

Laramie

Denver

SANTA FE TRAIL

ARAPAHO

Santa Fe

Rio Grande

NAVAHO

Skeleton Canyon
Geronimo surrenders

Tombstone X

Tucson

APACHE

Colorado R.

UTE

MOUNTAINS

Great Salt Lake

BANNOCK

SHOSHONE

NEZ PERCE

CENTRAL PACIFIC R.R.

Virginia City

PAIUTE

SIERRA NEVADA

Los Angeles

Seattle

Columbia R.

Portland

CASCADE RANGE

MODOC

COAST RANGES

Sacramento

San Francisco

and the East had become important. This commerce was creating depots like Cincinnati, Nashville, and Louisville, where gradually banks and small industries began to locate. Development of steam power was quickly followed by the rise of the steamboat in the 1820s and the railroad in the late 1830s, which further aided communication and commerce by increasing transportation's capacity for speed and mass movement of goods. What the Civil War did was to increase the demand for all types of goods and services, fueling an economic boom that was transforming the "Old West" from a rural area to an increasingly urban and industrial one.

When the War for the Union ended, the nation returned to its earlier ambition of conquering the West. Now the keynote was development, as the western lands offered enormous opportunities for private enrichment and national growth. The government encouraged these activities by its generous land policies and willingness to police the Indians. Recognizing the necessity of connecting California and the West Coast to the rest of the nation, Washington helped private interests build a transcontinental railroad that was finally completed in 1869. Following this first link, other cross-country railroads were constructed to further tie East and West, making western development easier.

Many did not wait for the railroad. Ranchers who saw the great market for beef in the East and knew that the Great Plains of Texas, Oklahoma, and Kansas offered a huge natural area for raising cattle began the range cattle industry in 1866. Stretching from the Rio Grande to the Canadian border, the "Cattle Kingdom" of the western ranchers prospered until the 1880s. Cattlemen drove their herds along the Chisholm Trail and other routes to railheads like Dodge City and Wichita, where the herds would be shipped to meat-packing centers like Chicago. The cowboy became the symbol of this effort, as he was later to become a symbol for the whole West.

That symbol included many black Americans, who were prominent in the advance of the western frontier, not only as cowboys, but as miners and homesteaders too. Heading west or anywhere "where gold is found more plenty," prospectors swarmed into any area rumored to hold rich deposits. Miners were often pathfinders who opened up new areas of the West. In their presence towns would spring up, serving whiskey or women or anything else the miners would buy, and then die as the prospectors left for newer, richer fields. When placer or surface mining gave out, companies moved in with the money and engineering skill necessary to bring the gold or silver out of its lode deep in the mountains. Silver City, Idaho, Dead-

Not all miners were solitary panners for riches like this grizzled prospector. Many used more sophisticated high-yield methods like hydraulic mining that involved crews and expensive machinery. This development gave the growing mining corporations of the West an advantage that spelled the end of the grubstaking forty-niner.

wood in the Black Hills of Dakota, and Denver, Colorado all grew up around mining areas. Those towns that did not die became magnets for homesteaders and western supply centers, "boosted" by businessmen and speculators determined to make "their" towns successful. Newspaper advertisements and propaganda campaigns to attract capital appeared, and enterprising businesses were launched. Six territories were added to the Union as a result of the mining frontier. "Go West, young man," urged one editor, for a man could make his fortune and be part of a great national movement for progress.

THE WILD, WILD WEST

For nearly four decades, this wide-open, speculative, go-for-broke atmosphere and attitude dominated the Far West. Life was hard, boisterous, risky, and frequently short in the mining towns and cow-towns throughout the frontier. Because there was little law and less government, violence was a part of living. As a young man Mark Twain had traveled west as secretary to his brother and later as a newspaperman. He recorded that to "be a saloon-keeper and to kill a man was to be illustrious," and that during one day in Virginia City, Nevada a "woman was killed by a pistol shot, a man was brained with a sling shot," and another was "disposed of permanently." In towns like Dodge City, Kansas, shootouts over stolen horses, card-cheating, and women were common, not to mention occasional sprees by drunken cowboys to "scare up" the townspeople.

Whatever local law there was took care of the more "important" crimes like bank holdups and train robberies, but until sheriffs could be elected or United States marshals brought in, most violence was met by more violence. Out in open territory justice was swift and usually dealt by the criminal's peers. Claimjumpers were shot by fellow miners and rustlers or horse thieves hanged by fellow cowboys. Townspeople joined vigilante groups, which served as judge and jury, often holding public hangings for sport and as a "warning to offenders." "Law and Order" was a favorite theme of western towns that were just being established and seeking "respectability." But the most outstanding example of violence in the West was the destruction of the last free American Indians, the Plains tribes.

"I WILL FIGHT NO MORE FOREVER"

The mounted, painted, buffalo-chasing, hard-fighting Plains Indians have become the "typical" American Indian of screen and novel. Ironically, their culture was affected by European influences more than any other group of tribes. Their late-flowering culture was made possible by the introduction of horses from the Spanish Southwest and guns from European and American traders. Even the beads on their colorful garb were imported. But in some ways the stereotype is justified, for the Plains Indian culture was both an amalgamation of many other Indian societies and an intensification of many of their traits: elaborate codes of combat and an emphasis on war, a strong religion based on rites and sacred objects, and an almost obsessive love of land and the free, migrant life. When this culture clashed with American settlers moving westward, the result was its destruction in the last Indian wars of the West.

As early as the 1830s, white trappers and hunters had penetrated deep into the lands west of the Mississippi. Uninterested in settlement themselves and bearing weapons, trinkets, and other commodities, the mountain men were generally welcomed by the Indians. Even when wagon trains of settlers bound for California and Oregon began to enter their lands, the Plains Indians were still more concerned with their own wars of Cheyenne against Comanche, and Sioux against Crow. The wagon trains were allowed to pass through. These intertribal conflicts were, however, a threat to Yankee commerce and dangerous to the wagonloads of settlers. In 1851 a United States Indian agent held a great council composed of about 12,000 Indians from most of the major tribes and all agreed on a general peace. The Indians were to stay within tribal areas and be considerate of the covered wagons, while the American government promised to keep its people under control.

That promise proved impossible to keep. During the late 1860s pioneers began to swarm into Indian territory. Petty arguments over a cow or a horse became small wars that engulfed others who had nothing to do with the original disagreement. Indians who watched prospectors following the scent of precious metals considered them as people gone insane. But where gold strikes were made, communities appeared. Land-hungry settlers and speculators filled the towns, and the buffalo began disappearing as the "Iron Horse" encroached on the Indian's hunting grounds. The Cheyenne and the Sioux, the Comanche and the Kiowa, would not give up those grounds without a fight.

There followed a vicious cycle of war and bloodshed. As Indian territory was invaded by white settlers, warriors fought to protect their homeland. It is ironic that the soldiers sent by the Great White Father in Washington to defeat the Indians included large numbers of black Americans. Then treaties were made that established new Indian reservations away from mushrooming white settlements, only to subject the tribesmen to further intrusion by a new wave of immigrants and another war. Wrote the most experienced of western Indian-fighters, "Greed and avarice on the part of whites . . . is at the bottom of nine-tenths of all our Indian troubles." The wars reached a climax in the 1870s when Lieutenant Colonel Custer's entire detachment of 265 cavalrymen was wiped out by Sioux led by Chiefs Sitting Bull and Crazy Horse. Americans were enraged and humiliated by the defeat, and Washington put forth a concerted effort that by 1880 utterly defeated the remaining Plains Indians. In 1890 an emotional religious revival that called upon the ghosts of dead warriors to help the living—the Ghost Dance—swept through many reservations. White hysteria led to the massacre of 200 Ghost Dancers at Wounded Knee in South Dakota (see Chapter 8, pp. 245–246 for details), and the movement died with the dancers.

In the Southwest, essentially the same round of events occurred. By 1890 the Kiowa, Comanche, Navaho, and Apache had all been killed or corralled onto reservations. None of the tribes, North or South, was treated properly on these Indian preserves. The Bureau of Indian

Affairs, despite the efforts of some well-meaning agents on the scene, was filled with corruption and hampered by red tape. Profiteers sold rotten beef or thin blankets to the Bureau for distribution to the Indians. Forced onto barren areas, decimated by whiskey, disease, and hunger, the tribes wasted away. Reformers like Helen Hunt Jackson, in her book *A Century of Dishonor*, (1881), protested the Indian's plight. In the 1880s Congress began passing a series of laws designed to eliminate tribal organization and bring Native Americans into white society as individuals, ostensibly for their own benefit. But the individual land allotments carved out of reservation lands were too small to support families. Moreover, the Indian knew nothing of modern, mechanized farming, and while he could sell his parcel of land, only a white man could buy it. In this way Indians were *legally* dispossessed of nearly 100 million acres of former reservation lands by the 1930s. Finally, this legislation contributed to the destruction of Indian culture by breaking down tribal customs and responsibilities that had governed the people's lives for centuries. The charge has been made that today the reservations are still areas of stark poverty and confusion.

Perhaps the plight of the Indians is best represented by Chief Joseph and his Nez Perces. After keeping a precarious peace with Americans for years, white encroachments and treaty violations forced Joseph to leave the reservation and try to lead his tribe to Canada. Tracing his way northward, he was hounded by three U.S. army groups sent to bring the Nez Perces back. Finally, brought to bay 30 miles from the Canadian border, he came to the army camp to surrender. "My people ask me for food, and I have none to give. It is cold, and we have no blankets, no wood. I have fought, but from where the sun now stands, I shall fight no more forever." Remarked the lieutenant who recorded the surrender, "I think that, in his long career, Joseph cannot accuse the Government of the United States of one single act of justice. . . ."

"OUR BROTHERS WHO WERE SOLD"

Another people found themselves becoming a persecuted minority in their own land. Spanish-speaking communities began to dot the Southwest during the 1760s. The half-century that followed witnessed an energetic planting of missions, presidios, and pueblos, before Spain relinquished her northern provinces to the revolutionary government of her former colony, Mexico, in 1823. For more than

four decades, the Mexicans ruled the Southwest, a region characterized by the Spanish priests' chain of missions, a system of large
ranchos worked by Indian laborers, and a generally sparse population spread across an immense expanse of land. As a result of the war
with Mexico in 1848, however, the American government obtained
the vast territory that later was carved into the states of Nevada,
Utah, California, Arizona, New Mexico, and a portion of Colorado.
Those Mexicans who chose to become American citizens were
guaranteed by the Treaty of Guadalupe-Hidalgo "the enjoyment of
their liberty and property." Although the final version of the treaty
deleted an earlier explicit safeguard of Mexican land titles (Article X),
American officials implied that their government would continue to
respect fully the newly enfranchised Mexican-Americans' rights of
language, religion, and property. Subsequent events were to prove,
however, that the spirit of the treaty signators would not be upheld.
Because the law itself was imprecise from a strictly legal point of
view, opportunists soon learned to circumvent the safeguards designed to protect the Mexicans.

The discovery of gold in California provides an excellent example
of the gradual betrayal of the intent of the Treaty of Guadalupe-
Hidalgo. After a century of slow population growth, California experienced in 1849 a great influx of people. More newcomers came
each day than had come in the previous decade. By 1852 these immigrants numbered almost a quarter-million, most of whom were of
non-Hispanic ethnic background. The original Californians, with
their Spanish-Mexican heritage, now found themselves a submerged
fraction of people, surrounded by 10 to 15 times as many strangers.
Although these "Californios" pointed proudly to their Spanish heritage, they were considered, according to one western newspaper,
"aboriginal Indians, and they must share the destiny of their race."
Like the Indians, the Californios were "in the way" of the Forty-
niners, and like the Indians, they were first defeated in war and then
deprived of many of their rights legally and extralegally.

Although many of the native Californians had pioneered in the
Gold Rush bonanza of 1848, it did not take long for their Yankee
cousins to take steps to restrict their activities. When the first legislature of the new state convened to meet, the state assembly asked
Congress to prohibit all persons of foreign birth from the mines, including any naturalized citizens. Such discrimination was echoed in
posters that appeared in mining towns, declaring that "foreigners"
must leave the mines immediately. At Hangtown 100 Gringos

claimed that the entire riverbed belonged exclusively to Americans who would "tolerate no foreigners." Vigilante groups were organized to deal swiftly with those who refused to comply. Whipping, branding, ear cropping, banishment, and hanging were commonly employed to impress upon the "Greasers" that they were no longer welcome. "To shoot these Greasers ain't the best way," one lyncher asserted. "Give 'em a fair jury trial, and rope 'em up with all the majesty of the law. That's the cure."

The fury of the Forty-niners cut a wide swath, but many of these efforts against Mexican-Americans were pursued through legal channels. The Treaty of 1848, for example, contained the implication that the citizens of the newly acquired territory of the Southwest would enjoy bicultural status, including equality in the use of language. Bilingual education was the hope of many Mexican-Americans, in order to promote the recognition of Spanish as one of the two official languages. As early as 1855, however, the state Bureau of Public Instruction declared that the schools must teach solely in the English language. This effort by the nativists was accompanied by another legislative act that suspended the publication of state laws in Spanish.

The rights of the Mexican-Americans to their ancient land claims were disregarded just as clearly as the language issue. In 1851 a senator proposed that all existing land titles should be carefully examined for any evidence of fraud or legal technicalities. The proposal easily passed the nativist-dominated legislature. To contest this law, the Mexican-Americans were forced into costly court litigation, and for those who chose to fight, it was often necessary to divide, sell, or give away parcels of land in order to pay lawyers' fees. The result was that by the mid-1850s landownership had drastically changed. Through the efforts of the legislature, the legal profession, financial manipulation, and outright force, Yankees had acquired huge tracts of land. Increasingly bitter, many Californios began to complain that they had been betrayed by the vague terms of the Treaty of Guadalupe-Hidalgo, and many people in Mexico berated their own government for "Our brothers who were sold."

The position of Mexicans in the Southwest did not improve in the latter part of the nineteenth century. The completion of the transcontinental railroads brought an even larger number of Yankees westward. A great "land boom" during the 1880s stimulated Anglo migration to California and greatly accelerated the process of "Americanization." In two years or so Los Angeles' census soared 500 percent, making the Anglos an overwhelming majority of the population. The exploitation of Spanish-speaking people in the Southwest was seen clearly by the turn of the century. It has been estimated that the number of Mexicans entering the United States between 1900 and 1920 in search of opportunity was equivalent to one-tenth of the entire population of Mexico. Most of these people, however, lived and worked at the edge of poverty. And yet, this persistent discrimination did not deter immigration into former Mexican territories now part of the United States. With depressed economic conditions at home, Mexicans responded to opportunities for work in such rising industries as railroad construction, mining, cotton and produce farming, and cattle and sheep raising. Had it not been for this source of cheap labor, the economic development of the Southwest would not have occurred as rapidly and dramatically as it did. Indeed, the Mexican contribution has been stamped permanently on the flavor of the West. From the Mexican *vaquero*, for example, came the American cowboy, with his Spanish horned-saddle, lariat, "chaps" or *chaparejos*, and similar gear used by horsemen even today.

Ironically, at the same time that Spanish-speaking people were

The Mexican *vaquero* herded large numbers of cattle in the Southwest long before the American cowboy appeared. The above illustration demonstrates that the methods and equipment popularly associated with the cowboy appeared earlier on the Mexican rancheros.

being largely disregarded, the "rediscovery" of the West's "Spanish past" began. The Anglos began to recreate in yearly celebrations or *fiestas* the glories of the "Spanish period," accompanied by a revival of architectural forms and a glorification of the Catholic missions. This vogue was subject to numerous distortions, minimizing the important Mexican influence and giving a romantic luster to the "Old Spanish Days." This cult enjoyed such popularity that the mistreatment of the Californios only a few decades earlier was conveniently forgotten. Nor were these mythmakers aware that there were still thousands of Spanish-speaking people in their midst. As one scholar has pointed out, "For only after they had reduced the real-life Spanish-speaking to the status of a foreign minority did the Yankees feel any deep compassion toward Spanish-American culture."

GARDEN OF THE WORLD

As the Indians were being forced onto reservations and Mexican-Americans were being made a minority on their own soil, farmers began the trek into the trans-Mississippi West. They followed trails that mountain men and other pioneers had made before them, settling down wherever they could find fertile land. In some areas ranchers and miners had preceded them; in others they were the first white settlers to see the land. Before the Civil War many had traversed the Oregon Trail and the Old Spanish Trail into Oregon and California, but most of the territory between Omaha and the Pacific Coast had never been touched by the plow.

Several factors were to change that, factors that created such a land rush that within a generation after the Civil War most of the western lands were settled. The most important cause of this agrarian westward movement was the appetite for land. Newly arrived immigrants, farmers whose lands had become unproductive or were too small to support their families, men (especially Southerners) uprooted by the war, and others who simply wanted to be more prosperous, all saw the West and its vast stretches of fertile soil as a land of opportunity. The catalyst that made this land accessible and set these people on the roads leading west was the Homestead Act of 1862. Sought by western leaders for years, the Homestead Act made it possible for a settler to own government land on the frontier merely by living on it for five years and making certain improvements. This incentive encouraged many to ignore old reports that described the prairies and the Great Plains as "dry and lifeless deserts," and those who settled there often found prairie soil as fertile as the meadows of Ohio. Western railroads also drew farmers out to the frontier by providing transportation and loudly advertising the West's opportunities, hoping in return to sell some of their own lands and promote business along the tracks.

Within about 20 years nearly all of the good western land was occupied and under cultivation. Many of the farmers were poor, their livestock and crops sufficient to eke out a fair living but little more. Moreover, the harsh conditions of the Plains forced farmers to develop advanced methods of raising crops and livestock. A western agrarian empire began to rise, supported by the more industrialized eastern area of the country that provided a market and a source of advanced farming implements like tractors and threshers. The United States was becoming the world's greatest exporter of farm commodities.

In the years following the Civil War, politicians and newspapermen began referring to the United States as a whole and the American West in particular as the "Garden of the World." This combination of the old agrarian myth, a belief in progress, and the concept of an American mission to lead the rest of the world, proclaimed that the nation's "boundless resources" would make it the world's benefactor

The cowboy has become a legend of the West. Despite the romance popularly attributed to his life, driving huge herds of cattle over a thousand miles to market was a demanding, dirty job that was not at all glamorous. It is not widely known that of the approximate 40,000 trailhands, 5000 of them were black-skinned. As the railroad took over the cowboy's role of moving cattle over long distances, white and black cowpunchers sought new jobs—whites in rodeos and on dude ranches, and blacks as Pullman porters on the new railroads.

Because both the railroad and the buffalo preferred gentle terrain, a clash between the Iron Horse and the shaggy beasts was inevitable. Roaming herds of buffalo, once estimated at some 15 million, were decimated by the hunters and settlers brought by the railroad.

and example. Echoing Jefferson at the beginning of the century, farmers were once again hailed as the country's pride and strength. But even as this utopia was being cheered it was being destroyed by that other arm of progress, the Industrial Revolution. With the help of machines, large-scale commercial agriculture was replacing the farms of the "sturdy yeoman." Wall Street financiers and railroad monopolists were gaining control of the farmers' very life by controlling loans and manipulating freight rates for his crops. Washington was favoring city over country, businessmen over farmers. The farmer became disillusioned with this gap between rhetoric and reality, and many joined the Populists' cries for reform after the depression of the early 1890s.

THE FRONTIER HYPOTHESIS

The year 1890 also saw a report by the United States Census that the West was so dotted with areas of settlement that there was no longer a continuous frontier line. Three years later, a young historian named Frederick Jackson Turner declared that "The existence of an area of free land, its continuous recession, and the advance of American settlement westward, explain American development." In short, Turner was saying that the nation's democratic institutions and the American character itself had been molded by the country's constant contact with and conquest of the West.

"Not the Constitution," he insisted, "but free land and an abundance of natural resources open to a fit people, made the democratic type of society in America." Because men had to depend upon themselves to succeed and not upon the privileges of class, contact with the frontier promoted individualism and egalitarianism. Given these two characteristics and the need for community cooperation against the hostile wilderness, democracy developed. The necessity of adapting to new ways that could cope with the frontier environment made Europeans into Americans. It also put a premium on material success and practicality. Free western land, Turner believed, acted as a "safety valve" for the poor and oppressed by offering them a place to escape to. Because there was an abundance of natural resources and land in the West, those who moved there could improve their own situation and rise in society. So many did move that Americans became a nation of travelers, as most visitors to the United States immediately noticed. The influence of the West and the frontier on Americans, Turner concluded, has been deep.

This "frontier hypothesis" has had a great impact on the study of American history. Today, most historians would say that Turner attributed too much to the influence of the frontier. They would point

It has been suggested that the American quest in outer space represents a new frontier to be explored and conquered. Indeed, it was President Kennedy's "New Frontier" program that set the goal of America's landing on the moon before 1970. Exploring this "frontier" requires, however, technological know-how and vast government subsidies that were scarcely necessary on the self-sufficient frontier of Daniel Boone.

out that American democracy also had its origins in certain traditional forms and laws brought over from England. Moreover, they
suggest that the frontier did not really act as a "safety valve" because, statistically, few of the poor and oppressed were able to take
advantage of the opportunity to head West. Mobility, some argue, is
more the result of good transportation and communication than a
by-product of the westward movement. Others feel that Turner did
not put enough emphasis on how much American development was
due to cultural baggage brought over by immigrants. They also point
out that Turner ignored one of the more negative influences of the
frontier—violence. Many historians believe that the American pen-
chant for violence (the United States has the highest crime rate in the
world) can be attributed to the unruly, brutal climate that dominated
the development of the West.

But even among Turner's critics there is general agreement that
the frontier's influence was extensive and of major importance. All of
the characteristics that Turner attributes to the result of interaction
with the West are at least partially the outcome of 250 years of contact with a frontier. When that frontier ended in 1890, profound
changes were bound to occur.

SUGGESTIONS FOR ADDITIONAL READING

Henry Nash Smith, *Virgin Land: The American West as Symbol and Myth*,
(1957). A study of the social and literary forces that have molded the image
of the American West.

Philip Durham and Everett L. Jones, *The Negro Cowboys*, (1965). An examination of the little-known contributions of blacks to the development of the
American West.

Bernard de Voto, *The Year of Decision, 1846*, (1943). A colorful account link-
ing American expansion westward, especially the Oregon issue, with
far-flung activities along the frontier.

William Brandon, *The American Heritage Book of Indians*, (1961). A dramatic,
general work on the cultures of the Indians in the Western Hemisphere,
and their effect on the conquering European and American peoples.

W.S. Greever, *The Bonanza West*, (1963). An excellent account of the western
mining frontier.

Lewis Atherton, *The Cattle Kings*, (1961). A study of the dominant years of the
cattle barons and the influence of the industry on western development.

Thomas Sanchez, *Rabbit Boss*, (1974). A novel that illustrates the culture
conflict between Indians and whites by voicing the Indian's vision of the
invader as a waster, "earth tourist," and thief.

CHAPTER FOUR

A CHANGING SCENE: SOCIAL AND CULTURAL RESPONSE TO THE INDUSTRIAL REVOLUTION

1874
Grange organized by farmers concerned over their low standard of living.

1885
United States becomes world's leading industrial power.

1886
American Federation of Labor formed; first successful national labor union.

1890
Sherman Anti-Trust Act passed to make big business more socially responsible.

1894
Pullman Strike threatens nationwide railroad paralysis before federal troops intervene to restore order.

1905–10
Peak years of immigration into the United States: over 500,000 annually.

THE PRICE OF POWER

The industrial revolution that swept the United States in the last three decades of the nineteenth century made America the wealthiest nation and the prime industrial power in the world. It literally changed the face of the nation as well. Urban life began to supplant rural life with the growth of new and bigger cities around centers of production and transportation. Attracted by job opportunities and an "exciting life," millions of Europeans left the Old World to come to America while thousands of farmers seeking the same things abandoned their country homes for the bustling city. The force that dominated these decades was change—constant change that brought new ideas, products, issues, conflicts, and new faces to life in America. Things seemed in perpetual motion.

This process put an enormous strain on American society. One observer of the scene felt that "new power"—power of machines, money and man's own organizations, but especially the power of change itself—was causing society to "disintegrate." The pace of industrialization and urbanization, though cheered and considered by many Americans as an indication of "progress," created at the same time much confusion, anxiety, and frustration. Old and cherished values, customs, and beliefs were being challenged, if not overwhelmed. During this period of American development problems surfaced that still face the country today—inner-city ghettos, crime in the streets, widespread corruption on all levels of government, and especially the conflict between business' freedom of development and the public welfare. To understand the scope of these changes and issues, it is necessary to acquire a feel for "village America."

VILLAGE AMERICA

America before the industrial revolution was a nation of village communities in a rural setting. Even in the country's few big towns life had a village flavor, with neighborhoods forming units that acted as though they were separate unto themselves. The expense and time required for travel combined with the poor state of roads made communication between communities difficult. This restricted interaction and dispersed political power over public policy. In fact, democracy was practically equated with local self-government. The people who lived in these communities shared common values and ethnic backgrounds, and they firmly believed that they could regulate their own lives as they chose. Although these villages and even

The lad in the foreground may not have grasped the significance of the railroad winding through his village community. As early as the 1850s the revolution in transportation wrought by the railroads was altering the face of rural America.

the farming countryside around them did rely on the outside world, they retained a sense of self-sufficiency.

This illusion was fostered by the slow pace of life in the village communities. Since farming was still the chief occupation, life revolved around the seasons. Change came at a slow, manageable speed. Nor did it seriously affect these communities' homogeneous makeup. Nearly everyone adhered to the Protestant ethic of modesty, morality, thrift, sobriety, and hard work. The prosperous were separated from the less well-to-do by fine gradations of status such as how well their home was decorated or how often the women of the house had fashionable new dresses to wear. With the exception of the doomed planter aristocracy of the South, none of these communities were typified by great differences in personal wealth among its members. Even in the cities, the elite of wealth and family usually congregated together in their own section of town to be among "equals."

Being uniform and somewhat self-contained, society in these communities was personal. Business transactions were made between people who knew each other as neighbors. A farmer temporarily in trouble because of a bad crop could go to the local bank and count on his reputation as a dependable and honest man to aid him in getting credit or a loan extension. Buying and selling may have been inefficient and even expensive, but it was on a personal level that gave people a sense of belonging. Politics reflected this same tendency. Whether a person was a Republican or a Democrat often determined his circle of friends and his enemies. Politics was in fact a national avocation, the justification for picnics, rallies, and social busy work. Yet national and state affairs were of only slight interest in themselves. Partisanship was local, identified with local interests and local problems.

"Local" might be the best description of village America. Believing themselves self-contained, secure in their homogeneous character, and insulated by the slow pace of life, these communities faced the future confident that it would not bring anything they could not handle. But the very progress that they sought to achieve was already beginning to change the nature of American society and to undermine their control over it.

THE FIRST SURGE

The first indications of change were the developments in transportation during the early 1800s. To make westward travel and communication easier several turnpikes were constructed connecting eastern centers with growing frontier communities. A boom in canal building began after the Erie Canal, connecting the Hudson River and Lake Erie, proved to be a great financial success. Along with the canal craze came the development of the steamboat. Soon these coal and woodburning craft were making regular runs up and down the Mississippi and Ohio Rivers, navigating the Great Lakes, and becoming larger carriers of goods and passengers than the canals. At the same time the American merchant marine was expanding the nation's markets abroad with the aid of the graceful clipper ship, and by the 1850s America could boast of the world's largest commercial fleet.

Last and most significant of the developments in transportation was the railroad. An invention imported from England, the steam-driven locomotive pulling a string of cars along steel rails quickly became a common sight in the United States. By 1840, only 13 years after the first railroad was built in Massachusetts, railroad mileage nearly equaled canal mileage. When Congress began to give grants of land to states to encourage construction, a boom occurred that made

30,626 miles operational by 1860. The railroad was the last link in the nationwide system of transportation that bound the country closer together. In 1816 it took 103 hours to make the journey from Philadelphia to Quebec by steamboat and stage; by 1860 the same trip took only 31 hours by railroad. The "iron horse" also expanded the horizons of businesses looking for new markets and encouraged foreign investment in American economic development.

This development continued despite the business cycles of boom and depression that plagued businesses in the United States from the 1820s to the 1850s. Westward expansion increased the material resources of the nation and provided new opportunities for growth. The discovery of gold in California added to the country's financial resources. An even more important financial factor was foreign investments, chiefly in railroads, which by the 1850s had grown to $381 million. Attracted by what seemed to be dazzling opportunities, Germans fleeing the Revolution of 1848 flooded into America as did Irish escaping a potato famine in their country. Joined by numerous Scandinavians, these groups swelled the tide of immigration into the United States. Growing manufacturing and industrial concerns benefited from this influx of labor. Production increases from the textile factories and from iron industries strengthened the economy. By 1860 America ranked second behind Great Britain in world value of manufactures. Nor did agriculture lag behind—production of cotton and foodstuffs increased even more dramatically than manufactured goods.

With the spreading idea that economic progress was good for the nation, the leadership of enterprising men willing to invest and take a risk, and the encouragement of government, the American economy began to experience an accelerated growth or "takeoff" that prepared the way for an industrial revolution of awesome proportions.

INDUSTRIAL TRANSFORMATION

That industrial revolution made the United States the world's leading manufacturing nation by 1885. The takeoff begun before the Civil War was boosted even further during the war years. Huge expenditures aided many businesses and the Republican administration in Washington passed legislation favorable to northern industrial and manufacturing interests. Inventions like the Bessemer process for refining steel became of fundamental importance to emerging industry, so much so that one English observer remarked that "the number of labour-saving appliances in use for almost everything is perfectly astounding." European investment continued to be important and the sale of agricultural products abroad provided even more foreign capital for development. As the immense resources of the West were discovered, they too spurred the accelerating growth of industry. Railroads connecting the east and west coasts and spreading into every corner of the land opened new markets and new sources of raw materials at the same time. Immigrants became both workers and customers to serve the expanding economy. Most Americans proudly hailed this industrial transformation, and great emphasis was put on the statistics of growth.

These statistics were impressive, if not staggering. Even though the value of agricultural produce tripled between 1860 and 1900, the value of industrial goods surpassed it by 1890, growing to eight times the 1860 figure. Between 1880 and 1900 the gross national product doubled to more than $37 billion. During the same period steel production multiplied over 100 times. The nation's railroad network made transportation so cheap that one businessman maintained that "a ton of goods can now be carried on the best-managed railroad for a distance of a mile, for a sum so small that outside of China it would be difficult to find a coin of equivalent value to give a boy as a reward for carrying an ounce package across a street."

The single group of men most responsible for these statistics were the entrepreneurs. Men like Andrew Carnegie, John D. Rockefeller, and J. P. Morgan built up great business empires (and equally huge personal fortunes) that transformed the American economy. Studies of these men have shown that they were generally native born of middle-class parents, bred in an atmosphere where business and relatively high social standing were closely associated with family life, and the recipients of a college education. Protestants by faith, they were highly competitive and self-confident, with a passion for their work. Rockefeller was so attentive to detail that he once revised the number of drops of solder used to seal oil drums to save money by eliminating one drop. J. J. Hill, the railroad magnate, left his private train one bitterly cold Minnesota evening to help his men shovel snow off the tracks. These men were in business for more than profits—they also sought challenge and adventure in what one of them called "The Great Game." They played "the game" by their own rules and were not above using bribery, political corruption, and vicious price wars to win regardless of the human or social cost.

"Cut-throat" competition like this meant dizzying changes in prices, costs, and profits that added to the instability that was natural in a dynamic economy. The business cycle took unpredictable turns, and 14 of the 25 years after 1873 were years of recession. Trying to smooth the economic ups and downs into a more steady (and more profitable) pattern of growth, the entrepreneurs moved to consolidate related industries into larger productive units known as *trusts* that could control the market for a product by monopolizing it. Standard Oil managed to corner 90 percent of American oil production before the turn of the century. Another trust, United States Steel, controlled 60 percent of all the steel and iron made in the nation when it was formed in 1901. Perhaps the most important and strongest trust was the House of Morgan, named after its director J. P. Morgan, which had access to millions of dollars for financial investment. Morgan's financial power and expertise were such that in 1893 President Cleveland appealed to him to protect the financial standing of the American government, which he did, making a tidy profit as a result of the transaction.

The economic power of these industrial and financial combinations allowed them to dominate the American economy. Although these economic developments reduced the cost of living and made more and cheaper goods available to the public, it also created an enormously rich elite. One such family, the Vanderbilts, had a mansion that required a staff of 30 servants. Most Americans rented a home and furnished it for less than the cost of a half-dozen of the Vanderbilt's imported salad plates. To complaints that this huge gap between the wealthy and the rest of society was unjust, John D. Rockefeller replied, "they have but to master the knack of economy, thrift, and perseverance, and success is theirs."

THE GOSPEL OF WEALTH

Rockefeller was not being cynical; he was merely voicing the tenets of a philosophy that was widely accepted in his day. Based on the rock of the Protestant ethic, this *gospel of wealth* simply stated that the rich were rich because they were more righteous than their fellow men. Opportunity was all around—one Baptist minister insisted that America was covered with "acres of diamonds" and that by "right thinking and right living" the secrets of wealth would be revealed. An Episcopal bishop wrote that "in the long run, it is only to the man of morality that wealth comes" and, bluntly, that "Godliness is in league with riches." Andrew Carnegie, poor immigrant turned millionaire, was one of the foremost advocates of the "gospel of wealth." But he maintained that responsibility went with fortune, and that the rich man should act as society's steward to return surplus money for the cause of the improvement of humanity. Only stewardship justified the acquisition of wealth. Carnegie practiced what he preached, building libraries and hospitals and supporting colleges across the nation. He was, however, more the exception than the rule. Most preferred the less sacrificing notion that since they made the money, it was theirs to spend as they chose. And they chose to spend it on themselves.

To people who required a more scientific explanation for the gap between rich and poor, apologists offered the natural law of "survival of the fittest" as adapted to fit the American social scene. The "fittest" were, of course, those entrepreneurs who had survived and prospered in economic competition. Yale professor William Graham Sumner and English economist Herbert Spencer applied the biological theories of Darwin to social and economic questions and popularized *Social Darwinism* in the United States. Concluding that economic competition was society's evolutionary test, these scholars maintained that those who succeeded were America's "fittest" and that their "natural selection" benefited both the nation and the race. To tamper with this "natural" state of affairs, Sumner warned, was "the greatest folly of which a man can be capable." The poor had simply lost the race. Government and society must allow evolution to right any existing injustices. "Perhaps," sighed one Darwinian, "in four or five thousand years evolution may have carried man beyond this state of things."

If most Americans accepted these arguments and "this state of things" it was because they expected or hoped to succeed and become one of the "fittest." Such emphasis was placed on financial and social achievement that philosopher William James announced the introduction of a new deity—"the bitch-goddess success." Handbooks on "How to Succeed" in all types of endeavors sold more copies than any other book except the Bible. Nearly as popular were the novels of Horatio Alger, whose young hero always managed to go from "rags to riches" with a combination of "pluck and luck" in books with titles like *Struggling Upward*.

All of these comments on the justice, or at least the righteousness, of the capitalist system as it was operating in America encouraged Americans to believe that with the right combination of morality and hard work they too could become Rockefellers or Carnegies. Actually, upward mobility at the time was limited mainly to moderate property accumulation. Moving up on the social scale was more difficult and far less common. Some Americans declined to accept the precepts of the gospel of wealth or of Social Darwinism. A California newspaperman named Henry George insisted that the "contrast between the House of Have and the House of Want" was unjust. He proposed a single tax on any increase in land value that was not a direct result of the owner's effort, thus returning to society what society as a whole was responsible for—the value of land. Another dissenter, Edward Bellamy, wrote a bestseller entitled *Looking Backward* about a socialist utopia tempered by humanitarianism and world peace. Though both George and Bellamy attracted a devoted following in the eastern United States, they were not as well in touch with the national temper as was Alger. For Alger told a people obsessed by the pursuit of success what they wanted to hear—that they could all be rich.

GROWTH OF THE CITY—THE URBAN FRONTIER

Industrialization wrought even deeper changes than providing more goods more cheaply and elevating a new social and financial elite to the top of American society. It also changed the basic scene of American life from a rural setting to an urban one. This switch had been made possible by advanced agricultural technology, which in the 1870s and 1880s allowed farms to produce enough to release most of the population from the necessity of growing their own food. Urbanization was also greatly aided by the railroad, which supplied the expanding city with the enormous amount of food and goods that it required.

Economic opportunity was what drew people to the cities. Older centers like New York and Baltimore with capital and labor already plentiful and with good railroad connections quickly became huge manufacturing centers for growing businesses. Newer cities like Denver or Chicago grew up around western industries like mining or meat packing that drew job-hungry Americans like a magnet. Chicago's development was typical of the process of urbanization throughout the country. When that city became an important rail center and marketplace in the 1870s, its population tripled in a decade. By the 1890s Chicago had become a major industrial town and the focus of many railroad networks, and its population had soared to over a million. One disgusted writer recorded that the making of money was Chicago's "genesis, its growth, its end and its object," and that everyone who came to the city came "for the common avowed object of making money."

The enormous influx of people that allowed cities like Seattle and Los Angeles to double their population and other cities like Denver and Dallas to quadruple theirs meant that growth was often haphazard and unplanned. New dwellings and industries mushroomed nearly overnight, faster than cities could take care of them. People in Philadelphia threw sink and slop water out onto gutters and sidewalks. Manufacturing wastes and sewer water were emptied into the Delaware River, where Philadelphia got much of its drinking water. Horse dung attracted swarms of flies to the city streets, especially in western towns where the horse remained the chief mode of transportation even into the twentieth century. Most streets consisted of dust or mud, depending on the weather. New Orleans had only 100 of its 500 miles of streets paved (with brick), and asphalt only came into use later with the introduction of the bicycle and automobile. There was little or no planning for open spaces. New York's Central Park, built in the 1850s, was a notable exception, but many cities used more land for cemeteries than for parks. Tenement dwellings sprang up to house workers in areas close to the factories, many of which had eight or more occupants crammed into one small apartment. The living room often served as the kitchen and even the bedroom for boarders, and the narrow alleys and streets served as recreation areas. One English visitor asserted that American cities were bland imitations of each other, differing "from one another only in that some of them are built more with brick than with wood, and others more with wood than brick."

Desperate city managers tried to ease some of these conditions and restore needed services to their residents. New York City created a board to deal with epidemics. From 1880 to the 1890s the number of public water works serving American cities increased five times. Various wonders were invented to improve city transportation: San Francisco's cable car, New York's elevated railroad, Richmond's trolley car, and Boston's subway. These developments enabled many of the urban well-to-do to leave the grim central city area for new suburbs in the countryside. Frequently, urban expansion would swallow these suburbs and new ones would spring up further beyond the city limits. In this manner cities slowly began to spread across the countryside. The only alternative was building up—Chicago built the first skyscraper in 1884.

Great social changes as well as physical changes were taking place in the city. For those who had left rural communities and come to the city, life was transformed. They were thrown together with a conglomeration of people with diverse origins, interests, and occupations. Complained one transplanted farmer, "there is no sense of common earth, a common fortune and a common fate." Thrown together with so many people, there was little privacy. Yet the bewildering array of differences and everyone's tendency to mind his own concerns made life impersonal. "In the city there is no sense of neighborhood," observed one clergyman. "You may be separated from your next neighbor by only a few inches and yet for years never see his face or learn his name." The poor families of unskilled or out-of-work laborers crowded into inner-city slums. A social worker in New York wrote concerning one family: "The man, his wife, and three small children shivering in one room through the roof of which the pitiless winds of winter whistled. The room was almost barren of furniture; the parents slept on the floor, the elder children in boxes, and the baby was swung in an old shawl attached to the rafters." Prostitution, crime, drunkenness, and gambling were widespread. The very pace of city life, with its constant change and emphasis on competition broke down the traditional social institutions of religion and family and made for anxious, insecure, and lonely living.

The churches were the first to recognize that these problems "threatened our Christian civilization." Religion wilted in the city as many workingmen left the church. When asked why he didn't attend services, a laborer said "the rich folks build their churches for themselves and they keep them for themselves, and I ain't never going to interfere with that arrangement." Sundays were fundays for workers, as religion seemed irrelevant to their lives. Aroused ministers and laymen alike urged their congregations to begin to meet the problems of poverty, crime, disease, and loss of personal worth that were "massed in the city." During the 1880s some clergymen began to challenge the Social Darwinists and the gospel of wealth with their own *social gospel*. Commented one minister wryly, "Jesus Christ knew a great deal more about organizing society than David Ricardo [an economist] ever dreamed of knowing. . . ." Groups like the Salvation Army, imported from England, began moving into the inner city to meet its people's physical needs as well as to preach Christianity. By

As the pace of industrialization continued in Gilded Age America, the gap between deep poverty and great wealth widened. The living conditions of immigrant tenement dwellers and the great entrepreneurs in New York City reflects this development at the turn of the century.

the turn of the century many churches were emphasizing that Christian ethics be applied to society and that Christians become active in social work and reform. But despite the efforts of Catholic and Protestant churches to meet urban problems, one group in particular continued to bear the brunt of inner-city life almost unaided—the immigrants.

IMMIGRATION "SALAD BOWL"

The immigrants who came to the United States between 1820 and 1930 were part of the largest mass migration in history. During this period more than 62 million people left their homes to seek new lands and a better life. Over two-thirds came to America, the "land of opportunity." Unlike most nations that have been peopled by immigrants (like Australia or Argentina, which were made up of a few nationalities), the United States has absorbed great blocs of many nationalities. They have been divided into two groups, the *old* and the *new* immigration. The *old* immigration originated chiefly in northern and western Europe, including Englishmen, Frenchmen, Germans, Netherlanders, and Scandinavians. It peaked in 1850 and never exceeded a half million a year until the 1880s. The *new* immigration came mainly from southern and eastern Europe, consisting of Italians, Greeks, Poles, Russians, and Slavs. It peaked between 1905 and 1910 with more than half a million entering the country every year.

They came in such numbers because the United States had a reputation as the land of opportunity and equality. Wrote one immigrant, "no one can give orders to anybody here, one is as good as another, no one takes off his hat to another as you have to do in Germany." Even with the new entrepreneur elite, American society was far less stratified than its European counterpart. The spirit of equality seemed to be catching—a disgruntled Italian landlord wrote that "the men who come back from America walk through the streets as if they were our equals." Many immigrants writing home to their relatives represented the United States in glowing terms as the home of the common man and the hope of the oppressed. Nor was the nation's image of having a wealth of opportunity for the industrious belied. Immigrants did more of the nation's work than natives in proportion to their numbers. During the 1880s they were one-third of the work force and only 13 percent of the population. "By reason of this incoming, our almost limitless resources have been partially developed, forests leveled, railroads built, and canals dug . . . and the wilderness

The pride and prosperity of an immigrant farmer in North Dakota are reflected in this photograph sent back to relatives in Norway. Large families were considered an excellent source of labor needed on midwestern farms at the turn of the century. This stern patriarch eventually fathered a total of 11 units of manpower.

has been made to blossom," exulted the *North American Review* in 1892. The Treasury Department estimated that each immigrant was equivalent to $800 in new capital; Andrew Carnegie felt the figure was closer to $1500. There were other less tangible benefits. A national magazine observed that "when the foreigner came in, the native engineered the jobs. . . . The American in every walk and condition of life has been the boss ever since." Immigrants who had been in the country longer also moved up socially and economically as new groups came in. All this reinforced social mobility. It also encouraged businessmen to mechanize to take advantage of the cheap labor provided by the immigrants.

Of all these advantages and benefits, the only one directly useful to most immigrants was a job. Usually it was in the least skilled, most menial task available. Women worked in "sweat shops," textile mills or, if more fortunate, as domestic servants for the middle and upper class. Men labored deep underground in dangerous mines, drove spikes with railroad construction crews, and did monotonous factory work requiring little skill. "If you could see the conditions of the Norwegians in America at present," warned one immigrant, "you would certainly be frightened; illness and misery are so prevalent that many have died."

Living conditions for these people were bad at best. They tended to collect in the big cities where, to preserve some sense of belonging and for self-protection, they clustered by nationality in neighborhoods. This tendency was a major factor in the process of urbanization—twice as many immigrants lived in big cities as did native Americans as a whole. The actual neighborhood in which they settled was generally a poor one because they could afford no better. Entire families lived in a single room in a tenement that had to share one toilet and one water faucet. Garbage piled up in the streets and disease was rampant. "My people do not live in America," wrote a despairing Slavic immigrant, "they live *under* America." Culturally isolated from their surroundings by their language and customs, immigrants were under intense pressure to conform. Germans living in Milwaukee were astounded to discover that native Americans regarded them as "drunkards" because of their traditional beer parties on holidays. The natural desire to become accepted led many to conform to dominant American patterns, but others firmly refused to abandon their old heritage. Thorstein Veblen's biographer wrote that Veblen's mother was so insistent that he and his brothers learn the Norwegian culture and language that they were unaware that she even knew English until they were almost adults.

Thus the *melting pot* thesis that immigrants were transformed into some sort of "standard American" is not accurate. Those who came to America from abroad brought varieties of food, language, religions, festivals, books, dress, dances, literature and theatre that have made American culture a colorfully rich and cosmopolitan one. Perhaps the process of assimilation is best described by one historian who refers to it as a "salad bowl," where "though the salad is an entity, the lettuce can still be distinguished from the chicory, the tomatoes from the cabbage."

RURAL REACTION

The effects of industrialization and urbanization were also reaching beyond city and factory into the rural farming areas of America. Inventions like the reaper and the combine harvester–thresher allowed greater acreage to be put into production, and the railroad made it possible for the farmer to get his crops to distant markets. The opening of the trans-Mississippi West brought immense new land areas under the plow, and new centers of wheat production in the Dakotas and corn production in Kansas developed. By 1880 the production of wheat was five times what it had been in 1860, and the corn crop doubled. A vast majority of farmers now concentrated on cash crops like wheat or cotton, and large commercial farms appeared. "Now the object of farming is not primarily to make a living, but it is to make money," declared the *Cornell Countryman*. "To this end it is to be conducted on the same business basis as any other industry."

Unfortunately, the business of farming was not doing as well as most other businesses in the United States. Farmers were now competing in a world market where a surplus of foodstuffs caused a decline in agricultural prices that continued to fall until the early 1900s. Dealers acted accordingly and the farmer had no choice but to sell for the offered price or make no sale at all—he had no control over the price of his commodity. When buying machinery or other manufactured goods, he also had to pay the asking price or go without the item. So the farmer was in a very poor bargaining position. He could not determine the price of his produce or the price of things he needed to buy. As agricultural prices continued to decline, farmers were faced with an increasing gap between their income and the cost of the goods they needed to purchase. Nor did they have any voice in setting the freight rates they had to pay the railroads to send their produce to market. Railroads would often be engaged in competitive struggles that caused the rates to fluctuate wildly, further angering farmers who could see no connection between the rates and market conditions. High loan interest rates (10 percent was not uncommon) also frustrated the farmers. Since most needed some sort of credit for buildings, fencing, or a water supply, they were frequently forced to mortgage their farms. By 1900 over one-third of all American farms were mortgaged. A bad year or a sharp drop in prices would mean disaster for a mortgaged farm. One sarcastic Nebraska farmer wrote that his state had three crops: "One is a crop of corn, one a crop of freight rates, and one a crop of interest."

Under these conditions it is not surprising that many farmers abandoned their fields for the more promising cities. On marginal New England land the exodus was startling—the New Hampshire commissioner of agriculture counted over 1440 abandoned farms in

1890. Many midwestern rural counties found themselves losing people even though their state as a whole was gaining. In the South, where tenant farmers and sharecroppers were always in debt and controlled by local banks or businesses that even told them what to grow, fewer could leave. Of those that did stay on the farm throughout America, more and more swelled the ranks of the Grange.

The Grange (or the Patrons of Husbandry) had been formed as early as 1867 to bring farmers together to improve their lot. By 1874 hard times and low agricultural prices had boosted Granger membership to a million and a half discontented farmers. Targets of the organization were railroads with their high freight rates and monopolies and middlemen who, farmers believed, were squeezing the profits out of farming. To place themselves in a better bargaining position with businesses, Grangers formed consumer cooperatives. These associations hoped to shrink the "surplus profits of middlemen," which they believed diminished their own gains, yet they generally failed due to poor management, inadequate credit, and a lack of the cooperative spirit. Granger attempts to get state legislatures to set fair rates for storage and transportation of their produce were more successful. Most of the regulatory laws were so weak, however, that corporations could get around them. With the temporary return of better times in the 1880s Grange membership declined and the organization devoted itself more to social and educational objectives. Similarly, the Greenback movement to bring cheap paper money into circulation, with which farmers could pay off their debts, lost steam in the 1880s.

But the economic woes that had sparked the Grange and the Greenback movement continued to plague the farmer. He was also well aware, through magazine advertising and merchandise catalogs like Sears and Roebuck's, that he was not reaping the full benefits of new comforts. Rural life still required long hours in the fields and was without the attractions of theatre, professional sports, and other amusements available in the city. "One of the chief difficulties," said President Teddy Roosevelt, "is the failure of country life, as it exists at the present, to satisfy the higher social and intellectual aspirations of country people." Rural life had not really become worse; rather country dwellers had come to expect better things.

EARLY STRUGGLES OF LABOR

Industrial workers, on the other hand, could complain that things had deteriorated. Working at monotonous jobs under dangerous factory conditions and living in slum tenements, they were both the backbone and the victim of industrialization and urbanization. After laboring sixty or more hours a week many workers still did not earn enough to support a family. A few factory owners had a *noblesse oblige* sense of responsibility for their workers' well-being, but most insisted on hiring and firing on their own terms. Labor was a commodity and therefore working people became a commodity, a thing to be manipulated.

The obvious answer to this situation was labor unions, but it was an answer workers themselves were reluctant to adopt. First, joining a union could cost a laborer his job since many employers made membership grounds for dismissal, or worse. "I have always had one rule," an employer stated. "If a workman sticks up his head, hit it." The very size and power of corporations and the surplus labor force made resistance futile in the eyes of many workers. Second and perhaps the key to the American laborer's reluctance to join unions was the fear of being labeled "working class." Nearly all working Americans expected to rise from their condition to new heights of success—they believed in the "gospel of wealth" and the American Dream. To be termed "labor" implied permanent occupation and status, a surrender of future hopes for success. These factors, including some government hostility to labor organizations, explain the fact that only five percent of the work force belonged to unions by the turn of the century. Even today only about 30 percent of all workers are organized. Those that did join union ranks in the last decades of the nineteenth century did so to preserve their humanity and sense of belonging in a system that threatened to destroy both. They continued to accept profit and property because they were "waiting for the break." In the meantime, unions served to improve working conditions and raise pay levels.

As early as the 1860s trade unions were developing among skilled workers, such as glass blowers and railway engineers. Ironworkers established the National Labor Union in 1866, and within six years it had a membership of 300,000. But the NLU could not dominate any trade and its goals were somewhat diffuse and idealistic. Founder William Sylvis hoped that by pooling their capital, workers could own their own factories, market their own product, and thereby collect their own profits. "By cooperation," he prophesied, "we will become a nation of employers—the employers of our own labor." His hopes were short-lived. The NLU fell apart in the business panic of 1873. Another group called the Knights of Labor attempted to build a stronger base. The Knights called upon all workers to join their organization, including blacks and women. Seeking to return to self-employed units in small businesses, the union declared itself "at war" with the industrial system. "There is no reason," maintained one leading Knight, "why labor cannot, through cooperation, own and operate mines, factories, and railroads." Through education, cooperation, and political action the union hoped to "abolish the wage system." Strikes were a last resort because the Knights hoped to gain public support, which was usually alienated by the tactic. Ironically, their successful strike against a railroad was what boosted their membership to 700,000 in 1885. But a year later when a demonstration for the eight-hour day in Chicago turned into a bloody riot in Haymarket Square during which seven policemen were killed, public opinion turned against the Knights. Though they were not responsible for the riot, they had sponsored the demonstration. Shortly thereafter a major strike against the same railroad defeated in 1885 (whose management had broken the agreement) was crushed. By 1900 the Knights had disappeared from the national scene.

Even as this organization floundered another rose to the surface. The American Federation of Labor was a trade union of craftsmen (carpenters, printers, brewers, and others) who had a better bargaining position than unskilled workers who could easily be replaced. Its goals were simple and basic—"the best possible conditions obtainable for the workers," explained one AFL leader. That included the now typical demands of recognition of the union as the employees' bargaining agent, better conditions, shorter hours, and higher wages. Union President Samuel Gompers, a former cigarmaker, said that "the trade unions are the business organizations of the wage earners. . . ." The AFL was politically cautious and did not officially endorse a presidential candidate until 1908. Its chief weapon was the strike, but the union had no quarrels with the capitalistic system itself. "Labor unions are *for* the workingman but against no one," insisted an AFL leader. "There is no necessary hostility between labor and capital."

Despite trade union emphasis upon gaining community sympathy and employer cooperation, strikes that ended in violence did occur. Typically, this happened when strikers tried to block strikebreakers from operating the struck facility or when extremist minority groups incited riots (as at Haymarket). The riots of 1877 against numerous railroad companies was one of the few instances where wage cuts, job cuts, and poor working conditions were themselves enough to cause spontaneous strikes and violence. An attempt by 300 private police

1F YOU DON'T COME 1N SUNDAY DON'T COME 1N MONDAY.

THE
MANAGEMENT

With few exceptions, management was totally unwilling to recognize the legitimate demands of the working class in the last decades of the nineteenth century. Such intransigence from the business interests often led to violent confrontations between striking workers and federal troops called in to "restore order."

hired to reopen the Carnegie steel mill at Homestead, Pennsylvania, was met by armed workers and a brief battle ensued, but the strike was eventually broken by 8000 National Guard troops. The Pullman Company provoked a huge strike by railway workers in 1894, tying up all railroads west of Chicago, when it refused to discuss wage cuts and fired union leaders. Once again the federal government, siding with management, intervened with troops to keep the trains and mails running. Such experiences convinced unions that violence alienated the public, "justified" harsh reaction, and won few strikes. Despite government hostility and management stubbornness, AFL and other trade unions continued their struggle for recognition and the right to organize.

In short, the union movement remained politically and economically conservative. It never adopted the belief of philosopher Karl Marx that only by controlling the means of production could the working class enjoy the just rewards of its labor. Only the International Workers of the World (IWW) insisted on a radical program of change along these socialist lines, and it remained a struggling minority on the labor scene. Socialism itself, which has been a standard response to capitalism and industrialization in nearly every other nation, never became a strong movement in the United States. One reason for this was that the fluidity of the social structure weakened class lines. Workers sometimes managed to accumulate enough money to own their own homes, or to enable their children to finish high school and become skilled laborers. People who hope to move up in society—and with reason for believing they can—do not develop much class identification. Since most workers could vote before they became unionized, they often decided political questions on the basis of their party affiliation rather than along economic or class lines. Socialism was also considered an "alien" philosophy associated with immigrants, and therefore aroused ethnic antagonisms that cut across class lines.

But the chief reason why socialism failed in the United States was that for most Americans capitalism *worked* sufficiently well. Real wages kept ahead of prices and Americans gained a relatively high standard of living. The Mosely Commission, made up of various English labor representatives, reported in the early 1900s that the average American workingman was "better educated, better housed, better clothed and more energetic than his British counterpart." One socialist summed it up well. He observed that "Americanism" consisted of "ideas like democracy, liberty, opportunity, to all of which the American adheres rationalistically much as a socialist does to his socialism—because it does him good, because it gives him work, because, so he thinks, it guarantees him happiness. America has therefore served as a substitute for socialism."

A FAILURE IN GOVERNMENT

Government in the United States may not have been faced with serious threats of a socialist takeover, but it was confronted by the twin challenges of growth and change. Industrialization and urbanization were creating stresses and strains on a political system designed and built to govern a rural society.

Nowhere was this more evident than in the cities. Rapid and haphazard growth had rendered most city administrations incapable of providing such necessary services as water, power, or garbage removal, much less of easing the shock of rural and foreign newcomers. Political bosses emerged to cope with this chaotic change and growth. By appealing to the need for order, the clannish solidarity of immigrant ethnic groups, and cultivating every faction in the city, the bosses built a political machine to support their rule. Hard-headed men of little education, no social background, and accustomed to violence, they acted as "godfathers," especially to their poorer constituents. In return for votes they found people jobs, distributed food baskets at Christmas and Thanksgiving, and dignified social occasions. This lent a personal touch in an impersonal city. But it also created a climate for corruption in which the political machine dealt out jobs, contracts, administrative offices, and franchises to perpetuate its own power. City government under the bosses was not particularly efficient, although this upset few people since the cities were widely considered ungovernable. Independent and powerful, the boss was a force to be reckoned with at the state and even the national level.

At those levels politics seemed to be rather bland. There was very little observable difference between the domestic policies of the Democratic and Republican parties. Actually, both were made up of numerous factions that were constantly shifting position and angling for influence. Neither major party had an integrated political program. Congress worked at a leisurely pace because little was expected of it, and because leaders felt that tackling tough issues would destroy party unity. Laws that were passed were general or advisory—local governments interpreted them and enforced them or ignored them practically as they chose. The Sherman Anti-Trust Act, passed in 1890 by Congress in righteous anger toward trusts and other combinations "in restraint of trade," is a good example. Its bold language was so vague that it was unenforceable except in a very limited sense. Government bureaucracies were either inefficient or undermanned (in the name of economy) or both. Presidents confined themselves to suggesting measures for Congressional consideration, presiding over their party, and setting a proper moral example for the nation.

The latter was difficult to do, since nearly all levels of state and national government were rife with corruption. Republican Vice-President Hamilton Fish accepted stock from a company that was seeking government subsidy in 1874. Democratic President-elect Grover Cleveland accepted responsibility for fathering an illegitimate child. During the campaign Republicans chanted "Ma, Ma, where's my Pa?" and after the victory exultant Democrats retorted "Gone to the White House, ha ha ha!" Though Cleveland's "sin" may have been more sensational, Fish's was more common. Business saw little wrong with influencing a legislator by giving him free railroad passes or cash "grants," especially if the business was located in the officeholder's constituency. A disgusted reformer remarked that "Standard Oil has done everything to the Pennsylvania legislature except refine it." Though each party tried to outdo the other in charging corruption, voters generally ignored it because it was expected. Politics as a calling was not highly regarded—saints entered the ministry and geniuses made a fortune in business. Government, despite a veneer of confidence and respectability, was neither willing nor able to handle the massive national problems resulting from the industrial revolution and the rush to the cities.

STRAIN ON THE FABRIC OF SOCIETY

That same veneer of confidence and respectability lay over all aspects of American society during the last three decades of the nineteenth century. Mark Twain called the period the "Gilded Age." But the bright gilt of multimillion dollar mansions, impressive figures of industrial production, and pronouncements of opportunity and success for all only covered deep and serious stress on the fabric of American society. Henry Adams wrote that "society here . . . is shaking. Men die like flies under the strain."

These strains were evident in the changing roles of men, women, and children in society. There was a high demand for female labor in factories and in service industries. Though the female population rose only 28 percent in the 1880s, the number of women working outside the home rose 50 percent. As higher education opened its doors to more women, they also made their way into the professions. Restaurants, packaged foods, and store-bought clothing also affected the role of women in society. In short, women were gaining more independence. This was not without its price. Women joined the struggle for better working conditions and pay in the Women's Trade Union League, and they were still faced with the domestic routine at

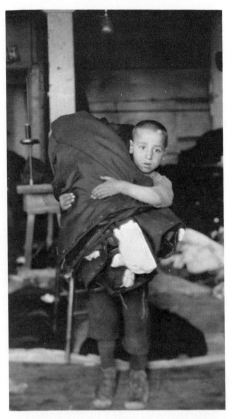

The working conditions that children labored under were no better and frequently worse than those of their fathers. The long hours and usually lower wages combined to deprive many urban youngsters of the childhood experiences that today are considered essential to normal maturation. Effective legislation governing child labor did not appear until 1916.

home in addition to outside work. Children also joined the ranks of the working class. By 1880 more than a million between the ages of 10 and 15 were employed outside the home and that figure went up by 75 percent in 10 years. At the same time American children were receiving a better education. All of this tended to loosen traditional family bonds, especially in the city where the family was not an economic unit as it had been in rural areas. The father had troubles exercising authority over a household where wife and even children might make the same wage as he, or replace him as family breadwinner if he was incapacitated. He might also find that children with a superior education and command of the English language tended to be independently minded. Family traditions were becoming confused.

In fact, American society was generally disorganized—a society without a core. Politics and government seemed largely irrelevant to people and so they lacked national centers of authority and information to give order to the accelerating rate of change. Institutions were still oriented toward community life and old patterns. Even business, which was supposed to be leading the rest of society around by the nose, suffered from the chaos. The range and complexity of corporate affairs made the trusts unmanageable. Even the factories were not particularly well-organized. Home offices were so swamped that company policy was often determined by local agents and officers acting on their own initiative. The shift from newly opened western areas to established urban centers as areas for economic growth and opportunity in the 1890s went largely unrecognized by business, resulting in a serious depression in 1893. Despite the trend toward centralization, haphazard growth and its resulting confusion still dominated the economy.

The village communities that had been characteristic of American society were changing and being absorbed. Though many people would continue to reside in them for a few decades, the community's ability to manage affairs within its own boundaries was gone. Some people still tried to understand the changing world in terms of the more settled and personal society based on village communities. They felt that something fundamental was happening to them —something that they had not asked for and did not want. They saw the dark side of the city, its corruption, crime, overcrowding, and dirt. Immigrants were regarded suspiciously as importers of "contaminating" morals and habits as well as dangerous philosophies like socialism and anarchism (which insisted that *all* forms of government are oppressive and should be overthrown). Monopolies were angrily attacked for making essential public services "the playthings of private profit." But what frightened people most of all was that these issues seemed to be beyond their control. Farmers were subject to changing freight rates, interest rates, and market prices all determined without their understanding or participation. The very existence of some cities depended upon industries owned by absentee managers, to whom appeals were made without success. Many workers not only depended upon their company for a job but for a home and goods supplied by company-owned towns. Helpless natives could only watch as immigrants who would work cheaper got jobs and "turned cities into decaying slums."

Many Americans saw tyrannical monopolies and subversive immigrants as the chief forces that were threatening the local community values and ways that they clung to. They began in the 1890s to strike out at these enemies in an effort to regain control of their lives and to preserve the society they knew.

SUGGESTIONS FOR ADDITIONAL READING

Blake McKelvey, *The Urbanization of America*, (1963). A study of the growing pangs of American cities during the period they came of age, 1860–1915.

Oscar Handlin, *The Uprooted*, (1951). A portrait of the psychological adaptations required of the European immigrants who settled in America.

Alexander B. Callow, Jr., *The Tweed Ring*, (1966). A study of the post-Civil War political machine that provided a model for later bosses in New York City.

Matthew Josephson, *The Robber Barons*, (1934). An indictment of the great Gilded Age entrepreneurs.

Jacob Riis, *How the Other Half Lives*, (1957 edition). A book written in 1890, attracting widespread public attention to the economic, social, and political problems arising out of slum conditions.

Copyright ©1973 by Herblock in the Washington Post.

CHAPTER FIVE

THE PEOPLE VERSUS THE INTERESTS: REFORM IN AMERICAN POLITICS

1892
Populist or People's party formed.

1901
Theodore Roosevelt becomes President; marks beginning of programs sponsored by the diverse Progressive movement.

1912
Roosevelt's "Bull Moose" third-party effort fails; Democrat Woodrow Wilson is elected President to carry on his version of Progressivism.

1920
Americans support "normalcy" with the election of Warren G. Harding.

1929
New York Stock Market Crash in October begins the Great Depression.

1932
Franklin D. Roosevelt elected President on his promise to restore prosperity.

1933
"Hundred Days" in which FDR receives Congressional approval for legislative acts that greatly increase the role of the federal government in American life.

1960
John F. Kennedy elected President to "get this country moving again."

1965
President Lyndon B. Johnson builds his "Great Society" programs.

1972
President Richard M. Nixon reelected and promises to return government to local levels through the "New Federalism."

A DEFINITION OF REFORM

The dictionary definition of reform is "to make better by removing faults and defects; correct." Its simplicity is deceptive. Just what it is in America that needs "correcting" has always been a subject for argument. Nor have people always been able to agree what the "faults and defects" are, much less how to go about "removing" them. For example, reformers before the Civil War offered a variety of prescriptions for the ills that plagued their society. (See Chapter 2, pp. 56–60 for details.) Similarly, all three of the candidates who ran for President in 1912 stoutly defended their own versions of reform. Despite these varied approaches, the idea of reform as the process of making America "better"—of securing the blessings of democracy, liberty, social justice, and (not incidentally) prosperity—has been a unifying theme in United States history.

Ever since the turn of the century this theme has played a dominant role in American politics. Whether the target was business monopolies, political corruption, social inequalities, or economic dislocation, reformers lashed out to destroy them in the name of the American people. Most often they sought to create some order out of the chaos wrought by industrialization and urbanization while trying to bring accelerating changes under control. The politics of reform embraced short-lived third parties as well as Democrats and Republicans. In the movement's ranks stood farmers, preachers, factory workers, business officials, educated professionals as well as the poor, and great numbers of middle-class people—a cross-section of America. How has reform played its part in national politics, and what is its future in the remainder of the twentieth century?

THE PEOPLE'S PARTY

The first nationwide reform movement began on the farms and gathered momentum during the 1880s. Farm problems had not died with the passing of the Grange as a reformist effort. A brief period of prosperity was quickly followed by declining prices, increasing debt, and loss of farms to mortgage companies. Farmers began to join local organizations that eased their social isolation and promoted agricultural interests. These groups united to form large unions in several southern states, and by 1888 they in turn had combined to form the Southern Alliance. Black farmers, not admitted to the white groups, formed their own Colored Farmer's National Alliance. Though separated, the two groups managed to work together to achieve some objectives. Farmers in the North were also banding together until by

1889 the Northern Alliance counted 400,000 members in several states.

Alliance organizations in Kansas, Nebraska, and the Dakotas chose to take their grievances into the political arena in the elections of 1890. Demanding government ownership of transportation and communication, a graduated income tax, abolition of national banks, and inflation through the unlimited coinage of silver, they soon realized that neither the Democratic nor Republican parties would accept them. So they organized independent parties and launched vigorous campaigns on their own. In Kansas, "Sockless" Jerry Simpson denounced the "bloodhounds" of wealth and Mary Elizabeth Lease suggested that farmers "raise less corn and more hell." Despite poor organization and a lack of money the Alliance farmers won a few resounding victories, and when Congress met in 1891 about 50 Congressmen were sympathetic to or supportive of its interests. Conservative Democrats and Republicans alike were frightened by this new sound and fury. It did not quiet their fears to hear that Kansas Alliancemen, convinced that they had won control of the state house of

Although the Populists generally restricted their activities to forming cooperatives and political action within the system, there were occasions when their sense of outrage compelled them to violate the law. Here Kansas Populists occupy the state legislative chambers, disputing the results of the off-year elections of 1890.

representatives, marched on the chambers with rifles and tossed out the resisting Republicans. The courts decided the dispute in favor of the Republicans, but the farmers retained control of the senate.

Encouraged by their victories, the Northern Alliance was now determined to form a nationwide third party to represent the interests of all "plundered people" in America. The Southern Alliance, which had had only limited success in working through the Democratic party, agreed to join. On February 22, 1892, representatives of the two groups met in a convention in St. Louis and, with the support of the Knights of Labor and other reform groups, formed the People's or Populist party. "We meet," declared the populist platform, "in the midst of a nation brought to the verge of moral, political, and material ruin. Corruption dominates the ballot box, the Legislatures, the Congress, and touches even the ermine of the bench." The solution was to expand the powers of government "as rapidly and as far as the good sense of an intelligent people and the teachings of experience shall justify, to the end that oppression, injustice, and poverty shall eventually cease in the land." Populists called for the free coinage of silver (which was expected to raise farm prices and help debtors), government ownership of railroads and telephone and telegraph lines, and a graduated income tax to force the rich to pay more to support the government. They proposed political reforms such as direct election of Senators by voters (rather than oppointment by state legislatures), a single term for the President, the right of the people to propose and approve their own laws (initiative and referendum), and the right to call a Senator or Congressman to account for his actions in a special election (recall). Basically, the Populists sought to return government to its true calling as the representative of all citizens and not just special interests, and then give government tight control over the economy to exercise on the people's behalf.

Here lay the real radicalism of the new party—the demand that government act directly upon areas of the economy that had been the preserve of private corporations. This was a direct rejection of economic individualism, the very center of American capitalism. Populists justified their position by insisting that a system which gave the farmer less money while he grew more crops and kept a hungry worker unemployed was plainly unjust. "People," observed one orator, "do not ask to be tramps." But their programs were still regarded as too radical by many Americans. Conservatives, especially on the east coast, ridiculed "simplistic" Populist proposals and labeled the Populists "country hicks." The dying Knights of Labor were too weak to give the party the urban support it required to gain a strong base. Rising trade unions like the American Federation of Labor were more concerned with wages and hours than with government ownership and social problems. Lacking an urban following of any size, the Populists lost the election of 1892 to Democrat Grover Cleveland. But their presidential candidate, James Weaver, did manage to poll a million popular votes, send several Senators and Congressmen to Washington, and gain control of three state governments. Thus encouraged, the Populists began to plan for the election in 1894 and the Presidential race two years later.

Cleveland aided their efforts by splitting his own party over a bill designed to protect Treasury gold reserves by preventing the purchase of silver for currency. When gold reserves continued to dwindle and hard times hit the country, an angry electorate repudiated the Democrats in 1894. Populist Jacob Coxey led a small army of unemployed and marched on Washington demanding work relief. After he was arrested for walking on the Capitol lawn, his followers dispersed. As the election of 1896 approached, the major issue became the currency question. Republicans endorsed the existing tight fiscal policy and nominated William McKinley for President. Dissident Democrats dumped Cleveland, chose the magnetic William Jennings Bryan, and drew up a program that gave the voters a choice. They called for tougher controls over trusts, a graduated income tax, and the free coinage of silver.

This presented the Populists with a dilemma. If they fielded their own candidate, they would split the vote on the silver issue so central to their program. After much debate most Populists decided to support Bryan in the hope that his victory would mean the adoption of the party program. This doomed Populism as a third party movement since most members were absorbed into the Democratic party. Bryan made a supreme effort, covering over 18,000 miles and making more than 600 speeches. But the Republicans conducted a highly organized campaign that dominated the press and spent 10 times more than the Democrats could afford. In the end McKinley won the election by carrying nearly all of the big states, although he only edged Bryan by 500,000 popular votes. His victory was the triumph of industrial over agricultural interests in the struggle for power in Washington.

THE RISE OF PROGRESSIVISM

It was a rather hollow victory. By striking out against the power of big business and its stranglehold on politics and the economy, the

Populists seem to have broken the climate of resigned helplessness that had enveloped the nation. Americans were no longer willing to accept as the "price of progress" crime, poverty, squalid slums, political corruption, and dictatorial control of vital public services like the railroads by socially irresponsible businesses. Labor union agitation for better pay and shorter hours increased in the late 1890s, and the Social Gospel that called for Christian aid to the impoverished and socially deprived became increasingly popular. The new philosophy of Pragmatism, popularized in the United States by John Dewey, maintained that people could and should use new techniques and ideas to deal with the problems of industrialized society. Contrary to the Social Darwinists, the Pragmatists believed that there was nothing "inevitable" about the course of evolution. Americans, they insisted, had both the right and the ability to create the type of society they desired. Professors studying the newly developing "social sciences" of economics, sociology, and psychology maintained that social change could be guided by scientific methods to benefit all the people.

By the turn of the century this sense of optimism had combined with a determination to tame business' power, eliminate corruption, and promote social justice—the product was Progressive reformism. The Progressive movement dominated the American political scene for 15 years, yet it was never embodied in a single political party as Populism had been. Progressives came from all sections of the country, represented all classes, and were partisans of both major parties. The movement included such diverse people as William Jennings Bryan from the Bible Belt of the Midwest and urban atheist Clarence Darrow. Socialist Eugene Debs and conservative William Howard Taft both embraced Progressive reforms. If the movement had a center it was in the cities among the large middle class, including white-collar workers and professionals such as teachers, lawyers, and newspapermen. Many Progressive leaders were young, well-educated, and from well-to-do families. Nevertheless, the Progressive reform movement has always defied the historian's efforts to categorize it. It remains one of the most diffuse reform movements in United States history.

Despite their diversity, Progressives did have certain characteristic attitudes and goals. Above all, they had an unshakable confidence in the common sense and morality of the American people. They believed that if Americans could regain control of their government they would have the ability and wisdom to make the necessary social and economic changes. So the first area of interest to the Progressives was political reform—making the government responsive to the will of the people. To this end they adopted most of the Populist political program (direct election of senators, initiative, referendum, and recall). "Democracy" was the movement's guiding light and it colored all of the Progressive programs. Since the "unholy alliance" between special business interests and government violated the democratic ideal, it too became a primary target for reform. A common creed upon which nearly all Progressives agreed was that "big business" had too much political power and that this was the source of most corruption in government. Their solution was first to return government to "uncorruptible" (fellow Progressive) representatives of the people and then invest a political bureaucracy with the power to regulate the business activities that vitally affected the public interest. This uphill struggle against the "interests" took place at all levels of government—local, state, and federal. Another goal was to get the government to enact social legislation like abolition of child labor (it was not uncommon for 10-year-old children to work 12-hour days six days a week), unemployment insurance, more enlightened prison conditions, and slum clearance. Most of this activity took place in urban areas where reformers could better exert their influence. The common denominator of all of these efforts was to focus the power of government on problems involving the general welfare of the American people.

Actually, since all Americans did not share reform sentiments, Progressive programs were more *for* the people than *of* the people. Most Progressive leaders, and many of the rank and file, were Anglo-Saxon Protestants who regarded themselves as spokesmen for "the people" and guardians of the American heritage. Many were resentful of the businessmen who were replacing them in power. Like the Populist of the 1890s, there was a strong anti-immigrant sentiment running through Progressivism. Alarmed that immigrant cultures seemed to be "diluting" the Anglo-Saxon American heritage, the *nativist* movement aimed to dam the flood of immigration. One "liberal" reformer compared the newly arrived immigrants from Southern and Eastern Europe to "the oozing of a sewer pipe into the clear waters of a well." Nor were most Progressives sympathetic to the plight of black Americans. In fact, when black southerners continued to vote for conservative candidates, Progressives helped white southern politicians who played on racial prejudice to win office and strip the blacks of their voting rights in the name of "reform." California

Progressives were no less harsh on the Oriental "intruders" in their state. Reformers also had a tendency to push legislation "for the good of the people" in spite of the people's wishes—when drinkers refused to abstain voluntarily from alcohol, Progressives passed Prohibition. Full of contradictions as it was, Progressivism was rising to the fore of American politics as the new century began.

ROOSEVELT, WILSON, AND PROGRESSIVISM

When the assassination of President McKinley in 1901 brought Theodore Roosevelt to the White House, Progressivism was already flourishing. It had made Robert M. LaFollette governor of Wisconsin, where LaFollette initiated a series of economic and political acts that made the state a "laboratory of democracy." Other states like California, South Dakota, and Iowa also elected Progressive governors. In cities like Detroit, New York, and St. Louis local Progressive movements fought to eliminate the corrupt political machines of urban bosses. Roosevelt himself had not been closely associated with the movement. As governor of New York he had shown only a mild inclination toward reform, perhaps because of the restraining influence of the party machine that had helped him win office.

But as President of the United States, Theodore Roosevelt came to personify the early Progressive movement. He was a young, well-educated man from an upper-class family who had a vigorous manner that made him a strong leader. Though he was ambitious and enjoyed the game of politics, he viewed issues in a moral light and regarded himself as "the steward of the public welfare." Roosevelt was well aware that the twentieth century had brought with it "many serious social problems" for which "the old laws, and the old customs . . . are no longer sufficient." He nevertheless believed that "the interest of the public is inextricably bound up in the welfare of our business." As President, Roosevelt therefore tried to tread the middle path. He distinguished between "bad" trusts which he tried to "bust," and "good" trusts which he left alone. At one point during the coal strike of 1902 Roosevelt reviled the "arrogant stupidity" of business leaders and later commented acidly, "Do they not realize they are putting a very heavy burden on us who stand against socialism; against anarchic disorder?"

This middle path of reform won Roosevelt some notable successes in his two terms as President. His campaigns against business monopolies and especially the suit brought against the enormous

"Action" was central to Theodore Roosevelt's political life. He roared through his terms as President (1901–1909), providing national leadership for the Progressive movement. When asked in 1912 whether his health permitted him to campaign for the presidency on a third-party ticket, he bellowed: "I feel as strong as a Bull Moose!"

Northern Securities Company railroad combine earned him a reputation as a "trust-buster," though in fact he instituted fewer antitrust suits than his successor. The point is that he brought the issue of corporate abuses clearly before the public. Roosevelt also showed a much fairer attitude toward labor than his predecessors by refusing to use federal troops to break up a coal strike in 1902, forcing the mining companies to negotiate with the workers' union. The Interstate Commerce Commission was given new powers to regulate railroad practices by presidentially-backed legislation. Other bills protecting the public from business practices dangerous to its health, like the Pure Food and Drug Act and the Meat Inspection Act, were pushed by Roosevelt. He also supported conservation programs to bring the nation's resources under scientific management and wise use for the benefit of future generations of Americans. Perhaps his most important contribution to the reform movement and American politics was to inaugurate a dynamic modern Presidency that acted as the initiator of legislation, the forceful representative of the people, and the guardian of the public interest.

Progressive journalists were another group that played the role of guardian. Given the nickname of "muckrakers" by Roosevelt, who disliked their habit of always "raking up the muck" in American society, they conducted a crusade in newspapers, magazines, and books against illegal and immoral business practices. Articles like Lincoln Steffens' "Tweed Days in St. Louis" exposed corruption in city government while others probed the power of big business over United States Senators. Ida Tarbell's landmark report on "The History of the Standard Oil Company" disclosed that corporation's social irresponsibility. Powerful novels told of squalid city living conditions, the impersonality of "the system," and of sickening conditions in the nation's food processing businesses. It was reported that Roosevelt did not eat sausage for a month after reading Upton Sinclair's *The Jungle*, which described the meat-packing plants of Chicago. These men and women alerted the public to dangers and issues vital to their well-being.

Americans used to the dynamic leadership of Theodore Roosevelt and the sensational articles of the "muckrakers" were less than enthused with the lackluster administration of Roosevelt's successor, William Howard Taft. Taft avoided the public and was such an inept politician that he managed to alienate both conservatives and progressives in his party, though he did retain control of the party machinery. He also angered his mentor Roosevelt by firing Gifford Pinchot, Roosevelt's close friend and co-worker, over a conservation dispute. Roosevelt then left the African bush where he had been hunting and returned to the United States. Seven months before the 1912 election, convinced that Taft had abandoned Progressive goals, he announced, "my hat is in the ring." Roosevelt's decision split the Republican party in two, the conservatives nominating Taft and the Progressives leaving the convention to form their own party and nominate Roosevelt. Proclaiming that he felt as strong as a "Bull Moose" in spite of his age, Roosevelt hit the campaign trail sounding more Progressive than he ever had.

The Democrats gleefully noted the Republican split and nominated their own reform candidate, Woodrow Wilson. Wilson was from an upper middle-class family with a strong Protestant background, and he had been president of Princeton College in 1910. Although an economic conservative, he had been a liberal governor of New Jersey and had fought for progressive programs. Wilson and Roosevelt soon dominated the 1912 campaign. As leader of the new Progressive Party, Roosevelt championed the full reform program—government regulation to control business and government legislation to bring about social justice—what he called the *New Nationalism*. Wilson argued in rebuttal that only a return to competition through anti-trust action would preserve economic democracy, and that more government legislation would only inhibit the self-reliant individual, who was the true source of social justice. He called this program the *New Freedom*. The voters, forced to choose between two methods of reaching the same goals, chose the New Freedom, because it appeared less radical. This general conservatism of the voters did not prevent Eugene Debs and the Socialist Party from capturing the votes of a million deeply dissatisfied Americans. But the Socialist appeal had hit its high-water mark without capturing national office.

The new President struck the keynote of his administration in his inaugural address: "We are facing the necessity of fitting a new social organization . . . to the happiness and prosperity of the great body of citizens. . . . But we can do it all in calm and sober fashion." Borrowing from Roosevelt's New Nationalism, Wilson concentrated on regulating business through the new Federal Trade Commission. One cabinet member wrote that the FTC was "a counsellor and a friend to the business world," not a club-wielding policeman. Congress passed the graduated income tax in 1913 and, six years later, the Nineteenth Amendment, which gave women the right to vote. Women like Jane Addams had been highly active in social reform and the amendment was the result of their work. Though Wilson was not particularly attracted to further social reform, Congressional pressure and the necessity of winning Progressive support in the 1916 election persuaded him to take a liberal position. Legislation was passed giving American seamen better living and working conditions, taking steps to eliminate the abuses of child labor, allowing workmen compensation for injuries on the job, providing low-interest loans to farmers and supporting an eight-hour workday. These programs won Wilson reelection in 1916 when Roosevelt became absorbed by World War I and the Progressive Party collapsed.

By 1916 the nation's attention had turned from domestic reform to the struggle in Europe and the attempt to stay neutral. Progressivism had achieved all it was going to achieve at the national level. Although it had made the political system more responsive to the public and therefore more democratic—most particularly by enfranchising women—it had excluded blacks as part of its constituency. Fewer blacks could vote by the end of the Progressive period than in 1900. Nor did the reformers alter the domination of corporations over the nation's economy. Many businessmen, anxious to bring some sort of order to the system, even supported federal attempts to regulate their industries—then exercised a dominant influence over the very government commissions designed to control them. Labor improved its relations with management only very little. All in all, the Progressives concentrated more on improving the existing system by making it operate more efficiently than on changing the system itself. Most of the programs Progressives proposed were of this nature, and most of them were enacted into law. To this extent, Progressivism was a success.

"NORMALCY" AND THE TWENTIES

In the 1920 election campaign Warren G. Harding set the tone for the postwar period: "America's present need is not heroics, but healing; not nostrums, but normalcy . . . not surgery, but serenity." With the abrupt end of World War I, the bitter partisan debate over the League of Nations, and the Red Scare that swept the country in early 1920, the American people had all of the excitement they wanted for awhile. Many considered their involvement in the war to have been a mistake and were tired of Wilson's "great crusade" rhetoric. They were also alarmed at the Communist revolution in Russia and what they saw as "radical stirrings" in the United States. Prosperity had shifted the nation's attention from reform to the business of making money. Harding's promise of "normalcy" was exactly what the public wanted to hear.

As President, Harding was not even master of his own administration. Three of his cabinet members were later convicted in the Teapot Dome Scandal of 1923 for taking a bribe from oilmen who wanted access to federal oil reserves. Attracted to dishonest friends, poker, bootleg whiskey, and a mistress, Harding contributed to the decline of the power and prestige of the Presidency although his warmth and good looks kept him popular. Under Harding, business was once

again permitted to go its own way with only minimal federal interference and the government returned to the habit of using troops to
end labor strikes.

When President Harding died unexpectedly, his Vice-President
Calvin Coolidge took the oath of office. "Quiet Cal" cleaned up the
administration and continued to follow the probusiness economic
policy begun by Harding. Coolidge sought and succeeded in making
his administration respectable and stable. This paid off in the 1924
election when the Republicans soundly beat both the Democrats and
resurgent Progressives. America "kept cool with Coolidge," as the
slogan said.

But the "cool" was only on the surface. Nativist groups fearful of
immigrant "contamination" of Anglo-Saxon American culture reduced the flow of immigration to a trickle through legislation by
1924. The Ku Klux Klan soared in membership in the South and
Midwest, proclaiming its "one hundred percent American" opposition to blacks, Jews, Catholics, and nearly every other non-WASP
group. More than 200 blacks were lynched between 1920 and 1925.
American intellectuals disillusioned with America and American
values were characterized as the "lost generation," and their attitudes were reflected in the works of Ernest Hemingway and F. Scott
Fitzgerald. The "roaring twenties" flaunted traditional manners and
morals as thousands of young people took up jazz, the Charleston,
speakeasies, and necking parties. Prohibition was a failure and criminal gangs like Chicago's Capone mob terrorized American cities.
Even though a majority of Americans clung to stability and refused to
join the "roaring," society seemed to be restless, nervous, and
vaguely dissatisfied.

Economic prosperity was also a surface phenomenon, though that
was not yet obvious even in 1928. Newly elected Republican President Herbert Hoover (Coolidge chose not to run in 1928) proclaimed
that, "Given a chance to go forward with the policies of the past eight
years, we shall soon with the help of God be in sight of the day when
poverty shall be banished from this nation." What Hoover did not see
was that the Republican policy of helping business had resulted in a
situation where the rich could invest in growing industries but the
poorer classes could not consume the mountain of goods produced.
Industrial production was up 50 percent, but the number of workers
remained static. Encouraged by surface prosperity, the stock market
climbed to incredible heights as speculators traded and bought for
quick profits. RCA shares soared from 85 to 420 points in one year.

But on October 29, 1929, after several days of confused uncertainty, stockholders panicked and sold more than 16,000,000 shares at ruinous losses. The Crash marked the end of an era and the beginning of the worst depression in American history.

FDR DECLARES A "NEW DEAL"

Wall Street's collapse sent deep shocks through the economy. Banks closely tied to the stock market through investment were shaken and those consumers who had bought on credit found themselves in trouble. The curtailment of credit reduced public purchases, and business began to decline. Since 39 percent of the nation's wealth was tied up in 10 percent of the country's families and these people tended to speculate or invest their funds, the Crash wiped out much of the national wealth in a few weeks. The prevalent economic theory—that the market would have to correct itself—prevented business and political leaders from acting to stop the spreading paralysis.

Hoover first diagnosed the whole problem as one of confidence. The economy, he firmly declared, was "fundamentally sound" and would return to normal if people would not panic. To restore confidence he worked with businessmen to maintain current levels of employment and wages. But as demand weakened the businessmen simply could not hold the line. By the spring of 1930 more than 4,000,000 people were out of work and the situation continued to deteriorate. Hoover began a program of limited federal intervention: an attempt to stabilize farm prices failed; the Reconstruction Finance Corporation could not lend enough money to banks and individuals to stem the tide; assistance to private welfare and charity organizations was inadequate; and federal work projects to relieve unemployment were too few. By 1932, 85,000 businesses and 5000 banks had failed. In the same period national income had dropped by half, while industrial production declined as much. Nearly one-fourth of the labor force was out of work. Bread and soup lines lengthened in cities across the nation and villages of shacks called "Hoovervilles" began to dot parks and dumpyards. People, looking for a scapegoat, blamed it all on Hoover.

So the Republicans faced the election of 1932 with scant enthusiasm. The Democratic convention nominated reformist governor of New York Franklin D. Roosevelt, who proclaimed that his party was now "the bearer of liberalism and of progress" and promised a "new deal for the American people." In a vigorous campaign the

The Depression fostered feelings of desperation that led to incidents of lawlessness. A Minneapolis newspaper in 1931 reported: "Several hundred men and women in an unemployed demonstration late today stormed a grocery and meat market in the Gateway district, smashed plate glass windows and helped themselves to bacon and ham, fruit and canned goods."

physically handicapped Roosevelt expanded little on that promise beyond saying that the government would take action to relieve unemployment and low farm prices. He also capitalized on Hoover's use of tanks, troops, and gas to rout members of the Bonus Expeditionary Force, about 12,000 World War I veterans who had marched on Washington to demand payment of a promised cash bonus for their service. Hoover warned that Roosevelt's program "would destroy the very foundations of our American system." But the electorate was not listening. Roosevelt won in a landslide that buried the Republicans under 12,000,000 popular votes. The nation responded to the warm, energetic Roosevelt with a confidence they had never given Hoover. When the new President solemnly told Americans in his inaugural address that "the only thing we have to fear is fear itself"—essentially what Hoover had said before—they believed it.

Franklin Roosevelt, therefore, was at the heart of the New Deal—to a large extent he *was* the New Deal. Although others contributed ideas and proposals, it was Roosevelt who led and vitalized the program and held together the Democratic political coalition that made it possible. A former Progressive who had worked for Woodrow Wilson's nomination, Roosevelt had been loyal to the liberal element in the Democratic party and had pushed through numerous reforms as governor of New York. He had always been impatient with ideologies and philosophies. "It is common sense to take a method and try it," he said. "If it fails admit it frankly and try another. But above all try something." As a reformist President, Roosevelt offered active, pragmatic leadership to solve the problems of the Depression.

Franklin Roosevelt used his charismatic leadership to bind together the diverse segments of the New Deal coalition and to win the confidence of the American people. Here in the first of his "fireside chats" during the banking crisis of 1933 President Roosevelt tells Americans that "it is safer to keep money in a reopened bank than under the mattress."

Congress soon learned just how active Roosevelt would be. In the famous "Hundred Days" from March to June, 1933, the House and Senate passed a record number of reform and relief measures that became the basis of the New Deal. First, the President stopped the run on banks that was destroying the nation's financial condition by closing all of them, shoring the weak ones up with loans, and then reopening them with assurances to the public that they were sound. People's confidence was restored—"capitalism," wrote one observer, "was saved in eight days." Then Congress established the Civilian Conservation Corps, designed to help young men by giving them jobs planting trees, establishing parks, and building dams. Under the Federal Emergency Relief Act government relief money went to help states support the unemployed, and later programs of work relief were started, though this barely made a dent in the relief problem. A Philadelphia social worker reported that "one woman said she borrowed 50 cents from a friend and bought stale bread for 3½¢ per loaf, and that is all they had for eleven days except for one or two meals." Conditions on the farms were little better since most farmers were deep in debt because of falling prices. The Agricultural Adjustment Act sought to raise prices by limiting production, and paid farmers for not growing crops. Critics protested that this policy encouraged the practice of slaughtering pigs and plowing under corn when people were starving. The Supreme Court later declared the measure unconstitutional. But other farm relief bills took the place of the AAA to help farmers keep their farms and give them a better return for their labor.

Perhaps the key measure in the early New Deal was the National Industrial Recovery Act (NRA) passed in June, 1933. Designed to help business and allow labor to share the expected benefits, the NRA involved government-business cooperation in creating a planned economy. Part of the measure created an organization to fund public works projects like construction of roads and bridges. But the most important section dealt with establishing "codes of fair competition" that would govern production, work standards, etc. A high-keyed propaganda campaign was conducted to attract business cooperation and public support. Stylized blue eagles proclaiming "We Do Our Part" symbolized the crusade. Yet NRA codes proved difficult to administer and nearly impossible to enforce. Labor, receiving new recognition, was enthusiastic, but business was only mildly favorable. Before it was finally struck down as unconstitutional by the Supreme Court, the NRA had become a political burden and proved itself a failure. One historian has likened its economic effectiveness to giving a sick person who needs an operation an aspirin instead.

Up to this point Roosevelt had tried to work with business and, with a few exceptions, within the bounds of political and economic tradition. Now, convinced that not enough was being done, Roosevelt directed the New Deal into more concentrated relief and recovery efforts that also included strong doses of reform.

LEGACY OF THE NEW DEAL

The first program in this "new" New Deal, although it belonged chronologically among Roosevelt's earlier programs, was the attempt to totally renovate the underdeveloped Tennessee Valley. The Tennessee Valley Authority (TVA) was authorized to build a series of dams that would control the raging Tennessee River, provide electric power, introduce new agricultural techniques to reduce erosion and increase fertility, and in general transform the valley from a backward area into a prosperous national showcase. It was the most successful program of the New Deal, and by 1940 TVA had achieved all of its objectives. The only reasons it was not copied in other areas was that business objection to government competition in power distribution was strong.

After the NRA and TVA, business became disenchanted with Roosevelt. The President in turn saw that moderate relief efforts were not enough. During the "Second Hundred Days," ending in August, 1935, Congress passed many relief measures and much basic social legislation to meet the continuing crisis in unemployment and poverty. The Works Progress Administration (WPA) sponsored thousands of work relief projects such as the construction of libraries, highways, and parks, as well as hiring artists and other professionals who could not find work. By 1938 over three million Americans were employed by the WPA. A proposal by California's Dr. Francis Townsend to give all persons over sixty $200 a month, and the "Share-Our-Wealth" plan of Senator Huey Long of Louisiana that advocated heavy taxes on the rich to give every family the necessities of life, sped the passage of the less radical Social Security Act in 1935. This act provided for old-age pensions and insurance, plus unemployment insurance and support for public health programs. Although the measure was conservative compared to Townsend's or Long's plans, it was so successful that it is still the basis of the government's social welfare program. In response to Long in particular, the administration passed higher corporate and estate taxes.

The area of labor relations saw the first President and Congress who actively promoted union organization and its goals. Child labor was abolished, minimum wages and maximum hours were set, and workers were given the legal right to unionize and bargain collectively with management. With this encouragement labor began a massive organization drive that, despite violent confrontations with stubborn businesses, finally put industrial workers (miners, auto workers, steel workers, etc.) in a union—the Congress of Industrial Organizations (CIO). Labor was now in a position to bargain with business as an equal. When part of the Great Plains turned into a "Dust Bowl" after a long drought between 1934 and 1936, Congress passed New Deal conservation measures designed to halt erosion and improve farm techniques.

To support all of this legislation, President Roosevelt pasted together a patchwork coalition of farmers, intellectuals, workers, and minority groups, cemented the rural and urban factions of the Democratic party, and thereby forged a strong political alliance. He held it together largely by the force of his own warmth, vitality, and skill. Despite the bitter opposition of conservatives and radicals alike, this New Deal coalition won the election of 1936 and presented Roosevelt with a 28,000,000 vote mandate. All barriers appeared to be overcome but one. Conservative judges on the Supreme Court had knocked down the NRA and AAA, crippling major parts of Roosevelt's program. It seemed that they might block even more reforms passed by Congress. Early in 1937 Roosevelt introduced a bill that would give him the power to add six judges to the bench, thus "packing" the court in his favor. This ill-considered maneuver united New Deal opposition, split the Democratic ranks, and handed Roosevelt his first major defeat. No longer able to use the party as a willing tool, the President found his coalition crumbling away at the edges. The innovative stage of the New Deal was over.

Though the New Deal did not restore full prosperity—it took the Second World War to do that by demanding full production for America's war effort—it had improved economic and social conditions from their low 1932 level. More important, it had restored Americans' confidence in their political, economic, and social system. Roosevelt had stolen the thunder from the radicals by implementing moderate versions of their own proposals. To do this, he had given the federal government more power than it had ever wielded before. Washington agencies now supervised nearly every major social or economic activity in the nation. It had invaded the field of private enterprise with the TVA project. The "welfare state" had been inaugurated with the Social Security Act. Progressive and Populist trends toward government responsibility for the people's welfare and security had been largely realized by the New Deal. Indeed, some individual Progressives were influential in forming New Deal policies. Like Progressive reform, New Deal reform did not seek to change radically the American system—it sought to "better" it. By distributing the benefits of the capitalist system more broadly, Roosevelt's New Deal helped Americans weather a bleak depression and restored their confidence in gradual change within the system.

A "NEW FRONTIER"

When the nation turned to war again in 1941 the New Deal became a secondary concern. Even Roosevelt declared that winning the war must come first. After the President died in office on April 12, 1945, Harry S Truman moved into the White House. With the end of the war the new President announced a liberal program that would extend the reformism of the New Deal. But a preoccupation with the Cold War and a conservative alliance between Northern Republicans and Southern Democrats frustrated his plans. A disapproving public coined the phrase, "To err is Truman," and returned a Republican Congress in the elections of 1946. Americans appeared to be turning toward conservatism as they had after the First World War. Despite being hampered by a splintered party, "give 'em hell Harry" beat the confident Republicans in a surprise upset in the 1948 presidential election.

Truman now sought to drive through his "Fair Deal," which included civil rights legislation, to create "a society which offers new opportunities for every man to enjoy his share of the good things of life." Congress, dominated by the conservative coalition, was indifferent at best. Public response seemed divided—one newspaper declared that the President's program "was the most frankly socialistic ever presented by a president of the United States." Little was accomplished. Some of the proposals—medicare, federal aid to education, and particularly civil rights measures designed to secure equal rights for black people—would form the essence of later reform programs. Even the "dynamic conservatism" of the Eisenhower Presidency reflected this influence by passing in 1957 the first civil rights legislation since Reconstruction. Eisenhower himself was more a reassuring, unifying national figure than a reformer. His administration did pass mild reform measures originating in Congress and used

federal troops to uphold the Supreme Court's decision against segregation in the nation's schools.

Unfortunately for the Republicans, Eisenhower's popularity did
not rub off on their candidate for President in 1960, Richard M.
Nixon. In the contest with Democratic nominee John F. Kennedy,
Nixon labored under the difficulty of Kennedy's engaging personality
and a Democratic majority among the nation's voters. The election
was close, but Kennedy held his party together and emerged victorious. During the campaign, the young candidate struck the keynote of
his Presidency—to "get this country moving again." "The torch has
been passed to a new generation of Americans," he exclaimed, who
were about to face a "new frontier." "The New Frontier is here
whether we seek it or not . . . uncharted areas of science and space,
unsolved problems of peace and war, unconquered pockets of ignorance and prejudice, unanswered questions of poverty and surplus."
Kennedy challenged Americans to explore this frontier and conquer
it. "The energy, the faith, the devotion which we bring to this endeavor will light our country and all who serve it, and the glow from
that fire can truly light the world."

The new President quickly created an administration of talent, including some of the most brilliant men in the world of business, law,
and education. He proposed legislation for aid to education, medical
care for the elderly, urban renewal, civil rights, a tax cut, and the
space program. All Congress let through was the space
appropriation—the old coalition of conservative Northern Republicans and Southern Democrats sidetracked the rest in committee.
Kennedy seemed unable to move the legislature through Congress.
The only major innovation his administration was able to produce
was the Peace Corps—and that by executive decree. Nevertheless,
Kennedy revitalized the office of the Presidency as the seat of national
leadership. During his brief administration, Washington was transformed into a cultural and social as well as a political capital
—poetry, painting, drama, chamber music, and a fresh sense of the
possible enlivened the city. It was all cut short by Kennedy's assassination in Dallas on November 22, 1963. The nationwide sense of loss
and the eulogies given to the fallen President at home and abroad
testify to the hope many felt he had carried for a better future.

LBJ'S "GREAT SOCIETY"

When a solemn Lyndon B. Johnson took the oath of office aboard Air
Force One after the assassination, he inaugurated a great change in

the national leadership. Johnson represented the rural Southwest as opposed to Kennedy's urban New England; projected an image of the common man, and could not match Kennedy's sophistication and charm. Under LBJ the White House took on a Texas flavor. Yet Johnson was a strong leader, a brilliant politician with firm ties to FDR's New Deal, which he had ardently supported. Above all a masterful manipulator of Congress, he liked to quote a passage from Isaiah as the key to his success: "Come, now let us reason together."

By a combination of reasoning, cajoling, and arm twisting, Johnson got Congress moving on the stalled Kennedy program. The same Southern Congressmen and Senators who had blocked it had an emotional commitment to their fellow Southerner's success. LBJ assigned the civil rights bill top priority, and it was passed in February, 1964. But the President was not content simply to follow Kennedy's program. During March he declared a "war on poverty" that resulted in the passage of the Economic Opportunity Act. This act created a multitude of new federal projects: the Job Corps, which like the ear-

VISTA (Volunteers in Service to America) was in the tradition of President Kennedy's personal activism and an integral part of President Johnson's "War on Poverty." Members would serve the public in such varied capacities as workers in the urban ghettos, classroom teacher aides, and vocational training instructors.

lier CCC provided work in conservation for young people but also trained school dropouts for technical trade positions; VISTA, a domestic equivalent of the Peace Corps; and "Head Start," an educational effort to give poor children a better chance to survive and learn in public schools. Success had its price, however. One newspaper columnist noted that Johnson "can make men do what he wants them to do, but he does not make them like it or him in the process."

The election of 1964 was only a brief interlude in Johnson's construction of a "Great Society." Republicans chose to give the American people "a choice, not an echo," and nominated the strongly conservative Barry Goldwater of Arizona. With Goldwater making statements such as the demand for "total victory" in the Cold War and a suggestion that the way to win in Vietnam was to drop "a low yield atomic bomb on Chinese supply lines in North Vietnam," Johnson had no difficulty labeling his opponent a "risky" choice for President. The country gave Johnson and the Democrats a landslide victory at the polls.

Johnson lost no time in pushing Congress to write the "Great Society" goals into law. He had astonishing success. The Eighty-ninth Congress proved to be the most productive since the New Deal: for aid to education, $1.3 billion; to fight poverty in the region of the Appalachian Mountains, $1.1 billion; for new housing, $7.5 billion; to clean up the nation's waterways and air, more than $3.7 billion; and $1.2 billion for urban development and the construction of "model cities." The civil rights bill of 1965 removed serious obstacles to black voters. Economically, the nation was experiencing an unprecedented growth and prosperity. General Motors alone made more gross profit than the entire GNP of the Netherlands. As a result of federal spending, a tax cut, and business cooperation, Johnson could proudly say in 1965 that "We are in the midst of the greatest upward surge of economic well-being in the history of any nation."

Yet by 1967–68 the "Great Society" was in trouble. Despite Johnson's assurance that the nation could afford both the war on poverty and the escalating war in Vietnam—"guns and butter"—the attempt to do so was beginning to create an intolerable tax burden on many middle-class Americans and resulting in serious inflation. John K. Galbraith, a Harvard economist, maintained that competitive capitalism had been replaced by a planned economy dominated by big business, advertising, and the government. Nor could the much publicized "war on poverty" show effective results—"the walls of the ghettos are not going to topple overnight," concluded one newspaper.

A now cautious Congress refused to fund adequately the President's domestic programs. But the final and decisive blow was Vietnam. As American casualties mounted and no end to the war appeared in sight, public protest increased. Students, who had played a prominent role in domestic politics since the early civil rights movement in the 1950s, led massive demonstrations against the war on campuses across the nation. Under the pressure of events, President Johnson finally decided not to run for reelection.

THE "NEW CONSERVATIVES"

Like Populism, Progressivism, the New Deal, and the New Frontier before it, the Great Society had sought to "better" the American system by removing its "faults and defects." That the system deserved saving was assumed from the beginning; earlier movements like socialism and more current ones like the "New Left," which dispute this assumption, have never gained more than a small voice in American politics. Adhering to the idea that the federal government is representative of the American people and guardian of the public interest, the Great Society followed its predecessors and sought their ends by granting the federal government a larger role in the economy and in dealing with social questions. Since the Great Society was Johnson's creation, it was expected that some of its programs would expire along with the term of their creator. But the trend toward a bigger, more involved national government that had been building since the turn of the century was expected to continue.

At first, this expectation appeared to be accurate. President Nixon, though a middle-of-the-road conservative, used the power of the federal government and especially that of the Presidency itself to a level not matched since Franklin Roosevelt. He invaded Cambodia in 1969, announced wage and price controls unprecedented in peacetime, and took upon himself the responsibility of deciding how much of Congressional appropriations could be spent without being "inflationary." Yet, after winning the 1972 election against liberal Democratic hopeful George McGovern by one of the largest landslides in American history, Nixon promised to end wage and price controls, return federal tax funds to state and local governments, and generally decentralize the powers and responsibilities of a "bloated" federal government. In his call for a return to the America that was "built not by government, but by people," Nixon appeared prepared to abandon "the condescending policies of paternalism" by cutting the funds for Great Society programs. The purpose, he maintained, was to balance the federal budget and inaugurate a "return to responsibility." This "New Federalism" was eclipsed by the deepening shadows of the Watergate scandal involving high officials and even the President himself (see Chapter 10).

Whether Nixon's goal of "reform" away from centralizing power and responsibility in the federal government will be reached remains to be seen. Regardless, it shows the influence of men like Daniel P. Moynihan, Daniel Bell, and Seymour Lipset of Harvard University who have been generally labeled the "new conservatives." These scholars have attacked the traditionally liberal point of view that proper programs and enough money can solve any problem. For example, Daniel Bell has written a book that persuasively argues that inequality of opportunity is the product not of educational differences but of pervasive family, ethnic, economic, and individual differences. Short of a quota system that would place people in positions regardless of merit—for which society would certainly suffer—inequality, Bell insists is inevitable. Similarly, Moynihan maintains, since money spent on educational improvement has been shown not to affect significantly students' learning, funds for education can be stabilized if not reduced. Other "new conservative" writers have suggested that local and state governments closer to the problems of their constituents should carry an increasing responsibility for economic and social reform without interference from the federal government.

This concept of reform runs contrary to the traditional liberal American ideas of reform that have prevailed in reformist politics since early in the century. Yet by 1972 the Nixon administration appeared ready to give the concept a trial in meeting the problems of pollution, urban blight, social welfare, crime, and apathy that plague society in the United States today. Nixon's resignation shifted the decision to President Ford, whose preoccupation with America's economic woes in early 1975 prevented him from taking any action on this issue.

SUGGESTIONS FOR ADDITIONAL READING

Richard Hofstadter, *The Age of Reform*, (1955). The classic account of the people involved in American political reform from the 1880s to the New Deal—their motives, dreams, and compromises with reality.

Eric F. Goldman, *Rendezvous with Destiny: A History of Modern American Reform*, (1957). A survey of the reform movement led by members of the declining, landed aristocracy.

Norman Pollack, *The Populist Response to Industrial America*, (1962). A description of the Populist crusade against the dehumanizing forces of industrialization, emphasizing the progressive and radical elements in the movement.

Lincoln Steffens, *The Shame of the Cities*, (1904). An attack against the bosses whose corrupt political machines dominated the big cities.

F. Scott Fitzgerald, *The Great Gatsby*, (1925). A novel revealing the hollow values of America's rich, ruling elite during the roaring twenties.

John Steinbeck, *The Grapes of Wrath*, (1939). A novel depicting the bitter world of the "Okie" migrants to California during the 1930s and the stubborn hostility and rejection they encountered there.

Michael Harrington, *The Other America*, (1962). A study of how the "other half" lives; influenced the War on Poverty.

CHAPTER SIX

THE EXERCISE OF POWER: FOREIGN POLICY OF THE UNITED STATES

1796
Washington's Farewell Address, warning America against "foreign entanglements."

1823
Monroe Doctrine announces special American interest in the western hemisphere.

1848
Treaty of Guadalupe-Hidalgo: height of Manifest Destiny sentiment.

1898
Spanish–American War makes the United States a world power.

1917
America enters World War I.

1941
United States "neutrality" is shattered at Pearl Harbor and America enters World War II.

1947
President Truman declares that the United States will support "free peoples" against attack; Russia and America begin the "Cold War."

1963
Russia and the United States begin detente with the Nuclear Test Ban treaty.

1965
America begins massive intervention in Vietnam.

1972
President Nixon visits China and the Soviet Union, with a truce concluded in Vietnam early the following year.

WHAT IS AMERICA'S WORLD ROLE?

The United States is currently involved in every corner of the world. Internationally, America wields such power that her chosen courses of action make waves in every major capital and vitally affect such global concerns as disarmament and the regulation of world trade. Exactly how Washington should exercise this power is a matter of hot debate. But it is not merely a question that should interest scholars and politicians. Actions of the United States in international matters also affect the domestic scene and the lives of ordinary citizens. Trade agreements with the Soviet Union or China can give a boost to the economy and raise the level of national prosperity—or the rate of inflation. The personal impact of the government's decision to wage war was brought home to many people who lost sons or husbands in the Vietnam conflict. Even those Americans apathetic toward their government's policies found their mobility threatened by Washington's energy crisis, triggered by the Arab oil embargo after the 1973 war in the Mideast.

America's choice of a world role should therefore be a matter of wide national concern since a poor choice will affect both the domestic and the international situation. Like every other nation, the United States chooses this role on the basis of its own interests as interpreted by the current executive and his advisors. Historically this interpretation has been characterized by a peculiar mixture of realism and idealism that has colored the whole nation's perception of the "outside world." How did this perception begin, and how has it influenced American foreign policy?

A NEW NATION'S DIPLOMACY

The American colonies were born during a time of intense international rivalry. European nations were engaged in a struggle for empire in the New World and their settlements were often pawns in this conflict. Many English colonists in America resented being drawn into a seemingly endless series of imperial wars in which they had little or no interest. At the same time, the New World settlers were beginning to acquire a sense of identity separate from their English brethren. When both were thrown together in an expedition against the Spanish port of Cartagena in the Caribbean, the British commander constantly referred to the colonials as "Americans" while they in turn labeled their English compatriots as "Europeans." Beyond feeling different, the American colonists regarded themselves as morally superior to the Old World societies. Even Benjamin Franklin shared this view of Old World corruption. Writing to his son about England in 1768, he remarked that "this whole venal nation is now at market, will be sold for about two millions, and might be bought out of the hands of the present bidders (if he would offer half a million more) by the very devil himself." The colonists were developing an exultant sense of difference. As the *New American Magazine* (note the name) expressed it, "A new world has arisen and will exceed the old!"

These attitudes crystallized in a determination to have as little to do with the wars and "immoral" societies of Europe as possible. A new medical school in Philadelphia was hailed for giving students the chance to study without having to set off "in pursuit of knowledge in a foreign country." When the seething troubles with Great Britain finally boiled over into war, Thomas Paine urged in his pamphlet *Common Sense* that "it is the true interest of America to steer clear of European contentions, which she never can do while, by her dependence on Britain, she is made the make-weight in the scale of British politics." Independence was the answer, insisted Paine, for it was only by completely severing the dangerous and corruptive ties with England that America could realize her full potential.

But independence did not solve the problem for the new nation's diplomats, who knew that they would have to have European aid to win their revolutionary war. France, being the habitual enemy of England, was of course the first country America turned to for such aid. Yet Congress remained aware that American interests were separate and distinct from European concerns. The model treaty it drew up for the instruction of its foreign diplomats emphasized that the only connection with European nations that Congress was prepared to approve was a commercial one. John Adams, who later became President, noted the first principle was that "we should calculate all our measures and foreign negotiations in such a manner as to avoid a too great dependence upon any one power of Europe—to avoid all obligations and temptations to take part in future European wars. . . ."

Americans were not without a certain sense of self-righteousness in maintaining their differences. When Adams himself was advised by a French diplomat to make the customary adjustments to European diplomatic niceties, he tartly retorted that "the dignity of North America does not consist in diplomatic ceremonials or any of the subtleties of etiquette; it consists solely in reason, justice, truth . . . [and] the rights of mankind."

This idealistic sense of difference between American and European interests did not prevent the leaders of the new nation from making realistic adjustments to necessity. Congress soon discovered that

France wanted America to commit herself to defend French possessions in the New World as the price for diplomatic recognition and
increased aid. Desperately in need of the supplies and military assistance Paris could send, Congress agreed to the conditions and signed
the Treaty of 1778 with France. That treaty led to Franco-American
military cooperation that eventually trapped Lord Cornwallis'
British army at Yorktown in 1781 and forced his surrender, bringing
an end to the Revolutionary War and guaranteeing American independence. But when the same treaty stood in the way of an advan-
tageous peace, the American negotiating team barely hesitated before they decided to violate its provisions and conclude a separate
agreement with Great Britain. The final Treaty of Paris signed in
1783 gave the United States ample room for expansion westward to
the Mississippi River and as much security as Congress could have
hoped for.

Unfortunately, Congress could expect little real security. Americans saw in their success the beginning of a "new order in the world,"
as the freshly minted Great Seal of the United States expressed it.
This was regarded with more contempt than wonder or awe in
Europe. "As to the future grandeur of America," wrote one leading
Englishman, "it is one of the idlest and most visionary notions that
ever was conceived even by writers of romance." The United States
was a republic in a world of monarchy, and a weak republic at that.
American statesmen had yet to prove that they could maintain their
nation in a hostile world climate.

ADOPTING NEUTRALITY

With this purpose in mind, the first United States government sought
to devise a strong foreign policy centering around two principles. The
first had been expressed by Congress even before the end of the war.
"The true interest of these states," Congress resolved, "requires that
they should be as little as possible entangled in the politics and controversies of European nations." America's treaty with France had
been a matter of necessity, but government leaders were determined
not to extend any further commitments. This decision was an emi-
nently practical one since the United States did not have the power to
become involved in the twists and turns of European diplomacy
without risking a war that could mean destruction. Yet it also had
strong elements of idealism. Americans felt that their high sense of
morality should be reflected in their nation's foreign policy. Thomas

Jefferson wrote that power and force may have been legitimate principles in the "dark ages," but he knew of only "one code of morality for men whether acting singly or collectively." He believed that America should adhere to that code and refuse to become enmeshed in Europe's power politics, which was "the pest of the peace of the world."

If this principle of noninvolvement had stood alone, then it might have led to an American policy of isolationism similar to that exercised by Japan during the same period. But it was modified by the second principle, accurately summed up by John Adams: "The business of America with Europe was commerce." The United States government avidly sought markets and trade wherever the opportunity for profit appeared. Such a policy was doubly legitimate—it was in the interest of merchants and farmers who depended upon trade for their livelihood, and it benefited the state by building a strong economy essential to the nation's stability and strength. Nor were commercial expansion and an aggressive trading policy beyond the strength of America, despite her weaknesses in the international political scene. Before the Revolution the colonies had been Great Britain's chief market and a vital link in her system of trade. American merchants had also carved out (somewhat illegally in many cases) a large part of the market in the Caribbean among Europe's colonies. These positions of strength could be used as levers to pry open other opportunities for profit.

Ideally, then, the new United States government hoped to steer clear of any political ties with Europe that could draw America into dangerous conflicts, and at the same time expand the country's commercial connections with that continent in the interests of its own citizens and in the interests of national strength. This two-pronged American version of neutrality immediately ran into difficulty. The United States could not hope to remain unentangled in European controversies as long as Europe retained strongholds in the New World. Great Britain still occupied a string of forts along the American-Canadian border after the Treaty of Paris had been signed and Spain still had a stranglehold on America's "back door," the Mississippi River. At least until these threats were removed the government would have to involve itself politically in European affairs. The main obstacle to commercial expansion was that the United States was outside the closed mercantilist trading systems of European nations that monopolized profitable avenues of trade. Even after the Constitution was adopted in 1789 and the power to make and execute foreign policy was concentrated in the federal government, President George Washington could not overcome these difficulties.

When the French Revolution brought on a general European war in 1793, the President's problems were compounded. America was still allied to France by the Treaty of 1778 and could be pulled into the conflict. Even Alexander Hamilton and Thomas Jefferson agreed that, technically, the United States would have to violate the treaty and remain neutral. Fortunately, the French believed that the United States would be more useful as a friendly neutral than as a weak cobelligerent. Britain reacted to the flourishing Franco-American trade that strengthened her enemy by instructing her Royal Navy to seize American ships and by inciting Indians against western settlers. President Washington sent John Jay to London to reach an accommodation on commercial practices and to avoid war. Jay came back with a treaty that was practically a surrender to British policies, but the United States reluctantly signed the treaty. Learning that America and Britain had reached an agreement, France exploded in anger and claimed the United States had violated the Treaty of 1778. The French navy began attacking American ships. United States diplomats trying to solve the problem were met by humiliating demands for a bribe by Paris officials. Americans in turn became angry and from 1797 to 1800 an undeclared war raged on the high seas between the two nations. Upon retiring from office in 1796, George Washington foresaw this danger and in his Farewell Address warned his countrymen that they should not entangle their "peace and prosperity in the toils of European ambition, rivalship, interest, humor, or caprice." He briefly reminded Americans that the "Great rule of conduct" for the United States in foreign relations was that "in extending our commercial relations" to other countries America ought "to have with them as little *political* connections as possible." It remained for President John Adams to end the war with France and cancel the Treaty of 1778, ending America's only formal connection to a European power. By the time Thomas Jefferson took office in 1801, international affairs appeared to have quieted down somewhat.

NEUTRALITY TESTED

President Jefferson was confident that he could make neutrality work. He observed that in times of peace American commerce thrived, and in times of war it could prosper as a "neutral carrier" of goods to the belligerents. Either way, Jefferson wrote, "the New World will fatten on the follies of the Old." None of the warring nations would attack America's rights to the carrying trade under international law for fear of antagonizing the United States' growing commercial power. The President also felt that since the border with Canada was quiet and Spain had given Americans the right to use New Orleans to ship out western produce, there was no reason to become embroiled in European rivalries. The United States could remain aloof from the "follies" and "corruption" of the Old World.

Jefferson's plan met a serious check when Spain turned the Louisiana Territory over to France and Napoleon prepared to incorporate the area into a new French Empire. New Orleans, which had become essential to America's western commerce, was closed to American use. Jefferson immediately began negotiations to purchase the city from France, fearing that the only other way to get it back would be to abandon neutrality and "marry ourselves to the British fleet and nation." Fortunately, Napoleon had so much difficulty in arranging to occupy Louisiana that in 1803 he decided to sell the whole area to the United States. Astounded, Jefferson agreed to buy it. At one stroke, western commerce secured vital New Orleans, the American domain doubled in size, and a potentially dangerous European power was removed from the continent. Neutrality had been preserved and peaceful prosperity could continue.

Even when war broke out between Great Britain and France shortly thereafter, America continued to thrive under the policy of neutrality. From 1803 to 1805, American commerce experienced a remarkable boom, and the United States became the world's greatest neutral carrier. British shippers resented this trade because they were losing business profits and because the trade was with England's enemies, France and Spain. After the battle of Trafalgar, in which Admiral Nelson smashed the Franco-Spanish fleet and established British naval supremacy, the Royal Navy began to crack down on American commerce. Then Napoleon won the battle of Austerlitz and gained virtual control over the entire European continent. With control of the seas, the British "shark" declared a blockade of Europe. Stalking the continent, the French "tiger" decreed that any ship that traded with England would be seized upon landing in Europe.

American commerce was entangled in this life and death struggle. It could trade with Britain only on stiff British terms and it could not safely trade with Europe at all. Both belligerents were breaking international law and violating America's neutral rights, and England was even forcibly taking seamen from American ships for service in their own navy. Each nation was committed to victory over the other, and was ready to do anything in its power to win the war. United States protests were ignored, but President Jefferson was as opposed in principle to war as he was to yielding any American rights. From a pragmatic point of view, he also recognized the hazards of war. He felt that economic coercion in the form of a boycott of foreign trade (or an embargo) would force the belligerents to respect those rights and bring a return to peaceful prosperity. From 1807 to 1809 all trade with the warring nations was shut off as the embargo was strictly enforced throughout the nation. One New Yorker noted that "the coffee-houses were almost empty; the streets near the waterside were almost deserted; the grass had begun to grow upon the wharves." Yet Britain and France stubbornly held to their war policies and the embargo failed. Jefferson left office knowing that the only alternatives were war or a meek surrender of the nation's rights.

For two more years the government tried halfhearted variations of the embargo, hoping the European war would end. The policy of neutrality seemed impotent, unable either to prevent British naval vessels from seizing American sailors and cargoes just outside their home ports or to stop England from encouraging Indian uprisings on the western frontier. "War Hawks" from the West and South in Congress demanded action. "Gentlemen," cried one, "we must fight. We are forever disgraced if we do not." They idealistically presented the question as a matter of national honor, as a choice between the humiliation of giving up American rights under international law or boldly going to war to defend those rights. At the same time, the "War Hawks" blatantly suggested that America could take Canada and the Spanish Floridas and thereby gain more valuable territory. Finally, when France appeared to change its anti-American policies in 1812 and the British still clung to theirs, Congress declared war against England.

The War of 1812 nearly proved to be a national disaster. Far from conquering Canada or the Floridas, America was blockaded by the Royal Navy, Maine was occupied, and the Capitol at Washington, D.C. was sacked and burned by British troops. But Americans took pride in a few naval victories against the "Mistress of the Seas," and Andrew Jackson's twelfth-hour victory at New Orleans (fought after peace had been made at Ghent, Belgium) gave them the illusion of having won the conflict. When Britain and the United States agreed to end the war in 1815, Europe grudgingly realized that America was not going to conform to its expectations and disintegrate. The United States had won a more secure place in international affairs.

"MANIFEST DESTINY"

From this position, America launched a policy of expansionism that lasted for 35 years and ended only when the country had stretched its borders "from sea to shining sea." One of the forces that powered this drive was nationalism. A perceptive government official observed that "the war has reinstated the national feelings. The people have now more general objects of attachment with which their pride and political opinions are connected. They are more American; they feel and act more like a nation. . . ." If this nationalism was the motivating power behind expansionism, then the desire to remove all Old World influence from the continent and avoid any future involvement in European problems 'justified' the policy. Washington policymakers believed that as long as Europe retained territories in the New World, it would be impossible for America to remain unentangled in Old World power politics. Since neutrality had become an American

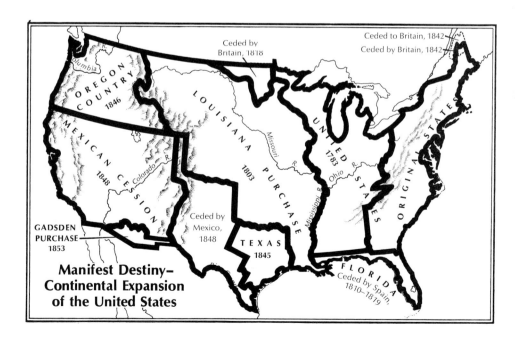

Manifest Destiny— Continental Expansion of the United States

dogma, successive United States governments sought whenever possible to oust European influence from the New World.

Spain was the first to feel the impact of America's new assertiveness. During the War of 1812 her province of West Florida had been torn away by a "popular revolution" orchestrated in Washington. President Monroe now demanded that Madrid yield East Florida since the Spanish government could not keep the area's Indians from raiding American settlements. Spain was already in a weak position, and when General Andrew Jackson moved into Florida with an army to "subdue the Indians," Madrid decided it had better compromise before it lost the province altogether. In the Transcontinental Treaty of 1819, Spain gave America East Florida and ceded her claim to the Oregon territory in return for a favorable Texas boundary. The United States was now a continental power, and Secretary of State John Quincy Adams exulted that "The acknowledgement of a definite line of boundary to the South Sea forms a great epoch in our history."

American attention then shifted to South America, where the Latin American patriots had all but eliminated Spanish influence by 1815. One Congressman reflected public enthusiasm for the movement, hailing "the glorious spectacle of eighteen millions of people, struggling to burst their chains and to be free." Soon after the United States recognized the new Latin American republics in 1822, rumors reached Washington that the Holy Alliance (reactionary European countries that were trying to suppress liberal dissent on the continent) was considering invading South America to restore the area to Spain. To compound this threat the Russians were moving into the Pacific Northwest. Great Britain, knowing that the United States would be alarmed and wanting to keep its profitable trade with the new republics, offered to join with America in opposition to these moves.

But Secretary of State Adams argued that it was time the United States announced its foreign policy principles and claimed a special interest in keeping the Western Hemisphere free of European influences. He convinced President Monroe that it would be more "candid" and "dignified" to act alone rather than to "come in as a cock-boat in the wake of a British man-of-war." Besides, he insisted, England would side with America in any case for reasons of her own. On December 2, 1823, the President in his annual message to Congress presented what became known as the Monroe Doctrine. It held that the "systems" of government of Europe and America were incompatible, and that the United States would regard as "unfriendly" any effort by a European state to extend its "system" to the Western Hemisphere. In return, America would adhere to its traditional policy and stay out of purely European affairs. European statesmen condemned the document as "blustering" and "arrogant," realizing that it was England's navy and not Monroe's Doctrine that discouraged the Holy Alliance's purposes. Initial Latin American enthusiasm waned when the United States did not follow up the President's statement with aid and declined to attend the Panama Congress called by the new republics to discuss inter-American interests in 1826. Washington still hesitated to involve itself directly in the chaotic politics of Latin America.

The federal government showed no such hesitation in expanding its influence in North America. A constantly growing agrarian populace demanded more land and sought it in every corner of the continent. The American merchant marine was now second in size only to Great Britain's, and commercial interests had their eyes on the natural harbors of Puget Sound and San Francisco on the west coast as keys that would command "the trade of the isles of the Pacific, of the East, and of China." A growing nationalism which held that America should take its democratic system to "less blessed" people on the continent encouraged these impulses for agrarian and commercial expansion. Public fervor for expansion grew to the extent that newspapers began to proclaim that it was America's "manifest destiny to overspread and to possess the whole of the continent which Providence has given us. . . ."

The United States government was not slow in responding to this cry. Indians that fought westward expansion were either destroyed or pushed onto temporary reservations. When American settlers swarmed into the Northwest and merchants eyed the harbor of Puget Sound, Washington contested Great Britain's right to the Oregon territory. The two governments eventually agreed to compromise and divide it between them. The disputes with Mexico proved more difficult. When Americans who had emigrated to the Mexican province of Texas revolted against their government, Washington allowed private companies to extend them financial aid that made possible the revolt's success. Later, in 1845, the United States annexed Texas over the angry protests of Mexico. President Polk renewed earlier American efforts to buy California, chiefly because of the fine harbor of San Francisco. But Mexico felt it had been robbed of Texas and was in no mood to sell. Unable to gain the province by peaceful means, Polk precipitated war with Mexico by sending an army to the disputed Texas–Mexico border.

The Mexican War (1846–1848) ended only when an American army fought its way into Mexico City. The Treaty of Guadalupe-Hidalgo gave the United States all of California and much of the present Southwest. Mexico received 15 million dollars in consolation for losing half her national territory. This settlement essentially completed the boundaries of the continental United States, filled the popular desire for land, gave American merchants the Pacific ports they wanted for trading with the Orient, and marked the height of "manifest destiny" sentiment. But it also opened the question of whether or not to extend slavery into the newly won territories, a question that increased sectional tensions and dominated the American political scene until it finally led to Civil War.

A NEW WORLD POWER

When the American states emerged united again after the Civil War in 1865, people were more concerned with national recovery and the development and settlement of the West than with further territorial acquisitions. While Washington was able to continue promoting commercial expansion in China in the 1870s and to maintain its influence in Latin America, the public would not support efforts to gain new naval bases in the Caribbean. "We cannot have colonies, dependencies, subjects," explained one newspaper, "without renouncing the essential conception of democratic institutions." Even Secretary of State Seward's purchase of Alaska from Russia was ridiculed as "Seward's folly" and barely passed Congress. For both ideological and practical reasons, Americans were not interested in overseas expansion.

By the 1880s, however, attitudes were beginning to change. The Darwinian concept of "survival of the fittest" was being extended to include nations and races, creating a vigorous international competition based entirely on economic and military power. This type of competition fed aggressive nationalism by making a country's power and colonial possessions the measure of its "fitness." All of Europe was engaging in the race for colonies and military power, and some Americans felt it was only realistic that America join them. Financiers and industrialists pragmatically argued that expansion was essential to the health of the American economy. Naval expert Alfred

Thayer Mahan pointed out the necessity of a large merchant marine and a big navy to protect it if the United States hoped to compete in the rush for markets and power, or even to protect itself from those nations that did. Other people reasoned from an ideological point of view, maintaining that the United States was obliged to bring Christianity and democracy to the "downtrodden pagans" of the world. In this atmosphere, America joined the rest of Europe on the imperialist path. Pacific coaling stations to serve the growing navy were obtained, and Samoa and Hawaii were brought under American dominance. Washington boldly asserted its primacy in the Western Hemisphere by invoking the Monroe Doctrine against Britain in a dispute with Venezuela.

Then an indigenous Cuban revolt against Spanish rule brought that island to the forefront of American concern in 1896. The Cubans pictured their revolution as a desperate effort to overthrow repression. The American press picked up this theme and presented it to the public complete with notes of its disruptive effects on trade and investments and with sensational stories of atrocities designed to sell copy. But President McKinley, after trying to buy Cuba from Spain and offering to mediate the conflict without success, declared that "we want no wars of conquest" and refused to intervene. Shortly after his statement the mysterious sinking of the American cruiser *Maine* on February 15, 1898 in Havana Harbor sent a wave of war hysteria through the nation. Rather than defy the public and risk the breakup of his party, the President asked Congress to declare war on Spain, although Madrid had already acquiesced to most of the demands contained in an American ultimatum two days earlier.

The war lasted only 10 weeks; one American called it "a splendid little war." Its biggest event was not the conquest of Cuba, whose independence Congress had already guaranteed, but the capture of the Philippines. A great debate followed in Congress and the press over what to do with the Pacific islands. Many Americans had sincerely approved the Spanish-American war on the humanitarian grounds of helping the Cubans. They expected that the Philippines would be given their independence just as Cuba had, and felt that making the islands a colony without their consent would be a violation of basic American ideals. Some religious organizations, however, insisted that it would be better for the Philippines to be "governed, educated, and civilized" by the United States. Advocates of naval and commercial expansion argued that the Philippines were needed as a stepping-stone to China and as a base to protect American commerce in the East. Bowing again to public pressure and private business interests, McKinley sided with the imperialists and the Philippines were retained despite a bloody struggle with Filipino patriots. An angry Mark Twain grimly proposed a new American flag "with the white stripes painted black and the stars replaced by a skull and crossbones."

The United States now had an overseas empire. "Our war in aid of Cuba has assumed undreamed of dimensions," marvelled one newspaper, "willy nilly we have entered upon our career as a world power." It was a career recognized by the powers of Europe and a course that would lead to a break with the traditional American policy of noninvolvement in European affairs.

BREAKING WITH TRADITION

Ever since George Washington had given his Farewell Address in 1796, the United States had been following a two-pronged foreign policy that stressed noninvolvement in European affairs—except when they intruded into the Western Hemisphere—and promoted commercial expansion. The assumption of this policy that the government could promote trade without becoming entangled in foreign political concerns had only been challenged once, by the War of 1812. Since then America's commerce had expanded unhindered, developing as the United States grew in industrial power until it was the equal of any in the world. By the early twentieth century America had assumed the role of "policeman" in Latin America, often intervening in the internal affairs of South American countries to "keep the peace." The construction of an overseas empire in the Pacific now opened an Asian market of 800 million consumers to American businessmen.

China was also being sought as a market by European nations, who tended to carve out chunks of territory for their own commercial development and to exclude other countries from these zones. Rather than concede such a huge potential market for surplus American production, Secretary of State John Hay sent diplomatic notes to the major European powers. These notes called for equal commercial opportunity for all countries trading with China and respect for that nation's independence and territorial integrity. Europeans scoffed at America's proposal, but in fact China did remain open because no single nation was strong enough to monopolize trade. Although Hay later admitted that the United States would not "enforce these

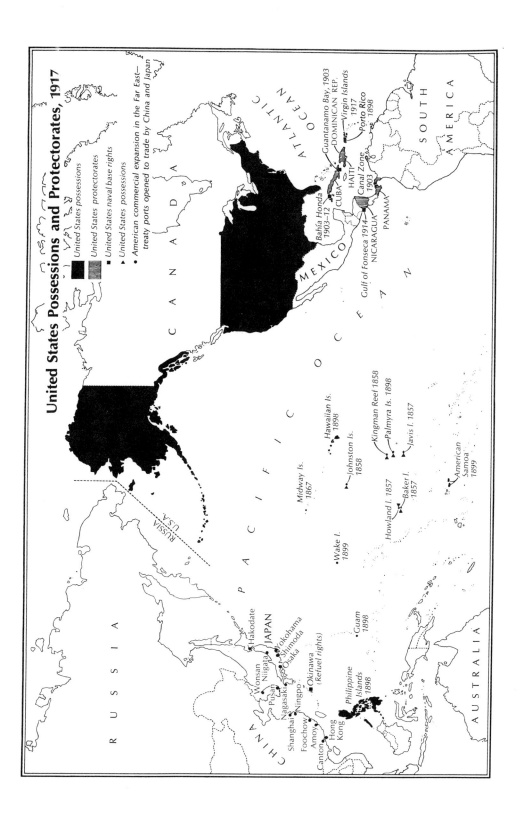

United States Possessions and Protectorates, 1917

■ United States possessions

▨ United States protectorates

■ United States naval base rights

▲ United States possessions

● American commercial expansion in the Far East—treaty ports opened to trade by China and Japan views" and insisted that this "Open Door" policy was perfectly in keeping with the principle of neutrality, the fact remained that the United States had involved itself in European policies to protect its commercial interests. It appeared that the scope of American commercial expansion had been enlarged to the point where Washington could no longer promote trade without becoming involved in foreign political concerns. This became even more obvious when President Theodore Roosevelt offered to mediate the 1904–05 Russo-Japanese War "in the interests of peace"—and to protect the Open Door.

The United States had extended its role in international affairs from "policeman" in the Western Hemisphere to "concerned businessman" in the Far East. In 1905 when Germany and France clashed over control of the North African state of Morocco, President Theodore Roosevelt broke the last of the taboos against interference in strictly European affairs and offered to mediate the disagreement, again "in the interests of world peace." Washington was still careful to maintain its freedom of action by refusing to tie itself to any European nation or alliance, but Roosevelt had established that the United States had an interest in world peace—an interest at least partially based on the knowledge that a major war would endanger American commerce. The desire for peace was pragmatic as well as idealistic.

But peace was a mirage. Intense competition between imperialist countries aggravated by aggressive nationalism had divided Europe into two armed camps: the Entente (France, Britain, and Russia) and the Central Powers (Germany and Austria-Hungary). The assassination of the heir to the throne of Austria-Hungary in June of 1914 sparked a series of actions and reactions that snowballed into war in August. Americans were appalled by the conflict, but since its origins were purely European they felt detached from it. "Luckily we have the Atlantic between us and Europe," observed one newspaper with relief. "It is their war, not ours." President Woodrow Wilson immediately proclaimed American neutrality. Despite confident European predictions of a quick war, the conflict soon degenerated into a prolonged and bloody stalemate.

As both sides stepped up their war efforts hoping to break the stalemate, the United States found itself gradually being drawn into the dispute. The Entente violated America's neutral rights by preventing all trade with German-held territory, but Britain was careful to conciliate Washington to avoid a break and to increase her ties to American businessmen by getting loans and buying huge quantities of supplies. The Central Powers also modified their originally strict submarine blockade of England, agreeing to observe the rules of sea warfare to conciliate President Wilson's strong stand on neutral rights. But Allied propaganda against German atrocities and incidents where German submarines sank ships with Americans onboard (like the *Lusitania* incident in 1916) angered many of Wilson's constituents. Efforts by the President and by private American citizens to mediate the war failed because neither side would accept "peace without victory." Wilson's own alternatives were narrowing because of his idealistic stand on the right of Americans to travel anywhere they choose and the principle of "free ships make free goods." In January of 1917 the Germans decided to make a final effort for victory by using the troops that had defeated Russia to attack the western front, and by resuming unrestricted submarine warfare. The resulting indiscriminate sinkings and the interception of a German note to Mexico (offering that country her former territories in the Southwest if she would go to war with America) were enough to persuade Congress to declare war on the Central Powers. America's break with the tradition of neutrality was complete.

President Wilson was determined that the break should be justified by nothing less than the creation of a new world order. Even as American money, supplies, and troops were turning the tide of the First World War and bringing about an Allied victory, Wilson declared his hope for "a universal dominion of right by such a concert of free peoples as shall bring peace and safety to all nations and make the world itself at last free." This idealism was not new—nearly a century earlier John Quincy Adams had said that America's heart was "wherever the standard of freedom and independence has been or shall be unfurled." The difference was that Wilson was determined to use the nation's power to champion peace and freedom, while Adams had warned against going abroad "in search of monsters to destroy." President Wilson thought he had his "concert of free peoples" and the key to future peace with justice in the League of Nations, established at Versailles in 1918. But many Americans were disillusioned with the Versailles Treaty's harsh terms for the losers and territorial gains for the victors. The world, it appeared, had been made safe for the winners rather than "safe for democracy."

Capitalizing on this national mood, Wilson's isolationist opponents determined to reject the collective security of the League for an "America first" policy. In the Senate they united with the Republican opposition to block United States membership in the League despite

In contrast to President Wilson, the leaders of Great Britain, France, and Italy had strictly practical ends in mind—the punishment of Germany, acquisition of new territories, and redrawing the boundaries of Europe to further their own power and security. It was these goals, not Wilson's idealistic ones, that shaped the Versailles peace treaty and disillusioned the American people.

the President's strong effort to push the treaty through. These isolationists who sought a return to non-involvement, though in harmony with American tradition, were at odds with the world role that America had created for itself over the preceding 20 years and that it had confirmed by entering World War I. The United States had had a decisive influence on that war and was responsible for the peace that ended it. By rejecting that responsibility the United States turned its back on the situation that the peace had created, a situation that would eventually result in another war.

THE FAILURE OF NEUTRALITY

Ironically, another war was precisely what American policymakers hoped to avoid by preserving their freedom of action. The 1920s and '30s were not really a period of isolationism as much as they were an attempt by various Washington administrations to champion the cause of world peace without committing the United States to enforcing it. A strong nationwide peace movement, sustained by the belief that financiers and munitions manufacturers had driven America into a wasteful First World War, demanded that the government promote peace but remain neutral. Washington sponsored a series of naval disarmament conferences that temporarily eased the naval arms race between Britain, the United States, and Japan. America also began to participate in the humanitarian efforts of the League of Nations, although she still declined to join. The crowning achievement of the peace movement came when 64 nations signed the Kellogg-Briand Pact outlawing aggressive war, an event hailed by the American public as a "thing to rejoice over . . . it is superb, it is magnificent!"

Then the illusion was shattered. The Versailles peace had created international inequities that were especially rankling to Germany, and even Japan (who was among the victors) was dissatisfied with the second-class status accorded her. In 1931 the nation of the Rising Sun began a policy of expansion into Chinese Manchuria and later attacked China itself. Asia was engulfed in war. At the same time, Europe also faced the specter of invading armies. Adolf Hitler's rise to power in Germany in 1933 on the platform of prosperity, national pride, and national power was paralleled by the creation of other fascist (rightist dictatorships) governments in European nations dissatisfied with the status quo. Mussolini's Italy joined Hitler's Germany in a policy of rearmament and expansion, intervening to help Spanish nationalists led by General Franco create a fascist government in Spain.

Initially, the American response merely acknowledged these threats to world peace by making diplomatic protests on the immorality of breaking treaties. To protect the nation from involvement, Congress passed a series of neutrality acts. One American policymaker flatly stated that the United States would not commit itself to "use its armed forces for the settlement of any dispute anywhere." But neither Japan nor Germany and Italy feared moral indignation or weak sanctions. The Japanese continued to swallow China and began expanding into Southeast Asia shortly after the Germans absorbed Austria and Czechoslovakia in 1939. President Franklin Roosevelt's attempt to warn the nation that these aggressions "are creating a state of international anarchy and instability from which there is no escape through mere isolation or neutrality" fell on deaf ears. "America wants peace," pleaded one newspaper.

Peace, however, was fast disappearing. Britain and France finally declared war on Germany after Hitler invaded Poland in September of 1939. A shocked America watched the Nazis launch a blitzkrieg (lightning war) in Spring, 1940 that conquered France and most of Europe within a year. The German air force showered Britain with bombs, and it appeared that Hitler was on the verge of winning the war. In the Far East, Japan joined Germany and Italy to form the Axis and put pressure on British and French holdings in Asia. Everywhere the Axis was triumphant.

President Roosevelt realized that the United States could not afford to stand by and watch most of Europe and Asia fall to the militarist Axis power. Gradually, the President guided the nation away from neutrality in an effort to aid the battered Allies. England received desperately needed war material on "loan," the American navy began patrolling the Atlantic against German submarines, and Washington placed strategic materials vital to the Japanese war economy on embargo to force Japan to halt her expansion. This measure forced Japan to reconsider her policy, but when faced with Washington's demand to withdraw from China, Tokyo secretly chose war in the Fall of 1941 rather than "humiliation." Congress and the American people, however, were still deeply divided over whether to go to war. Acting as "the arsenal of democracy" was one thing, suffering the casualties of a world war something else. Not until Japan struck with a surprise attack on Pearl Harbor on December 7, 1941, did the country unite behind a policy of total war.

Once again America's action proved decisive. By 1941 Hitler's invasion of the Soviet Union had been stalled at a tremendous cost in lives and material to the Russians, and Axis fortunes began to slide downhill. The United States and England together drove the Nazis from North Africa and pursued them into Sicily and Italy, knocking the latter out of the war in September, 1943. In early June, 1944, the Allies invaded German-occupied France as Russia advanced from the East. Aided by Allied air power, American, British, French, and Russian armies finally forced Germany to surrender on May 8, 1945. At the same time American sea and air power had turned the tide against Japan in the Pacific. Japan's naval arm was broken in the battles off Midway Island and in the Coral Sea near Australia. Despite suicidal Japanese resistance, by August, 1945 America had penetrated to the home islands. President Harry Truman made the decision to drop two newly developed atomic bombs on Hiroshima and Nagasaki to avoid a costly invasion and bring a quick end to the war. Stunned by the desolation that the A-bombs created, Japan surrendered on September 2, 1945. World War II was over. So was the traditional American policy of neutrality.

The United States was now ready, as it had not been after the First World War, to take responsibility for shaping the postwar world and for seeing that peace was maintained. American plans for the postwar world still included idealistic commitments to "freedom from want and fear" and "the right of all peoples to choose the form of government under which they will live." Washington policymakers were aware, however, that this would involve patient American leadership and the cooperation of the wartime Allies.

COLD WAR AND CONTAINMENT

Unfortunately, cooperation was lacking. As the Axis threat that had cemented the American-British-Russian alliance together receded, cracks began opening that endangered postwar harmony. The United States, Great Britain, France, and most of the other countries that had joined the United Nations against the Axis were chiefly concerned with the restoration of world peace and security. But the Soviets viewed "security" in a somewhat different light. Russia had been invaded twice in a generation by the Germans through Poland, and Moscow was determined not only to destroy German power but also to retain strong influence over Eastern Europe. Since the Slavic states were traditionally cool if not hostile toward Russia, Stalin forced upon them communist governments friendly to Moscow as the Red Army "liberated" Eastern Europe from the Nazis. Only Yugoslavia, which had beaten the Germans on its own, was able to set up a communist regime that was nationalist in character and not subordinate to Moscow.

This policy was totally unacceptable to the United States because it was inconsistent with the principle of national self-determination. President Roosevelt, however, was certain he could "handle Stalin" and eventually bring Russia around to the American point of view. Rather than threaten the Allied harmony that would be necessary if the newly created United Nations organization was to prevent future conflicts, Washington did not insist on hard and fast resolutions of disagreements at the final wartime conference of Yalta in 1945. But when the war ended and a new basis for understanding was needed, the disagreements widened instead. Washington wanted to end Allied occupation of Germany and reunite the Russian-occupied East-

In the last of a series of wartime conferences, Churchill, Roosevelt, and Stalin met at Yalta to hammer out the shape of postwar Europe. Soon after, the Soviets violated the provision calling for free elections in Eastern Europe. Though it has been charged that FDR was hoodwinked by the wily Russian dictator, Churchill himself later recorded that "Our hopeful assumptions were soon to be falsified. Still they were the only ones possible at the time."

ern zone with the Anglo-American Western zone. Moscow was determined to strip its zone of resources and organize it into another puppet state. America demanded that Russia live up to its promises to permit free elections in Eastern Europe. The Soviet Union countered that since elections would not result in friendly governments to which they were entitled for security reasons, there would be no elections. Stalin, wrote the American ambassador to Russia, could not understand America's stand on a principle: "It is difficult for him to understand why we should want to interfere with Soviet policy . . . unless we have some ulterior motive." Neither side would yield. An "iron curtain," in Winston Churchill's words, slammed down between Eastern and Western Europe.

Washington now faced the problem of developing a new policy to deal with the emerging East-West struggle that had destroyed hopes for peace through collective security. The American public would not abandon the principles of self-determination and freedom, and was frustrated because the Allies were losing the peace although they had won the war. United States policymakers realized they did not have the diplomatic power to "enforce" those principles without resorting to war, so they adopted a policy of "long-term, patient but firm and vigilant containment of Russian expansive tendencies" that would support America's principles short of an armed conflict.

Containment's first test was in Greece and Turkey. When the British warned Washington in 1947 that they could no longer help Greece fight off a communist revolt or counter Soviet threats on Turkish territory, President Truman announced that the United States would take over British responsibilities. "I believe it must be," he said, "the policy of the United States to support free peoples who are resisting attempted subjugation by armed minorities or by outside pressures." This Truman Doctrine provided a model for the Marshall Plan, which was designed to revive the nations of western Europe and thereby prevent the ominous growth of the communist parties that were thriving as a result of postwar economic stagnation. When Russian-supported communists took over Czechoslovakia and the Soviets began a blockade of Berlin, America participated in the creation of the North Atlantic Treaty Organization (NATO) as a military alliance against Communism in 1948. For the time being, the "Free World's" position in Europe appeared secure.

Its situation in the Far East, however, was shaky. In 1949, despite enormous American economic assistance, the decaying Chinese nationalist government fell to Mao Tse-tung's Red Army. Although the United States refused to recognize Mao's forces and continued to regard the nationalists as the legitimate government, China went communist. The long and bitter debate over this event revealed that many Americans regarded any communist gain as the result of a global Russian conspiracy for world domination. Communist North Korea's invasion of South Korea in 1950 seemed to confirm that belief, and Washington quickly extended the policy of containment to Asia. President Truman won United Nations approval for the movement of American forces into Korea to turn back the invasion. When the American effort triggered Chinese intervention and the "police action" became a frustrating stalemate, Washington adopted a "hard line." America opposed Communist China's membership in the United Nations, protected the Nationalist Chinese remnants on their Formosa sanctuary, and sought the participation of other Asian nations in containing the Red Chinese.

The French were only too happy to cooperate. In their colony of Indochina, a nationalist–communist coalition led by Ho Chi Minh was fighting against the restoration of French rule after World War II. Unlike Korea, this struggle was less an issue of military aggression than of a guerrilla war against remnants of European colonialism. President Roosevelt had planned to ease the French out of Indochina. But the President died in office, and Washington now regarded the war as part of a "single hostile front" against communism, pointing out that China was giving arms to the Vietminh (Ho's guerrillas). Even though the Eisenhower administration proceeded to underwrite 80 percent of the French war costs, the Vietminh inflicted a decisive defeat on French forces in 1954 at Dien Bien Phu. Desirous of a graceful exit, Paris turned the entire situation over to a convention of concerned nations at Geneva. The Geneva accords provided for the temporary separation of Vietnam into Northern (controlled by the Vietminh) and Southern (controlled by the French) zones pending a free election scheduled for 1956. The United States, though not a participant, assured the convention that it would not interfere with the settlement. France promptly left the area, turning her zone over to a Vietnamese government favorable to the West. Washington hoped this regime might counter Ho's influence and keep at least part of Vietnam from becoming communist. Eisenhower's administration supported the South Vietnamese government when it refused to hold the 1956 elections, which almost certainly would have resulted in a Vietminh victory. This action caused a renewal of the struggle for power in Southeast Asia between the Vietminh and American-backed forces. The fighting spread outside Vietnam into Laos and Cambodia with the Vietminh slowly gaining the upper hand.

Containment was also running into problems in the Middle East and Latin America. Washington had hoped to win over the Arab peoples to the Western position, securing the strategic Middle East from Soviet penetration and insuring Western access to Arab oil holdings. But the Arab nationalists mistrusted the United States. They were still skeptical of the imperialist record of the western powers and nourished great anger toward Israel, which was supported from its birth by the United States. Into this unstable scene stepped the Soviets, whose influence in the Middle East grew as the

Arab states seesawed back and forth between the American and Russian sides. In Latin America, the United States faced the first challenge to its dominance since the Monroe Doctrine when a Cuban revolution against a repressive Havana regime placed pro-Soviet Fidel Castro at the head of its new government.

THE END OF THE OLD ORDER?

A "Third World" was emerging in Asia, Africa, and the Middle East from states that were former colonies of the European powers. In these areas, the people were primarily concerned with independence, economic advancement, and social reform. The Cold War began to assume a new shape, with both the Soviet Union and the United States vying for the favors of the Third World. The bipolar world, characterized by firm East–West divisions and conflicts, was disintegrating. In its place was rising the familiar, pre-Cold War polycentric pattern, in which many nations now demanded that their interests be respected. Moscow, for example, was becoming more worried about its relations with Red China and Eastern Europe, and Washington was concerning itself more with its NATO troubles with France and its Latin American relations. There were a few more sharp Russian-American confrontations (over Berlin, culminating in the Berlin Wall and over Laos, ending in that nation's precarious neutrality), which reached a peak during the Cuban missile crisis of 1962. Moscow had tried to alter the strategic nuclear balance by sneaking missiles into Cuba, but American spy planes discovered them. President Kennedy reacted firmly, demanding that the missiles be withdrawn and instituting a blockade of the island. The Soviet Union was forced to back down. Premier Khrushchev, who had lost his Cuban gamble and whose domestic policy was failing, was ousted and replaced by a less adventurous leadership.

From 1963 on, the United States and the Soviet Union began a slow detente (an easing of tensions). Both had been sobered by the Cuban confrontation, which had brought them to the brink of war. Each nation felt that "peaceful competition" would be more safe and effective than perpetual crisis. The first step came with the Nuclear Test Ban Treaty of 1963, limiting atomic weapons testing to underground sites. President Johnson and the Moscow leadership held a series of meetings to explore areas for further agreements. But it remained for President Nixon to produce the startling breakthrough. In 1972 he became the first American President to visit the Soviet Union, and

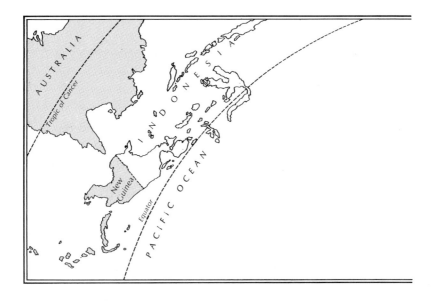

came back to the United States with a promising trade agreement and the first Russian-American arms limitation treaty. Months earlier Nixon had made an historic trip to Red China, which marked the end of the American policy of ignoring that nation since 1949, and opened the way for establishing formal relations.

These signs of progress were encouraging, but areas of tension still remained. Russia had demonstrated its determination to keep Eastern Europe within the Soviet sphere of influence when it invaded Czechoslovakia in 1968 to suppress a liberal communist regime in Prague. The United States, too, had indicated its aim of preventing any further spread of communism in Latin America by forcibly suppressing a nationalist–communist revolt in the Dominican Republic in 1965. Washington modified its policy somewhat when it chose not to openly oppose a new leftist government legally elected in Chile in 1971, but did use economic subversion to undermine that government. In short, both nations were committed to holding onto their own areas of dominance. Where these commitments came into conflict, as in the Middle East, each side refrained from actions that could force a confrontation. When the Arab-Israeli hostility broke out in a Seven Day War in 1967, Washington and Moscow avoided direct involvement and instead watched their favorites fight on a limited scale. Despite a renewed threat of open confrontation when the Arab-Israeli conflict resumed in October, 1973, both the Soviet Union

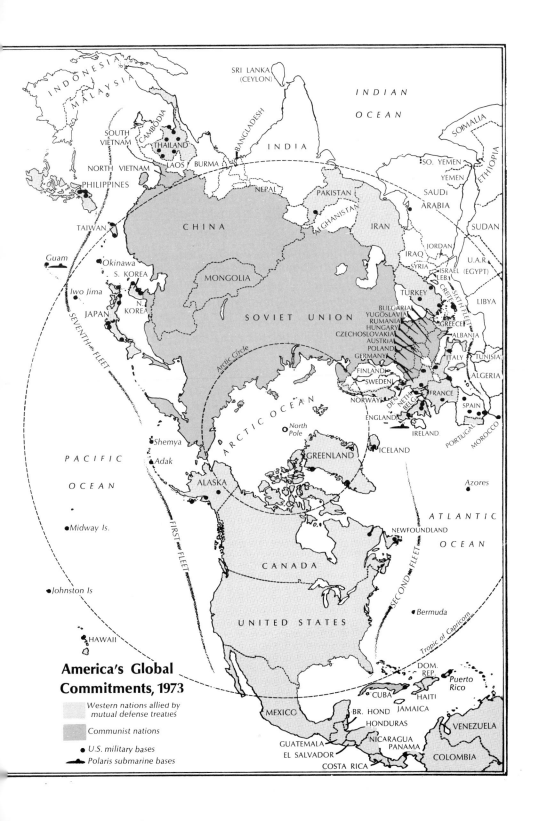

INDONESIA

MALAYSIA

SRI LANKA
(CEYLON)

INDIAN

OCEAN

SOMALIA

SOUTH
VIETNAM

CAMBODIA

THAILAND

BANGLADESH

INDIA

SO. YEMEN

ETHIOPIA

NORTH VIETNAM

LAOS BURMA

NEPAL

PAKISTAN

AFGHANISTAN

IRAN

YEMEN

SAUDI
ARABIA

SUDAN

PHILIPPINES

TAIWAN

CHINA

JORDAN

IRAQ

SYRIA

U.A.R.
(EGYPT)

ISRAEL
LEB.

Guam

Okinawa

S. KOREA

MONGOLIA

TURKEY

LIBYA

SIXTH FLEET

CRETE

Iwo Jima

JAPAN

N.
KOREA

SOVIET UNION

BULGARIA
YUGOSLAVIA
RUMANIA
HUNGARY
CZECHOSLOVAKIA
AUSTRIA
POLAND
GERMANY

GREECE

ALBANIA

ITALY

TUNISIA

ALGERIA

SEVENTH FLEET

Arctic Circle

FINLAND

SWEDEN

NORWAY

DEN.
NETH.
BELG.

FRANCE

SPAIN

ENGLAND

ARCTIC OCEAN

North
Pole

IRELAND

PORTUGAL

MOROCCO

Shemya

PACIFIC

Adak

GREENLAND

ICELAND

Azores

OCEAN

ALASKA

ATLANTIC

FIRST FLEET

Midway Is.

NEWFOUNDLAND

OCEAN

CANADA

SECOND FLEET

Johnston Is

Bermuda

HAWAII

UNITED STATES

America's Global
Commitments, 1973

Western nations allied by
mutual defense treaties

Communist nations

● U.S. military bases

Polaris submarine bases

Tropic of Capricorn

DOM.
REP.

*Puerto
Rico*

CUBA

HAITI

JAMAICA

MEXICO

BR. HOND

HONDURAS

VENEZUELA

GUATEMALA
EL SALVADOR

NICARAGUA
PANAMA

COSTA RICA

COLOMBIA

and the United States showed restraint and even cooperated in bringing the warring parties to a Middle East peace conference.

In Southeast Asia, however, direct American involvement was more difficult to avoid. The United States had committed itself to containing any further communist expansion there during the Truman and Eisenhower administrations. President Kennedy had extended that commitment in 1962. Faced with the choice of either seeing South Vietnam fall or increasing American involvement he never really acted on his statement in 1963 that "in the final analysis, it is their war . . . . They [the South Vietnamese] are the ones who have to win or lose it." Washington still saw the Vietminh as an instrument of communist (Russian or Chinese) expansion, not as an independent national movement like communism in Yugoslavia. Similarly, although President Johnson stated that he would not send American troops to fight in Vietnam, by 1965 the United States was again faced with the choice of either seeing the Saigon government fall or escalating American involvement. Johnson chose massive intervention with American ground, air, and naval forces, which by 1968 numbered more than a half-million men. Still the war dragged on. After the Vietminh (now called the Vietcong) launched a strong offensive during the Vietnamese Tet New Year holiday in 1968, Washington began to reexamine its position. That Spring, President Johnson announced the beginning of peace negotiations in Paris and his own withdrawal from the Presidential race as a consequence of rising war dissent in America. After the 1968 election, the new Nixon administration began a policy of withdrawing American ground forces while increasing air and naval support for the strengthened South Vietnamese armed forces. In an effort to force North Vietnam to make peace and release American prisoners of war, President Nixon escalated the war by invading Cambodia, raiding Laos, and mining Hanoi's harbors while at the same time reducing the American conditions for peace. North Vietnam replied with a massive invasion of South Vietnam in early Spring, 1972 that gradually ground to a halt because of American air power. Action then shifted from the battlefield to the peace negotiations in Paris where Special Assistant to the President Henry Kissinger held a series of private talks with North Vietnamese delegates. In January, 1973, after several breaks in the negotiations and a resumption of heavy American bombing of North Vietnam, a final peace agreement was reached. Though the war continued to rage intermittently between the South Vietnamese and the Vietcong, America's direct role was over.

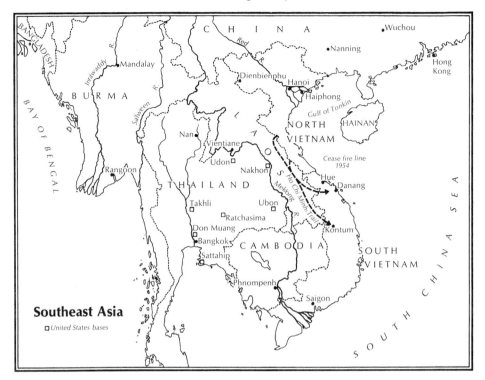

Southeast Asia

□ *United States bases*

The Vietnam struggle sparked unrest and dissent in the United States. Many argued for a reduced American world involvement, claiming that the United States had extended itself beyond its powers and that other Western nations should contribute their share to world security. Others maintained that since the Soviet Union was now as strong as the United States militarily and growing stronger, America must continue to play an active global role. The Nixon administration appeared to favor a return to the "balance of power" system in which the United States would act as the balancing nation between vying groups and retain its independence of action. One of the most successful examples of Nixon's approach was the stunning triumph of Secretary of State Henry Kissinger's mission to disengage Arab and Israeli armies following the October, 1973 war in the Mideast. This diplomatic success put the Middle East on the road to peace, and greatly increased American prestige and influence among the Arab peoples. At the same time, however, critics abroad wondered if the administration's tendency to "go it alone" would result in agreements made at their nations' expense. Skeptics at home insisted that real detente must include a relaxation of repression of dissident intellectuals and Jews within the Soviet Union. It may be years before the Nixon-Kissinger approach can be evaluated, especially since President Ford's administration continues to rely upon Dr. Kissinger to guide American foreign policy.

SUGGESTIONS FOR ADDITIONAL READING

William Appleton Williams, *The Tragedy of American Diplomacy*, (1959). An indictment of United States foreign policy for its tendency toward imperialism.

Daniel M. Smith, *The Great Departure: The United States and World War One*, (1965). A study that interprets American participation in the Great War as the result of Wilson's mix of pragmatism and idealism.

Robert A. Divine, *The Reluctant Belligerent: American Entry into World War Two*, (1965). An excellent survey of American foreign policy from Manchuria to Pearl Harbor.

George Kennan, *The Realities of American Foreign Policy*, (1966). An analysis of American foreign policy, arguing that the United States should exercise greater restraint and respect in its dealings with other nations.

Walter La Feber, *America, Russia, and the Cold War*, (1967). A "revisionist" view of the origins of the Cold War, critical of American policy toward the Soviet Union.

David Halberstam, *The Best and the Brightest*, (1972). An incisive account of the failure of the architects of America's Vietnam involvement to understand the conflict, highlighting how the bureaucracy tends to suppress data critical of accepted policy.

CHAPTER SEVEN

THE IMPACT OF WAR ON AMERICAN LIFE

1775
Battle of Bunker Hill, where the legend of the invincible American "Minuteman" was born.

1801
U.S. Military Academy at West Point is created to give America a professional fighting force.

1848
Congressman Abraham Lincoln charges that the United States began an unjust war with the invasion of Mexico.

1935
First in a series of neutrality laws passed by the U.S. Congress; reflection of disillusionment and the sentiment to avoid future wars after World War I.

1941
American entry into World War II ends further consideration of New Deal reforms.

1942
Creation of the War Production Board begins military–business cooperation that lasts long into the Cold War.

1945
United States drops the first atomic bomb over Hiroshima to end World War II and usher in the Nuclear Age.

1954
Postwar Red Scare reaches its high point when Senator Joe McCarthy of Wisconsin charges the Democratic party of Roosevelt and Truman with "twenty years of treason."

1961
President Eisenhower warns against a "military–industrial complex" with extensive influence on modern American society.

1969
War protest peaks with the killing of several students by National Guardsmen at Kent State University in Ohio.

AMERICANS AND WAR

The United States was forged in the fire of a revolutionary struggle and has since fought nine major wars and numerous "police actions." With the exception of the ill-fated Southern Confederacy, the country has managed to avoid widespread devastation and abject defeat. Yet every war has left its imprint upon American society. Some have sparked patriotism and national pride or encouraged economic growth, and others have brought disillusionment in their wake or quenched the spirit of political and social reform.

Americans as a people have always been somewhat ambivalent toward war. Thomas Jefferson considered resorting to armed conflict "barbarous," and Benjamin Franklin once commented that "there has never been a good war or a bad peace." The idea that war is merely an extension of diplomacy is traditionally alien to Americans. Instead it is seen as a break with "normalcy," a last resort after diplomacy fails. No President involved in a conflict abroad has ever been free of dissent at home. Yet the United States has launched aggressive wars of expansion against neighboring countries and native Indians, dealt harshly with domestic protest and "dangerous aliens," and glorified their war heroes by making seven of them President. American feelings toward the military have been similarly mixed, a blend of caution and suspicion, pride and support.

To understand the impact of America's wars on the nation's evolution, to see how and why the United States has gradually grown away from a small volunteer army and built up a huge military establishment allied with private industry, American attitudes toward war and the military must be traced from the beginning.

THE MINUTEMAN MENTALITY

English colonists who came to the New World found themselves surrounded by foes—the French in Canada, the Spanish on the Florida border, and Indians everywhere. But this did not make all colonists expert marksmen and able soldiers. In fact, their everyday lives were only occasionally interrupted by the call to arms and then only for a brief time. Battles with the Indians were on-again, off-again affairs. Not until the frequent skirmishes and raids erupted into major wars did the brunt of battle shift from frontiersmen in the struggle's immediate locality to the now-threatened settlers in farms and villages closer to the East coast. Then all able-bodied men would form a militia to defeat the "savages" and retire to their own affairs as soon as the emergency was over, usually serving no more than a season.

Colonists met the French and Spanish threat in the same manner. When European conflicts between the colonial powers spilled over into the New World, English settlers relied once again upon the militia. These struggles, however, rarely generated much enthusiasm. Colonists tended to call the wars after the current monarch—Queen Anne's War or King William's War—and identify them with Europe's concerns rather than their own. Whenever the colonists took part, they made sure the objective was worth their effort. Asked in 1690 to mount an expedition against Quebec (capital of French Canada), New England militia instead decided to attack Port Royal, a haven for privateers who were sinking their ships and ruining their commerce. They took the port and were satisfied with that.

The English monarch sent little aid to his colonies in any of these struggles, chiefly because he had little to spare. Frontiersmen and militia fought their own battles. Not until the French and Indian War began in 1754 and shaped up as a contest for dominance in North America did colonial militia and British regulars campaign together in large numbers. It was not a happy alliance. One English commander called his colonial soldiers "the dirtiest, most contemptible cowardly dogs that you can conceive." The British regulars were accustomed to strict discipline, fine uniforms, and fighting in tight lines as though they were on the plains of Europe. Colonial militia were a more independent, motley lot who saw that tactics practiced in Europe simply were not effective in the forests of America. Disasters like the defeat of British troops under General Braddock at the hands of Indians and French rangers in 1755 convinced them they were right. But colonial hostility to the presence of British regulars went beyond disagreements over tactics.

Colonists mistrusted standing armies. As soon as France had been defeated and ousted from Canada in 1763, the New England assemblies requested that London withdraw its troops from America. They felt that the regulars were not only a needless burden, but were a threat to their local liberties and freedom of action since the troops could be used to strengthen the King's authority. The regulars left, but later returned to Boston under the Quartering Act of 1774 (one of the Intolerable acts mentioned in Chapter 2, p. 42), forcing Bostonians to house and supply the very soldiers sent to subdue them. When the Revolutionary War finally broke out at Lexington and Concord in 1775, it was now British "redcoat" against American militia.

Even with their lives and independence at stake, American patriots were suspicious of a professional army. Militia continued to make up

During the outburst of patriotism that followed the American Revolution, one painter offered his version of "the Spirit of '76." This idealized image of the invincible militiaman helped to mold Americans' dependence on a volunteer citizen's army that persisted until the Civil War.

most of the American forces, electing their own officers and serving for one to three months. These volunteers were not for the most part sharpshooting frontiersmen but farmers, mechanics, and day laborers. Yet when this "rabble in arms" met trained British regulars at the Battle of Bunker Hill in 1775 and gave more than they got, the legend of the invincible Minuteman was born. So superior were Americans, the myth went, that a farmer could put down his plow, pick up a rifle on a minute's notice, and still beat the best England could send against him. The legend, however, did not hold true in reality—militia generally fought poorly in pitched battles. Had it not been for General Washington's own persistence in creating regular Continental Army units from the few who volunteered for longer service, the American army might have lost the Revolution. Despite the fact that these Continental regiments aided by the French bore the brunt of fighting during the war, the myth persisted that it was the Minutemen who brought the United States into being by their victories.

Those victories were not attained by any "war machine." The American war effort was disorganized, halting, and plagued by a lack of cooperation between the states. Congress in Philadelphia had to beg, borrow, and steal supplies and soldiers necessary to sustain the American armies. Wrote one organizer, "it is a melancholy fact that near half our men, cannon, muskets, powder, cloathes, etc., is to be found nowhere but on paper." Many states, cautious about giving

Congress too much power and suspicious of standing armies, kept their money and militia for their own local defense. Lack of money to pay the Continentals nearly resulted in a rebellion in 1783 when Congress had to refuse army officers the barest relief from wartime inflation. The angry officers published the Newburgh Address and ominously hinted that "in any political event, the army has its alternative." Washington calmed the men in an emotional and patriotic appeal and eventually got them pensions. Later, perhaps remembering this affair, Congress declared that "standing armies in time of peace are inconsistent with the principles of Republican Governments, dangerous to the liberties of a free people, and generally converted into destructive engines for establishing despotism." Nevertheless, many of those who had served in the Continental Army regarded it as a symbol of national unity and later were among the nationalists who served in the central government.

Nationalism itself was at a high point during and immediately after the Revolution. Those who remained loyal to England, estimated at anywhere from one-third to one-half the population, suffered harsh persecution. Called Tories or Loyalists, they lost their civil rights, frequently their property, and even the right to work in some states. Nearly 80,000 were forced to leave America to find new homes in England, Canada, or the West Indies. Nor were Americans ready in most cases to honor the terms of the Peace of Paris, which called upon them to return confiscated Loyalist property. Anti-Tory feelings were especially high in the South, where Loyalist volunteers fighting with the British had nearly turned the tide of war against the patriots. Faith in the revolution was the one creed rebel Americans insisted upon.

The War for Independence made its impact chiefly in the social and political spheres of American life. Since many Tories were of the upper class or "aristocracy," their exile removed a source of conservatism and tradition. Often their lands were broken up and distributed to returning soldier–patriots, increasing the numbers of the small landowners. Politically, besides having won her independence, America would now be served and led mostly by the men who had made their marks as war statesmen or soldiers.

PROTEST AND PROFESSIONALISM

First among these men was George Washington, the unanimous choice of his countrymen to be the first President of the United States. Despite the turmoil in Europe caused by the French Revolution,

Washington managed to keep America out of a foreign war. He had little choice—America had an army of 676 men and no navy. But when faced with arrogant French attacks upon American commerce in 1798, his successor John Adams revived the navy and sent it out to conduct an undeclared war with France on the high seas. As the ocean battles revived the navy, harsh repression of dissent was also revived at home. Adams' Federalists enacted the Alien and Sedition Acts, which clamped down on Republican political opposition and protests against the war. An army was raised both to prepare for operations against French Louisiana, and, as one Federalist senator put it, "to enable us to lay hands upon traitors" who opposed Adams. However, the army never marched, the disagreements with France were settled, and the Alien and Sedition Acts so angered the nation that they backfired and helped Republican Thomas Jefferson to win the election of 1800.

Jefferson immediately set out to scrap the navy and disband the army, both of which he considered expensive and unnecessary. He felt that America's opportunity lay in commerce, not only with England but with all of the foreign ports that had been closed when the United States had been part of the British Empire. Beginning in the early 1800s American merchants entered a period of unparalleled prosperity. In the Mediterranean this commerce was threatened by the Barbary pirates operating from several North African states. To nearly everyone's surprise, the pacifist-inclined Jefferson ordered the navy to be rebuilt and sent against the pirates rather than increase the tribute demanded by the Barbary states. Like Adams before him, President Jefferson conducted the affair himself without a Congressional declaration of war. In this brief encounter the American Navy was born, and before it was recalled from North Africa the new warships had forced the pirates to moderate their demands.

The reason that President Jefferson had recalled the vessels was that the incessant Anglo-French conflict was heating up again and threatening to involve the United States. When a British frigate fired upon an American warship and took off three alleged "deserters" to serve in England's own navy, war fever swept the country. Rather than give in to this sentiment, Jefferson won Congressional support for a halt on all American commerce with Europe. This embargo gave port authorities practically dictatorial powers of enforcement in the hope that a military struggle with England could be avoided. The measure prostrated the commercially oriented Northeast and sent a wave of protest throughout New England. Jefferson, to his credit, restricted himself to stiffening the embargo and sought no new Sedition acts. But the effort failed to change Britain's policies and Jefferson passed the problem over to James Madison, leaving office in 1809. President Madison eventually took the nation to war against England in 1812.

Southern and Western Congressional "War Hawks" led the war movement. They confidently expected to eliminate the Indian problem by removing British "agitators" in Canada and the "incompetent" Spanish in Florida, thereby adding those areas to the United States. To reach these military objectives they counted upon the invincible Minuteman and especially the formidable American frontiersman. Conquering Canada would be a "mere matter of marching," and War Hawk Henry Clay thought it could be done with a thousand Kentucky riflemen. But frontiersmen and militia units alike were commanded by generals who were senile or incompetent or both. The American armies fared poorly. Disaster was barely averted in the North, while a British force defeated American troops defending Washington, D.C. and burned the capitol. The only good news came from the high seas, where the American Navy won several ship-to-ship battles against the "Mistress of the Seas."

Even this ray of hope was overshadowed by the British blockade of American ports. New England's commercial economy was hard hit, and northeastern Federalists angrily opposed the war. They withheld support from the government and even traded with the British in Canada. Outside of the New England area, where they were a majority, the Federalists were harshly persecuted. Pro-administration mobs in Baltimore killed and mutilated several outspoken dissenters in the summer of 1812. As the war dragged on, northeastern Federalists convened a protest convention in Hartford, Connecticut and sent delegates to President Madison with demands that included a veiled threat of secession. By the time they reached Washington, however, news of General Jackson's victory at New Orleans and the signing of a peace treaty at Ghent made their mission look ridiculous. The Federalist party was branded as unpatriotic and defeatist, and it never recovered from the blow.

A nationwide thrill of pride at having stood up to the world's greatest power ran up and down the United States. Jackson's victory with a ragtag army against British veterans wiped away the shame of earlier defeats and renewed confidence in the "invincible" American fighting man. The government learned a lesson from its early military fiascos. It strengthened the navy and expanded the army to a peacetime force of 10,000 men. It also began training more officers at the United States Military Academy at West Point, which had been established in 1801. The United States now had a small but professional fighting force.

EXPANSIONISM AND THE MILITARY

That force was to prove invaluable in the next 45 years. During this period the United States embarked on an era of territorial expansion and internal development freed from European entanglements. Another swift naval victory against the Barbary pirates in 1816 swept the Mediterranean of threats to American commerce, and the merchant marine entered a period of vigorous growth. With the nation at peace, the corps of engineers assisted in river and harbor improvements and the construction of canals and roads, while topographical engineers like John C. Fremont explored Western lands.

As the ideas of Manifest Destiny sparked expansionist sentiment and both settlers and merchants began to look toward the West, America's military arm became increasingly useful. The regular army, augmented by state militia units, fought Indians who resisted the tide of settlers moving onto their ancestral hunting grounds and also policed reservations created for the defeated tribes. As an instrument of national policy, the military became a tool of expansionism. Since Manifest Destiny was a favorite slogan of merchants seeking Pacific ports as bases for trade with the Orient, America's professional fighting force was tied to domestic economic interests. The government had always considered commercial expansion one of its prime goals and, as an arm of the government, it was only natural for the military to take a similar attitude. Naval vessels visiting the port of San Francisco reported that it had "the best harbor in the world" and that it was "the key to the Pacific." Traders dealing with Santa Fe demanded and won army protection of their wagon trains.

When the American desire for California and a larger Texas finally drove the country to war with Mexico in 1846, the military was called upon to bring this latest expansionist crusade to a successful conclusion. It was a drastically different force from the one that had gone confidently to war in 1812. The navy had been enlarged and modernized and was led by younger officers who had gained experience in the Barbary affair. By 1847 the new Naval Academy at Annapolis was training midshipmen. The army was built around a strong core of regulars led by young officers who had been trained at West Point and had experience in the Indian wars. It too was modernized and well-equipped and augmented by the ever-present state volunteers. Not all of these men were hell-bent on war. Once the shooting started, however, the Americans piled up a string of victories. The Mexican forces, poorly trained and led, were defeated in a long series of engagements that ended with General Winfield Scott's capture of Mexico City on September 13, 1847. Just as the War of 1812 had seen the birth of an American Navy, so the Mexican War saw the maturing of an American Army. Expansionists won all they had hoped for with the signing of the Treaty of Guadalupe-Hidalgo in 1848—California and the Southwest.

But this war also had its dissenters. Captain Ulysses Grant called the whole conflict "unholy" and regarded the American march to the Rio Grande as "an act of hostility." Many Northerners saw it as a Southern plot to extend slavery into the Southwest. Congressman Abraham Lincoln embarrassed the administration by implying that the Americans had begun the war by invading Mexican soil. Henry David Thoreau went to jail rather than pay taxes that supported the war. Shortly thereafter he wrote *Civil Disobedience*, insisting that in this unjust war "the true place for a just man is prison." One minister even said that if he had to fight in the "damnable war" he would fight on the side of Mexico. Because dissent was centered in the opposition party, it could not be easily suppressed and it even hurried Polk's efforts to end the war. Political battlelines were then drawn up over what to do with the newly won territory. As the North and South drew farther apart on the question of slavery, those political fronts became real battlegrounds in a civil war across the nation.

AMERICA'S FIRST TOTAL WAR

"The war," wrote one combatant, "was a very extraordinary affair. Nothing like it ever occurred before, and I doubt that anything like it will ever happen again." At the outset all was chivalry and proud patriotism. Several hundred army officers were allowed to resign their commissions and join the Confederacy, men like Robert E. Lee who were to prove brilliant commanders. When both governments called for volunteers they were swamped by more men than they could immediately arm or equip. Northerners fought for "our sacred Union and the Constitution of our Fathers," while Southerners did battle for "our homes, our families, and our rights." Some soldiers wore brilliant uniforms and cavalry charged with trumpets blaring

Many young men who marched off to war anticipated exciting adventure and quick victory. Too often, however, the romance of war was replaced by the drudgery of camp life, or death on the battlefield. As a witness to many stirring, bloody battles, General Robert E. Lee said: "It is well that war is so terrible—[else] we should grow too fond of it."

and swords drawn. But after several years and tens of thousands of casualties, the nature of the conflict changed.

Civil war became total war. Invading Union armies ravaged the Southern countryside, burning homes and farms and pillaging cities. General Sherman's "March to the Sea" from Atlanta to Savannah cut a swath of destruction nearly 60 miles wide. Confederate troops leveled the town of Chambersburg, Pennsylvania when it could not raise a ransom of $500,000. Sieges like the one at Vicksburg, Mississippi caught civilians in the horrors of war. Trench warfare foreshadowing World War I dominated the 1864 campaign in Virginia. The conflict also touched the homefront as no other war had. A need for mass armies forced both governments to institute the draft. In New York City, poor people angry at the rich who were buying draft substitutes took to the streets for four days, destroying an immense amount of property. The riots ended when troops fired on the crowds, causing more than a thousand civilian casualties. Just behind the battlelines, hospitals were swamped with wounded from the battlefront. Prisoners of war camps were death traps on both sides, and the exchange system broke down in 1864. All of this may not have lessened patriotism, but it did produce a war weariness that almost defeated Lincoln's bid for reelection in 1864 and increased Southern criticism of Confederate President Jefferson Davis.

Poor New Yorkers were outraged at the rich man's draft exemption and bitter over social injustices aggravated by the war. Over 50,000 dissenters took to the streets in July 1863 in four days of rioting against the draft law.

In the massive effort to win, both sides mobilized all of their material as well as human resources. The South's effort to build a war industry necessary to support its armies eventually failed for simple lack of skilled workers and material. By 1865 the Southern economy was a total wreck, having lost at least three billion dollars in capital. Complete recovery was slow; even as late as 1932 the South was referred to as the nation's "economic problem number one." But in the North, where business and industry had been strong before the war, the economy thrived. Lincoln's administration favored business by passing protective tariffs, reforming the nation's monetary system, and by encouraging the immigration of skilled labor. Pressed by the necessity of supporting a tremendously increased military force, the government spent huge sums buying everything from shoes to warships. Many business fortunes were founded upon war contracts: Armour in meat packing, Carnegie in iron and steel, and Rockefeller in oil were a few. These ties of contracts and cooperation between government and business continued to grow until, even after the war had ended, critics would call the national administration "a businessman's government."

The war also had its political and social effects. Most of the social reform movements active in the 1830s and '40s were swallowed up by the conflict, not to emerge again for nearly a half century. The infant American Peace Society was fragmented by the choice of war or disunion. Both Lincoln and Davis were faced with opposition to the war. The Confederate President was mostly helpless to counteract it, while Lincoln used harsh measures (like jailing persons in Maryland without charging them in court for a crime) only when he deemed it absolutely necessary. Politically, with the exception of Grover Cleveland, the war kept the Democratic party out of the White House for 50 years. In each election following the war Republicans would "wave the bloody shirt," reminding the electorate how "traitorous" Democrats had tried to break up the Union. The theory of secession went down to defeat with the Confederacy in 1865, but the concept and practice of states' rights remained. As late as the 1960s, states continued to defy the federal government over civil rights and other questions. Although slavery was abolished and blacks were nominally given equal rights with whites, the attitudes of racial hatred and the reality of discrimination—North and South—were not altered by the war or by Reconstruction.

Yet something else had changed. The fact that America's process of peaceful political change had been broken, the long years of conflict that killed more men than all of America's other wars combined, the destruction of the Southern culture, and the accelerated industrialization that was altering Northern society brought "the end of American innocence." Wrote one famous historian, "The Civil War . . . introduced into the national consciousness a certain sense of proportion and relation. The world seemed a more complicated place, the future more treacherous, success more difficult."

CONQUEST, CRUSADE, AND CONSEQUENCES

American experience during the next quarter of a century seemed to belie that conclusion. During this period the remaining Western lands were settled, Civil War veterans drove the last Indian tribes into extinction or onto reservations, American engineers and immigrant labor crisscrossed the continent with railroads, and a rapidly industrializing economy had thrust the United States into a new era of problems, prosperity, and potential world power. American businessmen had already entered the race for world markets, and Europeans accustomed to American dominance in agricultural produce now found they were faced with stiff competition in manufactured goods as well. Admiral Alfred T. Mahan's influential writings, which pointed out the necessity of a large navy to protect and secure markets abroad, helped convince Congress to appropriate funds for a modern fleet. In the heady spirit of nationalism that possessed the country, the new navy "showed the flag" overseas and gained influence in governmental circles as a symbol of national pride. This influence was shown during the 1891 dispute with Chile over a riot that killed two American sailors in Valparaiso, when one Washington diplomat noted that the Navy "practically made" policy regarding the affair.

Another naval incident, the sinking of the battleship *Maine* in Havana harbor, brought long-standing disagreements with Spain over Cuba to a boil and precipitated the Spanish-American War in 1898. Neither side was prepared. America once again had to resort to volunteers like Teddy Roosevelt's Rough Riders to augment the small number of regulars and make up an army to invade Cuba, Puerto Rico, and the Philippines. Once again the navy provided headlines by destroying Admiral Cervera's fleeing ships off Santiago and by defeating the Spanish fleet stationed in the Philippines. But the question now arose, what should America do with the islands? Peace groups that had been overwhelmed by war fever now joined with anti-imperialists to stem the tide of annexation sentiment. Their defeat on this issue was discouraging; but discouragement turned to anger when the Filipinos resisted and American forces sent to pacify the islands used torture and concentration camps in a brutal effort to suppress the insurrection. After the conflict, military influence shrank again, although the size of the armed forces themselves grew—with the exception of the Navy. Beyond outraging a minority of Americans, the Spanish-American War and its aftermath left only a faint imprint upon society at large.

It had, however, made the United States a world power. No longer could the country remain entirely unaffected by overseas events. In the Caribbean and Central America, United States warships and Marines became common sights as the government sought to "police" the Western Hemisphere. When European politics led to confrontation and war between the Central Powers and the Allies in 1914, America immediately became involved through its trading connections with both sides. At first the government tried to act with impeccable neutrality. When President Wilson read a newspaper report alleging that the War Department was drawing up contingency plans for war with Germany, he angrily ordered that any officer who participated be removed from command and thrown out of Washington. Gradually, as German submarine attacks began to infringe upon America's rights as a neutral, Wilson faced the agonizing choice of giving up those rights or going to war. He finally chose war, and in 1917 the nation went with him despite the efforts of peace groups and pacifists like Senator Robert LaFollette to persuade the public otherwise.

Although the nation followed Wilson into war, it was not unanimously popular. To promote national unity and mobilize enthusiasm for the war effort, a Committee on Public Information was created. Its leader, George Creel, enlisted armies of artists, writers, and educators to flood the country with patriotic propaganda presenting the struggle as a "war to end war," "a war for democracy," and a battle for "honesty and decency" against "despotism." A draft system was instituted in conjunction with patriotic appeals to enlist. The government also set about smothering protest and dissent. Laws were passed against "false reports or false statements" that could hinder the war effort and later included any spoken or written attempt to bring "the form of government . . . into contempt." The Secretary of State declared that "there are men walking about the streets of this city tonight who ought to be taken out at sunrise to-

The suppression of dissent during World War I was echoed by the postwar fear of Bolshevik subversion in the United States that created the Red Scare of 1919. This cartoon reflects the paranoia of many who approved of Attorney-General A. Mitchell Palmer's crackdown on suspected radicals and the subsequent deportation of 600 people to Russia.

morrow and shot for treason." Both the press and movies were censored, and all pacifist films were ordered burned. Along with federal pressure, local pressures upon dissenters was also a strong force for conformity. Those who resisted, like socialist Eugene V. Debs, were sentenced to lengthy prison terms and required to pay hefty fines. But all of this patriotism only made the abrupt end of the war and the failure to gain the nation's idealistic aims for a "just and lasting peace" more emotionally devastating. Disillusionment set in and there was the suspicion that the whole effort had been wasted. This mood produced the "lost generation" of the 1920s, energetically seeking pleasure and deeper purpose yet pessimistic about finding it.

American participation in World War I also had economic side effects. It had been necessary to begin mobilizing all industrial resources as well as public sentiment to support the war effort. Because pressure for an enormous amount and variety of goods had begun to produce rampant inflation and chaos in the economy as early as 1915, Washington planned to coordinate the economic aspects of war support as soon as the prospects of staying out of the conflict started to narrow. A War Industries Board established production priorities, fixed prices or controlled them by agreement, and taxed surplus profits, generally seeking to increase the efficiency of wartime production and supply. Businessmen cooperated with this unprecedented interference of government in the economy because the only alternative appeared to be chaos. Herbert Hoover's policies as head of the Food Administration proved highly beneficial to both farmer and consumer as well as to the war effort. Industry generally benefited from this government coordination and scientific management, and labor also profited from higher "real wages" and better bargaining power. After the war ended and the government abruptly dropped its efforts to manage the economy, however, competitive chaos resumed between industries, and labor found itself the target of business attacks upon the privileges it had gained during the conflict.

This reduction of the government's role in the economy was matched by similar retreats from other areas of participation at war's end. Disillusioned by failure to achieve war aims, tired of crusading rhetoric and anxious to enjoy postwar prosperity, the American people sought "a return to normalcy" and political peace and quiet. Their political conservatism on the one hand and the changing manners and morals of the "Jazz Age" on the other combined to bury Progressivism. It also brought about a decline in the power and prestige of the Presidency, which had been so greatly enlarged by Roosevelt and Wilson. The centralized power that war had placed in the hands of government went unused during the period of Republican ascendency.

GROWTH OF A MILITARY-INDUSTRIAL COMPLEX

That era of the 1920s and the early 30s saw a bitter backlash against American involvement in foreign wars. A Congressional committee chaired by Senator Gerald Nye found a pattern of war-industry lobbying and huge profits that convinced many Americans that the nation had gone to war in 1917 to secure the profits of a few "merchants of death." Peace movements were at the height of popularity and influence, spurred on by personal memoirs detailing the horrors and stupidity of war like Remarque's *All Quiet on the Western Front*. Washington's foreign policy mirrored this sentiment. The United States refused to enter into any commitments that might lead to war and launched a series of disarmament conferences. To insure noninvolvement, Congress passed a series of neutrality laws in the 1930s.

So America watched from the sidelines as Japan swept over China and began expanding into Southeast Asia while Hitler's Germany won concession after concession in Europe from war-weary France and England. Not until war erupted in Europe and the Axis blitzkrieg had overrun nearly all of the continent to leave Britain standing alone did America respond with action. Ironically, it was President Franklin Roosevelt—elected on the domestic issue of fighting the Depression—who had to deal with the crisis. Roosevelt utilized fully the powers of the Presidency and the federal government in general to vigorously expand the government's role in many areas of national life. He used this power to lend money to Britain, transfer 50 over-aged destroyers to London, and even to cut off strategic exports to Japan to force that nation to halt its expansion. These moves evoked mixed reactions from the American people. Not until the Japanese struck at Pearl Harbor did the country unite firmly behind the President and a policy of war.

Once again the nation mobilized for total war. Steps had already been taken in some areas. The fall of France to Nazi armies in 1940 demonstrated that the less than half-million men in the armed forces would not be enough for national defense. Congress responded by creating the first peacetime draft. Ever since World War I the military's condition had been deteriorating, and measures were begun to bring its equipment and tactics up to modern standards. But it was in the area of industrial production that President Roosevelt, borrowing an idea from Wilson's War Industries Board, really exercised governmental powers of direction and control. Industrial production was the key to victory. As one British general observed, "God now marched with the biggest industries rather than the biggest battalions."

In January, 1942, the President responded to the need for more and more efficient production by creating the War Production Board, which set goals for manufacturers and gave general direction to private industry. Wage and price controls were imposed. The government also loaned money for expansion to key war industries and in some cases even built the plants for them. All sorts of war-related scientific research were subsidized or entirely supported by the government. Some government agencies and the industrial management they were guiding developed such an identity of interest and outlook that for all intents and purposes they merged. This process forged in the heat of war a complex between business and governmental interests, both of which were directed toward satisfying military needs for weapons and supplies. A partnership between corporations and the military was encouraged, and it occupied thousands of officers and business executives. The cooperation was a resounding success; American industry produced an overwhelming quantity of high qual-

An awesome product of the partnership between science and government was the mushroom that appeared over Japan in August 1945. The development of atomic weaponry inaugurated a new age that required a heightened sense of human restraint and responsibility. The alternative remains nuclear holocaust.

ity war material that enabled the Allied forces to totally defeat the Axis powers. American military leaders had their equipment, Washington had its victory, business had its profits, and the nation had a military-industrial complex.

Other changes in American social and political life were brought about by World War II. Government subsidy of scientific research on the nation's campuses saved many universities and colleges financially. It also subtly altered their nature. On the positive side, new courses in international relations and cultures were introduced, facilities were upgraded, higher standards were set for teaching, and more emphasis was placed upon physical education. A controversial move after the war was the widespread introduction of Reserve Officers Training Corps on campus and a new emphasis on war-related research. Many historians also regard the war as a turning point in American race relations, a point where blacks were no longer willing to accept discrimination in housing, employment, and even in military service. They took the "war for democracy" seriously and identified their racial demands for reform with this ideal. The cynicism that labeled the struggle a "white man's war" was accompanied by both a hope that change could come and by a determination to bring it about. Black organization of a march on Washington (cancelled when Roosevelt met some of their demands) was a symbol of growing militancy. Black leaders observed a "growing bitterness" and a black newspaper stated "experience has taught us that we must rely primarily upon our own efforts." During this period the seeds of the civil rights protest movement of the 1950s and 60s were sown. (See Chapter 8, pp 232—233 for details.)

Politically, the war marked the end of New Deal reform. Roosevelt announced that he had ceased consulting "Dr. New Deal" and was now following the prescriptions of "Dr. Win-the-War." "I am not convinced," he remarked, "that we can be realists about the war and planners for the future at this critical time." Since the President was the heart of New Deal reform, when the heart stopped the program died. Liberals helped to undermine their own cause and contribute to the conservative resurgence by not opposing the suppression of dissent or even the forced evacuation of Japanese-Americans into "relocation camps." A combination of New Deal measures and war direction had given the federal government and especially the Presidency enormous power and influence over everyday domestic matters as well as foreign policy. Nor could that power and the extent of the governmental role in society be relaxed as it had been after World War I. That role became an integral part of postwar American society, both because of its own inertia and public insistence that the government continue it. Americans also expected that the Allied victory over the Axis would usher in an age of national security and world peace under American and United Nations guardianship.

PERPETUAL WAR FOR PERPETUAL PEACE

Two events operated to frustrate that goal—the introduction of atomic weapons and the growing gulf between the Soviet Union and the United States. They turned the Allied triumph into a bittersweet victory without peace. With the first flash of atomic fire over Hiroshima on August 6, 1945, global war or peace became a matter of the extinction or survival of mankind. Russian-American antagonisms over the shape of the postwar world quickly became a series of confrontations and clashes called the "Cold War." The constant tensions created by this struggle that threatened to spark a full-scale war had a profound impact upon the United States.

First, it meant that the emphasis on meeting military requirements for national defense that had dominated government during World

War II would continue under the headings of "preparedness" and "deterrence." Despite America's historic suspicion of standing armies in peacetime, the large military establishment built during the conflict did not dissolve as it had after World War I. Not only was the draft continued, but military strategy played a dominant role in containing communism after the war, thereby expanding the influence of the armed forces in Washington. This constituted a milestone in American attitudes toward the military.

At the same time, the continued need for new weapons and more equipment made the war industries that had grown up during World War II a permanent feature of the American economy. Cooperation between business and government also continued, and soaring defense requirements gave the military and business common interests. Equipment needed by the military drew automatic support from industries seeking profitable contracts for themselves. Income from these contracts became the lifeblood of over one hundred corporations, just as the material produced became essential for the defense establishment. This military-industrial complex grew to such large proportions that President Eisenhower felt compelled to warn the nation. Speaking in 1961, Eisenhower declared that its "total influence—economic, political, even spiritual—is felt in every city, every state house, every office of the Federal Government. The potential for the disastrous rise of misplaced power exists and will exist. We must never let the weight of this combination endanger our liberties or democratic processes."

American society was also affected by the Cold War confrontation. Russia's launching of the Sputnik satellite in 1957 did more than cause the United States to begin its own space program under the National Aeronautics and Space Administration (NASA). It also created the fear that there was an "education gap." Washington's reaction was extensive Federal aid to schools that raised the quality of education in the nation. Throughout the 1950s, economic prosperity and technological advances gave Americans the highest standard of living in the world. Yet the constant Cold War tensions and fear of a hot, possibly atomic, war also created a security-conscious "silent generation." One magazine summed up the ambitions of the younger generation of the fifties by saying that they wanted "a good, secure job with a big firm, and with it, a kind of suburban idyll." Everyone seemed to be concerned with getting "well fixed," complained one writer. Young people were accused of being intellectually "stodgy," of "not speaking out for anything," for never "losing their heads," and for not expecting more out of life. "Youth today," declared one magazine in 1951, "has little cynicism because it never hoped for much." Even the "beatniks," who condemned the "rat race" of American life and dropped out of society to places like Greenwich Village in New York were accused of practicing "only another kind of conformism."

One reason for this attitude was that many Americans felt under attack by an insidious communist menace that threatened every aspect of the "American Way." Dissent, criticism, and even ordinary reformism were branded as disloyal or "un-American." The people accused of such activity faced more than social ostracism. Senator Joe McCarthy's angry campaign against those within government and education whom he considered to be "traitors" or "soft on communism" made it highly dangerous even to be "controversial." The Cold War tendency to paint everything in black and white—"Free World" vs. "Iron Curtain" slavery—encouraged the idea that all was well and good in American society. Political conservatism and defense of the status quo dominated the era. Right-wing groups such as the Minutemen and the John Birch Society flourished. This forced reform-minded liberals and the black civil rights movement to face even more determined opposition than they might otherwise have had. The "crisis politics" of the Cold War, which required quick and decisive action, combined with the precedents set by Roosevelt during World War II, contributed to the further growth of presidential power and Congressional willingness to allow that growth. Another result of Soviet-American antagonism was the expansion of an intelligence community responsible for espionage abroad and surveillance of "un-American" groups at home. These agencies, including the Central Intelligence Agency (CIA) and the Federal Bureau of Investigation (FBI), employed 200,000 persons by the early 1960s. They operated in secrecy and had budgets practically invulnerable to Congressional scrutiny—an "invisible government" functioning largely outside public control.

The issue of civilian control also came up in relation to the role of the military. Its responsibility and influence in government had grown with its size and importance in relation to Cold War objectives. During the 1950s civilians in the Department of Defense most frequently limited themselves to choosing policy alternatives presented by the Joint Chiefs of Staff. The case of General Douglas MacArthur became a symbol of military-civilian conflict. MacArthur rejected the concept of limited war in Korea and publicly insisted that "there is no substitute for victory." President Harry S Truman finally resolved the conflict by removing MacArthur from his command. But the General received a hero's welcome from New York to San Francisco. His solution of "victory" appealed to many Americans frustrated with fighting "brush-fire wars" and tired of maintaining a perpetual state of war-readiness when no resolution appeared in sight. To many people, waging a continuous series of "police actions" and coping with crisis after crisis seemed like being caught up in an exhausting "perpetual war for perpetual peace."

THE VIETNAM WAR

Nevertheless, the Cold War–military outlook still prevailed. Eisenhower's decision to aid the Diem regime in South Vietnam against insurgent Vietcong guerrillas reflected this outlook—that "brush wars" were all part of the communist attempt to subvert the underdeveloped nations of the world. Vietnam, in particular, was felt to be the geopolitical key to Southeast Asia. According to the "domino" theory, if it fell to the communists so would the whole area. Determined not to see it fall, a series of American governments escalated the nation's commitment to Vietnam's defense until in Lyndon Johnson's presidency the United States sent over a half-million men to the area and was spending nearly 20 million dollars a day on the war.

This put an enormous strain upon the economy. President Johnson chose to continue his "war on poverty" (which required great expenditure of government funds) while vastly increasing military spending for the war—without raising taxes. America could afford both "guns and butter," Johnson maintained. While the increased spending created more jobs and offered fatter defense contracts to many industries, it also caused a rampant inflation in prices and huge budget deficits ($25 billion in 1968). Wages stayed about even with prices until the 1970s, but the rise in both helped to make American goods even less competitive with those of other nations and to create a balance of payments deficit (more money going out of the country than coming in). Neither an increase in taxes nor budget cuts, such as were made in the space program, seemed to be able to stem inflation. In fact the NASA cuts created a serious unemployment problem in the aerospace industries. Even wage and price controls instituted by

President Nixon did not halt the inflationary spiral. At the same time government-business interaction, especially within the military-industrial complex, continued to grow until one observer complained that "instead of a free enterprise system, we are moving toward a government-subsidized private profit system."

Political and social reaction to the war was even more far-reaching in its consequences. As the 1950s faded into the 60s, the "silent generation" did a turnabout. Invigorated by the challenge of President Kennedy's Peace Corps and angered by conservative white opposition to the black civil rights movement, many young Americans joined the effort to aid impoverished foreigners abroad and persecuted minorities at home. There was a new idealism, sparked in general by the contradiction between the promise of American life and the reality of poverty, discrimination, and alienation. Impatient for the political system to act on these problems, students and liberals reacted. Using tactics developed during the civil rights struggle, they initiated petitions, strikes, sit-ins, marches, and other demonstrations to dramatize their grievances. The Free Speech Movement at the University of California at Berkeley in 1964 quickly spread to other campuses as students demanded a larger voice in college rules and curriculum.

But the key issue after 1965 quickly became the war in Vietnam. As it continued to escalate and American casualties mounted, with no end in sight despite government statements to the contrary, Americans grew tired, disgusted, and outraged with the conflict. For many observers it symbolized all that had gone wrong in American society. Critics charged that the "corporate state" and the military-industrial complex were continuing the conflict because it brought profits. An anonymously published book, *Report from Iron Mountain*, purported to be a government research report that found war to be necessary to the nation's prosperity. Others accused the government of betraying democracy by not telling the public "the truth about the war" and by not heeding the growing voices of opposition. To minority groups, the war seemed the reason why more money and attention were not being devoted to critical problems at home. Most dissenters were convinced that the Vietnam war was a costly overcommitment of American resources or an immoral use of power or both. During the late 1960s both protest and repression escalated. ROTC and research facilities were targets of dissidents on many campuses. In October 1967, more than 100,000 demonstrators marched on Washington to

Although the war was half a world away, it was brought home daily by the media to the American people. Televised newscasts and a free press depicting the inhumanity of war made a major contribution to the antiwar movement.

THE PRICE OF PEACE

THE DEAD

CIVILIAN ABOUT 1,000,000

MILITARY

ENEMY 926,541

SOUTH VIETNAM 183,719

U.S. 45,940

U.S. DOLLARS

MILITARY AID $138 BILLION

ECONOMIC AID $8.5 BILLION

The cost of American military involvement went beyond the statistics of casualties and aid—though even these figures (determined by early 1973) may rise if the war resumes or the United States commits itself to the reconstruction of both Vietnams. In addition, the war caused deep rifts in the American body politic and destroyed the fabric of Vietnamese society.

demand peace. Protest and suppression peaked during the nation-wide college strike against the American invasion of Cambodia in 1969 when several students were shot and killed by national guardsmen at Kent State University in Ohio. The Vietnam war had seriously divided the country.

It also created new divisions within the political system. Criticism of his policies forced President Johnson to announce in 1968 that he would not seek another term. The Democratic party divided over foreign and domestic policies that the war brought to the surface. Out of the confusion in the Democratic party emerged a third political force labeled the New Left. Made up of disaffected liberals and radicals, this group sought drastic changes in the shape of American society. Wrote one New Leftist, "America is reaching a point of bankruptcy and decay so complete that . . . reform has failed. Our victory lies in progressively demystifying a false democracy, showing the organized violence underneath reformism and manipulation." Events were to reveal, however, that the nation's political sympathy remained in the moderate tradition. For example, most Americans were not willing to regard the draft evaders as heroes in the 1960s, but by 1974 many citizens were ready to accept amnesty and Lincoln's appeal "with malice towards none, with charity towards all, let us bind up the nation's wounds." With the end of the Vietnam war a new era began, the effects of which will be felt as the government reevaluates its foreign policy and American society recovers from the war's long-range social and economic consequences.

SUGGESTIONS FOR ADDITIONAL READING

John Kenneth Galbraith, *The New Industrial State*, (1967). A vivid account of the realities of the modern American economy.

Arthur Ekirch, *The Decline of American Liberalism*, (1955). A study of the effects of World War II on the efforts to continue New Deal political and social reform.

Ernest Hemingway, *A Farewell to Arms*, (1929). A classic novel of the experiences of an American deserter during World War I.

Dalton Trumbo, *Johnny Got His Gun*, (1970). A strongly antiwar novel of a young man and his struggle to communicate after losing his limbs, sight, and speech during World War I.

Samuel Eliot Morison, Frederick Merk, and Frank Freidel, *Dissent in Three American Wars*, (1970). An insightful study of the nature and extent of modern American antiwar protest.

Anonymous, *Report from Iron Mountain*, (1968). A "true" study by Pentagon think-tanks, concluding that continuous conflict is necessary to American economic prosperity.

CHAPTER EIGHT

WE SHALL OVERCOME: THE CRUSADE FOR HUMAN RIGHTS IN AMERICA

1619
First captured Africans arrive at Jamestown, Virginia.

1789
Slavery sanctioned by the new Constitution.

1882
Chinese immigration to the United States forbidden by Congress; not lifted until 1943.

1895
Booker T. Washington gives his "Atlanta Compromise" speech, encouraging a gradual approach to black civil rights.

1919
Nineteenth Amendment gives women the right to vote.

1942
Over 70,000 American citizens of Japanese ancestry forcibly evicted from their homes and interned in "relocation camps."

1954
Brown v. the Topeka Board of Education: the Supreme Court declares separation of the races unconstitutional; black civil rights movement accelerates.

1955
Four million Mexican immigrants deported without legal due process, including many American citizens of Mexican descent.

1966
Stokely Carmichael states that black people must look to themselves for improvement, beginning the Black Power movement.

1967
Cesar Chavez and the United Farm Workers begin a nationwide grape boycott to win recognition and better working conditions.

1973
American Indian Movement occupies Wounded Knee to force government action on Indian problems.

" . . . WITH LIBERTY AND JUSTICE FOR ALL"?

Although many Americans would agree that the ideal of equality contained in the Pledge of Allegiance has not been fully realized, they are generally unaware of the origins of racial prejudice and the pervasive legacy of discrimination in more modern times. Despite evidence of lessening prejudice in recent years, it has been argued that racial, ethnic, and sexist discrimination continues to be a harsh reality for many people in American society.

Such attitudes have persisted in the United States, supported not only for economic reasons but by less tangible psychological motives as well. An examination of American history suggests that society has always required that the various minorities keep their "place." Only in this way could uncertainty and fear of them be contained. Thus the history of each "oppressed" group in the American experience has been one of having its position in society defined and, in the process, its rights circumscribed. This process has borne two major results. First, the impact of discrimination has had a profound psychological effect on its victims; second, the official sanction given the exercise of discrimination has simply confirmed and reinforced prejudice.

Although most scholars today would agree with this view, inadequate attention has been given to the role played by the racial minorities and women in America's historical experience. Such an oversight is particularly unfortunate because of the wide variety of peoples who have participated in the nation's development. Most historians and popularizers of history have presented a one-sided view that has failed to do justice to the contributions and suffering of these people. If conventional history books have slighted their presence, then a reexamination of this aspect of American history may be useful. This is especially true in an age that has witnessed such a militant demand for human rights by peoples around the globe.

Yet the drive for human rights that dominated the headlines in the 1960s is not new nor is it a fad. Indeed, historically this quest has been a lengthy although not a constant one. During the last century it has been subject to many changes. The goal of its participants may have been the same, but the underlying philosophy propelling the movement and the means employed to secure those rights have been altered greatly through the years. Submission, accommodation, and working within the System were replaced by protest and other extra-Establishment methods such as revolutionary rhetoric and riots. Some glimpses of America's underside can aid us in comprehending the rise of human consciousness and the energetic drive toward full citizenship in the United States. Moreover, by examining the twentieth-century efforts of blacks, other racial minorities, and the feminist movement, our understanding of the phenomenon of protest in this country can be furthered.

EUROPEAN AMERICA'S FIRST TARGET: THE INDIAN

The special bias of our historians appears in sharp relief in their discussions of the early discovery and colonization of the New World. Although conventional history tells of the explorers' efforts, very few commentators have confronted squarely the justice (or injustice) of their quest. But the expansion of Europe into various parts of the world involved moral and legal implications that cannot easily be ignored. For example, to the extent that the colonizing nations were concerned with the legal ethics of possessing Indian lands in the New World, their primary concern dealt not with the rights of the original inhabitant but rather with the claims of rival European powers. This is revealed by the Treaty of Tordesillas sanctioned by Pope Alexander VI in 1493, which divided the world between Spain and Portugal (see Chapter 1, pp. 6 for details). The treaty was deemed necessary to prevent a potentially dangerous competition among Christian nations for areas of the world not yet conquered by Europeans.

But the conquest of Indian lands did not occur immediately. Nor was the Indian response to the arrival of Europeans initially a hostile one. The earliest chronicles of English-Indian contact are lavish in their praise of the welcome accorded the first colonists. Although the settlers were impressed with Indian hospitality, their gratitude was directed to God. A sentence from an early diary—"God caused the Indians to help us with fish . . ."—mirrors this attitude. Seventeenth-century Europeans gave thanks to their God, not to their fellow man. Thus, cordial relations between the woodland tribes of the eastern seaboard and the first English colonists were short-lived as issues of conflict began to surface.

Central to the disputes that arose between the European settlers and the natives of North America was the clash of cultural values. The colonists frequently assumed that ulterior motives accompanied Indian "kindness," somehow transmuting that trait to one of "treachery." If Indian customs could not compare with the more "civilized" European way of living, the Indians would be subjected to the charge of "barbarism." And because they did not seem to subscribe to the Protestant Ethic of hard work—a century-old belief thoroughly imbued in the European—it was difficult to avoid the conclusion that Indians were a "lazy" people. Europeans traveling in eighteenth-century America constantly referred in their diaries to the "indolence" of the natives. A Frenchman in 1700 observed:

I am again struck by the dominant preference of these tribes for indolence. They will go without things that we regard as absolutely necessary merely because it would require a little effort to get them.

In other words, the belief in the ethnic superiority of European culture permitted white Americans to condemn any values different from those of their own "civilized" world.

The Indian's air of indifference toward the European's conviction that work was man's most sacred calling created an additional misunderstanding involving the concept of land ownership. The Indian relied heavily on the idea of cooperation in the common use of the land. The white man, on the other hand, had a seemingly endless appetite to possess the land (and as much of it as possible) for himself. Here were the ingredients for a clash in values that would bear very serious consequences for those who would not emerge successful from the conflict.

The primary argument used to remove the Indian from his native soil was the one of "utility," which came to be known as "usofruct" or "use-of-the-land" argument. The main idea was that man's right to the land depended on the condition that he use the land, cultivating it not only to further his prosperity but also in obedience to the Biblical admonition that man "have dominion" over the land. Since Indians were usually regarded as wandering hunters with no permanent habitation, their title to the land was contested. To live as vagabonds on the land was simply too wasteful in a world in which other nations faced (or thought they faced) problems of overpopulation. This argument provided an extremely popular justification during the eighteenth and nineteenth centuries for dispossessing the Indians of their land. As a result, one late eighteenth-century observer noted: "It is plain as day that they have no right to the land and it is permissible to drive them out at will." The idea that a hunting and gathering society could be forced to submit to a more agricultural economy imposed by force by an alien people was voiced by many influential spokesmen, from John Locke in the late seventeenth century, to Theodore Roosevelt—our first twentieth-century president—who said: "The settler and pioneer have at bottom had justice on their side. This great continent could not have been kept as nothing but a game preserve for squalid savages." It was clear that those who wasted God's land by being nomadic hunters had now lost whatever "natural" title they may have had earlier.

Is it safe to assume, however, that "usofruct" provided a valid rationale for taking Indian lands? Were the Indians in fact roaming vagabonds? Of course, there was a certain amount of nomadism among the Indians of the eastern coast, but agricultural pursuits played a far more prominent role in their economy and society. In general, the usofruct argument conveniently overlooked the fact that these Indians were primarily village dwellers. It is ironic that graphic depictions by European visitors of seventeenth-century Indian life often show substantial dwellings, palisaded villages, well-planned streets, and garden plots.

The attitudes that took root in colonial America did not diminish in the years following the birth of the new nation; on the contrary, during the nineteenth century they led the Indian down the path of subjugation. Thomas Jefferson, who wove the principle of human equality into the Declaration of Independence, found the issue of white men on Indian lands a thorny one. As the westward movement rapidly swept away Indian settlements in the early nineteenth century, some jurists and theorists recognized the moral dilemma that resulted from the white man's repeated violation of solemn treaties respecting Indian sovereignty over their own lands. Other Americans, however, were able to resolve this question easily. In 1874, for example, Lieutenant Colonel Custer frankly admitted that the Indian could not be "civilized": "Nature intended him for a savage state; every impulse of his soul inclines him to it." By the end of the century, a young Theodore Roosevelt admitted that Indians were clearly not the equal of white men: "I don't go so far as to think that the only good Indians are the dead Indians, but I believe nine out of every ten are, and I shouldn't inquire too closely into the case of the tenth. The most vicious cowboy has more moral principle than the average Indian." Finally, the Supreme Court in 1902 declared that earlier treaties gave no absolute protection over reservation lands, that reservation lands could be sold—in spite of treaty stipulations to the contrary. In effect, this meant that reservation Indians possessed no property rights.

By the early twentieth century the Indians had been subdued. Not only was much of their land taken from them, but they were ravaged by the white man's diseases and spoiled by his liquor. The original American was now a fallen warrior. As a result, a new image of the

An anonymous artist's rendering of an Indian town. One expert states that Indians "who had been for generations town-dwelling farmers, as were the majority of North American Indians, came to be characterized as raggle-taggle nomads, interested only in keeping their lands as 'hunting grounds,' which, of course, made it easier to justify seizure of their lands."

Indian began to emerge. Even the American scientific community was quick to engage in race stereotyping; a series of supposedly objective studies appeared claiming that the Indian was clearly of an inferior race.

Increasingly, the "real" Indian, who had been for so long an able adversary of the white man, was left to wither away on the reservation. In his place the mythical red man was created, the subject not only of "scientific" studies but also the convenient victim for countless literary heroes. The West and its earliest inhabitant became a two-dimensional source of entertainment for three generations of Americans in magazine stories, novels, on the Hollywood screen and on television. As one writer observes, "in the popular mind the Indian evolved from a troublesome heathen to a mortal enemy to an unfortunate ward of the state to a non-person."

THE BLACK MAN IN A WHITE MAN'S COUNTRY

The discovery of America required that the Indians surrender their lands to its new proprietors. Intent upon establishing an agricultural society across this broad expanse of land, the settlers faced an urgent need for labor. In a society with an abundance of land, few would work as hired hands on another's property. This economic necessity dictated the fate of black Africans, who soon became pawns in an international slave trade. One should not assume, however, that the appearance of black slavery in America was either immediate or inevitable.

Because of the planters' preference for white laborers, they encouraged immigration from the British Isles. By fixing a definite term of indenture of five to seven years (see Chapter 1, pp. 20 for details), the planters hoped to stifle rumors drifting back to the homeland that desperate conditions in the colonies had led to indefinite servitude. The system of indentured servitude therefore had the effect of guaranteeing favorable prospects for the white man willing to come to America. It was far otherwise for his black counterpart. Every improvement in the status of the white servant served to widen the gap between him and the African, who slowly found himself sinking into a system that was virtually the same as slavery.

This state of legal indecision persisted for about 40 years after the first blacks arrived in 1619. During this strange twilight period there was still reason for hoping that blacks would not find themselves in a state of perpetual slavery. But the decade of the 1660s

Few white people during the colonial period were sensitive to the inhumanity of the African slave trade. One company engaging in slave commerce instructed its ship captain to pack his vessel with "negers" and "Cattel" together. These crowded conditions doubtless increased the incidence of disease and epidemics during the voyage to America. The result was a shocking mortality rate, sometimes exceeding 50 percent of the black cargo.

witnessed a decline in the Southern economy that threatened the black man's future. Recovery from a serious drop in tobacco prices did not occur for another 20 years. As the margin of profit narrowed and as costs rose, small-scale tobacco production was seriously hampered. The planters came to realize that profits could be restored only by expanding production, and they decided to rely on a large work force whose labor could be depended on over the long term. Therefore, it was argued that lifetime black servitude must be written into law. In 1662 the Royal Company of Adventurers was founded to encourage the importation of black slaves. This symbolized the planters' hope that slave labor would be the wave of the future in the southern colonies.

Of course there were numerous examples of discrimination against the black man in English America long before slavery was legally codified in the 1660s. The most essential feature of slavery appeared as early as the 1640s when court records refer to the sale of blacks for life. Moreover, black labor was generally regarded as more valuable than its white counterpart. But this difference between white and black servitude did not mean institutionalized slavery for the black man. Instead, it merely signified that blacks were discriminated against more seriously than whites. Although the institution of slavery itself may not have existed through most of the seventeenth century, it is clear that black people were being subjected to increasing discrimination as time passed. By the opening years of the eighteenth century, this trend became much more explicit when blacks were defined legally as property, to be bartered and bargained for.

When the American legal system acknowledged black inferiority—and hence racial inequality—it contributed to the attitude of American society toward the black man. The trend became more apparent when Thomas Jefferson's antislavery section was deleted from the proposed Declaration of Independence. This bias was reflected a few years later when the Founding Fathers meeting in Philadelphia in 1787 wrote the Constitution, which not only circumscribed the black man's rights but recognized the institution of slavery itself. These laws were reinforced by certain economic developments including the invention of the cotton gin in 1783 and the introduction of a new type of cotton seed early in the nineteenth century. Cotton soon became the largest American export, vital to the economy of the South.

Obviously there was a contradiction between the ideals of equality contained in the Declaration of Independence and the reality of black exploitation. During the pre-Civil War period the passage of much proslavery legislation such as the Fugitive Slave Act of 1850 contributed to the demise of Jefferson's doctrine of equality. Moreover, historians generally agree that the institution of slavery effectively stripped the transplanted Africans of their cultural identity. Not only were their personal freedoms such as marriage and education seriously hampered, but their employment opportunities, responsibility, and self-respect were geared to a very low level. These restrictions contributed to the development of black inferiority, a concept reinforced by other sources of authority right down to the middle of the twentieth century.

For example, the courts of the nation, theoretically the final interpreter of justice and the law, helped to ingrain in American thought the notion of racial inferiority. In the Dred Scott case of 1857 the U.S. Supreme Court determined that blacks were not American citizens. In this decision a majority of the justices suggested that the framers of the Declaration of Independence and the Constitution never intended that black men should participate in American political life. The process of excluding black men from the rights of American citizenship persisted after the Civil War despite the passage of the Fourteenth and Fifteenth amendments to the Constitution, which were designed to safeguard those rights. Indeed, during the last three decades of the nineteenth century the Supreme Court handed down a series of decisions that rendered these amendments meaningless.

The trend toward the segregation of the races climaxed in the 1896 Supreme Court case *Plessy v. Ferguson.* Stripped of its legal jargon, the conservative, states rights-minded Court stated that blacks and whites may be separated. In this way a system of segregation emerged in America, fully sanctioned by the highest court in the land. Furthermore, the legal subordination of black Americans was not simply a regional phenomenon; although Americans often looked disapprovingly upon the South for its Jim Crow laws, it should be noted that seven of the nine justices who decided the *Plessy* case were from the North. It is clear that the segregation laws that appeared by the early twentieth century enjoyed the approval of the entire nation. Indeed, it was during these same years that the facilities of the national government itself in Washington, D.C. were segregated. Finally, the full impact of the *Plessy* decision can be understood only if one realizes that the "separate-but-equal" doctrine contained in the 1896 case would remain the official law of the land until 1954, when it was overturned by the landmark case *Brown v. the Topeka Board of Education of Topeka, Kansas.*

Thus, the contest between the forces of equality and racial inferiority that had been raging for more than a century following the American Revolution was finally resolved. By the opening years of the twentieth century America was unequivocally a white man's country. This reality was recognized by Booker T. Washington—the black man's most prominent spokesman at the turn of the century—when he gave his famous "Atlanta Compromise" address. Aware of the diminishing options open to his race, Washington counseled patience and manual training to his black brothers until white people were willing to accept them as fellow Americans.

The lawmakers and justices of the courts were not alone in reducing black Americans to second-class citizens. During the first decades of the twentieth century spokesmen from other influential areas of American life contributed to the tightening ring of control that defined and circumscribed the black man's freedom. Journalists were quick to stereotype black behavior in the most degrading terms. A literature appeared that portrayed the ex-slave as a bumbling child-like Sambo.

These vicious distortions were mirrored in the scientific community's prolonged effort to dehumanize blacks. In 1906, for example, a well-known zoological society in New York City proudly announced a new exhibit that demonstrated the theory that the black man was much closer to anthropoids than to the Caucasian on the evolutionary scale of Charles Darwin. Hundreds of thousands of curious sightseers flocked to see a five-foot African "pygmy" named Ota Benga together in the same cage with an orangutan. Organized protests by local black clergymen to free the African failed, eliciting the bland reply that this was a "purely ethnological exhibit." This shocking ignorance of Africa and its people was echoed in 1909 by President William Howard Taft, a learned man and later Chief Justice of the United States, when he stated that Africa had no history at all "... except that which we trace to the apes."

Even historians were partners in this conspiracy against black Americans. Concerning the topic of slavery, for example, two prize-winning American historians write in 1930: "As for Sambo, whose wrongs moved the abolitionists to wrath and tears, there is some reason to believe that he suffered less than any other class in the South from its 'peculiar institution.' " When a second edition of this widely read volume appeared 20 years later, these comments on the slave remained virtually intact.

During the course of many decades, the black American gradually found his place in a nation governed by white men. In spite of the efforts to guarantee his political character and humanity after the Civil War, he was effectively stripped of that protection and, instead, found himself the target of stereotypes and misunderstanding of great magnitude. The negative image that emerged was that of the "nigger," and stamped on that image was the phrase "Made in America."

THE MEXICAN: A STRANGER IN HIS OWN LAND

The history of the Mexican-American has a parallel with his Indian counterpart. Each became a minority not by immigrating or being brought to this country as a subordinate people, but instead by conquest. Like the Indian, the exploitation of the inhabitants of the Southwest was also a result of the white man's appetite for land. In this sense, the early history of Mexican-Americans, beginning in the nineteenth century, is a repetition of the treatment of the Indian that began two centuries earlier.

The earliest confrontation between Mexicans and Americans occurred when the great area of the Southwest was still under the sovereignty of Mexico. In just a few decades a floodtide of Americans swarmed into the area containing present-day Texas, New Mexico, and California. By 1836 Americans in Texas had successfully revolted against the Mexican government and established the independent republic of Texas. (For a more complete discussion of Mexicans and the nineteenth-century westward movement, see Chapter 3, pp. 78–81; 87–91.)

To conquer the land and dominate its inhabitants required, of course, a rationale justifying their subjugation. Racial myths about Mexicans appeared as soon as their earliest encounters with the Anglos. As early as the 1830s and 1840s, Mexicans were regarded scornfully as being "lazy," "cowardly," "corrupt," and "cruel." Although the concept of "race" is especially difficult to apply to the Mexicans, who are largely the result of mixture of at least two peoples, yet the above-mentioned traits were considered characteristic of the Mexican "race." Distrust of this ethnic group was widespread and reflected in a statement appearing in the *Atlantic Monthly* in 1899: "No one can tell what a Greaser thinks; no one can say what masked batteries of passion lie back of his well-mastered eyes. To trust a Greaser is to take a long jump into utter darkness."

During the nineteenth century, the Mexican-American was exploited for his ancestral lands. After 1900, he found his fate tied to the economic development of the Southwestern states. The rise of agricultural technology coupled with the development of large reservoirs for irrigation purposes created heavy labor requirements. Irrigation farming led to a demand for cheap Mexican labor for work in cultivating, carting, packing, processing, and shipping. Workers were also needed in cotton production and on the railroads.

The racial stereotypes that had developed provided a convenient excuse to explain a division of labor in which the Mexicans were usually at the bottom. Although this source of labor enjoyed an initial welcome, the appearance of an increasing number of brown-skinned people with different customs and living habits heightened the racial fears of the new Anglo majority.

By the 1920s a deepening agricultural crisis culminating in the Great Depression of the 1930s made the Mexican's position in his ancestral lands much less secure. As the Dust Bowl migrants from the Midwest came westward seeking jobs, the amount of agricultural work available to the unskilled ethnic was drastically reduced. Gradually, newspapers and magazines began to devote more space to the presence and danger of the Hispanic element. Racial fears were now accompanied by charges of unfair economic competition. Patriotic societies and labor unions began to demand that the goverment must "close the back door" in an effort to restrict the continued immigration of Mexican nationals into the American Southwest. Besides preventing the influx of additional Mexicans, there was a move to "repatriate" those who were already residents of the United States. Between 1930 and 1934, for example, more than 64,000 Mexican aliens were forced to leave the United States without formal legal proceedings. Indeed, these fears flared anew in late 1974 with the blunt statements of the U.S. Attorney General, who declared "open season" on illegal Mexican aliens. Mexican-American spokesmen claimed that the Mexican aliens were being made scapegoats for American economic woes. They insisted that, unless these pressures were resisted, Mexicans would be required to carry identification tags like the Jews in Hitler's Germany; "only rather than yellow stars, we will be set off by the color of our skin."

The coming of World War II, with its manpower emergencies, altered the economic situation once more and created again the need for Mexican labor. In 1942 the *Bracero* (contract labor) program was established. After the war, agricultural employers exerted their influence to continue the Bracero program. They argued that there were not enough domestic workers and that native Americans were generally unadaptable to the stoop labor needed in the fields.

Responding to the need for farm workers, Mexican immigration increased rapidly in the 1950s. This influx reached such proportions that a wave of anti-Mexican sentiment swept through the Southwest, leading to a repetition of the repatriation of the Depression era. "Operation Wetback" was designed to deport these aliens who had entered the country illegally; however only a small fraction of the almost four million immigrants deported during the mid-1950s received the right of a formal legal hearing. In the process, the civil rights of hundreds of thousands of American citizens were violated. The legacy of this emotionally charged government policy was to provoke greater distrust and alienation in the Mexican-American toward "establishment" America.

WHITE AMERICA AND THE "YELLOW PERIL"

Anti-immigrant sentiments were also directed against another people. By 1851 recently arrived Chinese "coolies" in California found themselves at the bottom of the heap along with the Mexicans. Most had been brought over, some by contract with Chinese warlords, as railroad labor. Like the Mexicans, these Asians were also required to pay the foreign miners' tax and to beware of overzealous vigilantes. Anti-Chinese sentiment gained momentum during the 1870s among the laboring classes in California who were suffering from a business depression. Soon fear of the "Chinks" spread to regions in America where the Chinese had never been seen. As early as 1869 a New York newspaper described the threat to traditional America:

It is then a flood of this sort of population that is just beginning to sweep over America. Already the Chinese are supplanting Americans and even the Irish in all sorts of manual labor in California. How shall we assimilate this element? How shall we maintain our boasted civilization, how maintain the reputation of our country as "the land of the free and the home of the brave?"

Within 10 years Chinese immigration totaled 100,000, and agitation for exclusion of these foreigners from American shores increased. The debate that ensued focused on arguments that were frankly racist in nature. One aspiring presidential candidate in 1879, speaking in favor of exclusion, concluded that ". . . either the Anglo-Saxon race will possess the Pacific slope or the Mongolians will. . . . We have this day to choose whether we will have . . . the civilization of Christ or the civilization of Confucius." President Rutherford B. Hayes indicated that as a result of our discouraging experience with the Indians and blacks, he would be willing to support "any suitable measures" to prevent further Chinese immigration. By 1882 the clamor against the Chinese reached such proportions that Congress passed an immigration exclusion law that was made successively even more ironclad in 1888, 1902, and 1904.

The need for Chinese laborers in the railroad construction crews and in the mines of the West did not last for very long. Soon they came to be seen as an alien and nonassimilable element. Undesirable socially and unwanted in the job market, the Chinese became the target of a series of immigration restriction laws enacted during the last decades of the nineteenth century.

As a result of the exclusion legislation, those who chose to remain in the United States found little opportunity for success. They lived in ghettos called "Chinatowns" and their children often were required to attend segregated schools. Finally, in 1943, Congress decided to repeal the 60-year-old immigration legislation, hopeful that by doing so the morale of America's wartime ally in the Orient might be boosted in the fight against Imperial Japan. In the meantime, however, the damage had been done, and their pattern of life had been established during the century since the first Chinese had responded to the call for labor on America's west coast in the 1840s.

Of course, both the Chinese and the Japanese who came to America later suffered from disadvantages that did not plague immigrants from Europe. The "ideal" newcomer was expected to be white, Anglo-Saxon, Protestant, and from a nation friendly to the United States. Neither "yellow" peoples could claim these traits. Instead, they were nonwhite, Asian, and non-Christian. In the case of Japan, that nation later engaged in all-out war with the United States. Moreover, the Japanese encountered adversity as a result of the previous Chinese experience. After 1885 thousands of Japanese men came to the continental United States from their homeland, often via Hawaii. Following on the heels of decades of harrassment, acts of violence, and legal restrictions levied upon Chinese immigrants, it should be no surprise that the 22,000 Japanese who had come to America by 1900 were confronted with a variety of challenges.

The "Yellow Peril" had become such a specter that in 1906 the San Francisco school board ruled that Japanese-American schoolchildren must attend special schools, although it was later revealed that only 93 children out of a school population of 25,000 were Japanese. The supporters of this school segregation order—including labor groups and patriotic organizations—advanced a variety of arguments to support their view. Like other minority groups, the Japanese were seen as different in their "values" from those of the white majority. One Congressman charged that there were no words in the Japanese language for such western concepts as "morality," "sin," "home," and "privacy." "The concept of 'commercial honor' is almost totally devoid in the Japanese mind," he added. Other concerns were also expressed. The sexual fears of the white majority were stimulated by a California politician who announced his determination to prevent "matured Japs with their base minds [and] lascivious thoughts" from sitting in the classroom "next to the pure maids of California." To men of this mind, the exclusion of the Japanese was obviously necessary.

The uproar over the school order had international repercussions. The suggestion of inferiority elicited angry protests from Japan. To avoid the possibility of a break in United States-Japanese relations, President Theodore Roosevelt convinced the San Francisco school board to withdraw the segregation ruling if he would end further Japanese immigration. This he did through a series of diplomatic notes with the Tokyo government in 1907–1908, resulting in the so-called Gentleman's Agreement. This was made more concrete in 1924 when pressure from such groups as the American Legion, the Native Sons and Daughters of the Golden West, and the American Federation of Labor forced Congress to exclude the Japanese from migrating to American shores.

The insecurity of Japanese life in America hardened when the two nations went to war. The surprise attack by Imperial Japan upon Pearl Harbor had disastrous results for Japanese citizens of the United States. By the spring of 1942, 70,000 American citizens of Japanese ancestry, as well as some 40,000 aliens, were forcibly evacuated from their homes on the West Coast and interned in several "relocation centers" in the interior. No formal charges were made against these people, simply because no laws had been violated. Why did this extralegal action occur?

Economics is one factor that can not be ignored in explaining Japanese internment. For many years one of the few avenues of opportunity open to the Japanese immigrant had been in farming, especially in California. By 1941 the Japanese produced 42 percent of the state's truck crops. Their success had antagonized the Caucasian vegetable growers and shippers, who sought the expropriation of their land. But a narrow economic interpretation does not adequately explain the government's action against these people.

It is difficult to avoid the conclusion that racism played an important role in the decision to evacuate the Japanese from the Pacific Coast. In Hawaii, for example, none of the Japanese population was evacuated, although the proportion of Japanese and the possibility of Japanese espionage there were greater than on the mainland. Relocation occurred despite the lack of any evidence of espionage or sabotage by the Japanese on the mainland. At the same time, individuals of German and Italian ancestry were not disturbed, although the governments of Germany and Italy were also at war with the United

While Japanese-Americans were summarily accused of disloyalty and shut-
tled off to "concentration camps" surrounded by barbed-wire enclosures and
machine guns, many of their brothers and sons were defending their country
in both theaters of the war. Their fighting units — comprised solely of
Japanese-American soldiers — were among the most decorated units in
United States military history.

States. Moreover, internment was advised not only by the military,
but by influential persons in civilian life as well. Liberals such as then
California governor Earl Warren supported the action, which was
upheld by the Supreme Court.

The legacy of wartime evacuation and internment was deep. Established family patterns were disrupted and psychological studies

show that feelings of hopelessness, personal insecurity, and inertia overcame many individuals who formerly had been an enterprising, energetic people. When the war ended, the internment camps had affected many of their inmates in a way similar to the reservations' effect on the American Indian. There were also economic consequences. In a poll taken in 1945, when asked if Japanese-Americans should have the same opportunity for jobs as white people after the war, 61 percent of those polled replied negatively. Furthermore, many Japanese families were financially ruined by internment. Their property left behind on the West Coast was lost, sold, or confiscated. More than 25 years later, only a fraction of the lawsuits initiated by Japanese–Americans to recover a portion of their property losses has been satisfactorily resolved in the courts.

PAST, PRESENT, AND FUTURE

These glimpses of America's underside suggest that racism in America has cast a long shadow, stretching down to the postwar atomic age. The systematic denial of full human rights gained the support of lawmakers, the courts of law, men of science, and also writers of popular literature. One should not assume, of course, that racial minorities merely tolerated this exploitation and mistreatment at the hands of the white majority without resistance. Indeed, throughout the history of the United States there are numerous examples of nonwhites who fought long and hard for the realization of their constitutional rights. In large part, however, their efforts did not bear fruit during their own lifetimes. But that ongoing struggle did contribute to the growing momentum of the human rights movement that has appeared in the past 20 years.

. Although many groups have rallied to this modern banner, historically black people have been in the vanguard of the movement. To a very large extent, it has been their efforts and experiences that have provided a blueprint of inspiration and change for other groups who more recently have seen themselves as the victims of institutional oppression in American life.

EARLY STIRRINGS TOWARD EQUALITY

By the twentieth century, Jim Crow legislation had been enacted throughout the South, reinforcing the economic deprivation and political disenfranchisement of black people. The black man himself had played a role in the gradual decline in his economic, political, and social status, reflected by Booker T. Washington's "Atlanta Compromise" address in 1895. But Washington's gradual approach to the racial problem was not welcomed by all. Over a period of a few years some blacks and their white allies began to advocate more militant methods to gain equality. Calling themselves the Niagara Movement, in 1909 they met to create the National Association for the Advancement of Colored People (NAACP). Although most of the officers of the organization were white, its guiding spirit was W.E.B. DuBois, a black man who stridently demanded an equal place for his people in American life. To him, nothing less was acceptable. Challenging Washington's role as a spokesman for black people, DuBois claimed that the Alabama educator's approach "has tended to make the whites, North and South, shift the burden of the Negro problem to the Negro's shoulders . . . when in fact the burden belongs to the nation. . . ." The NAACP, with its black–white liberal alliance, became the most influential organization designed to serve black interests. It later continued its work primarily through lawsuits in the federal courts. But progress, both economic and political, was painfully slow. In fact, during the early twentieth century lynching became an even more widespread means of controlling or intimidating blacks.

The violence and bloodshed perpetrated against blacks aroused a powerful force after World I that anticipated the Black Power Movement of the 1960s. It is estimated that as many as a half-million black people became followers of Marcus Garvey, the charismatic founder of the Universal Negro Improvement Association. Rejecting the politics of compromise and cooperation with whites that characterized the NAACP, Garvey instilled pride in his followers, insisting that "we of the UNIA do not want to become white." Though Garvey was later convicted and imprisoned on charges of fraud, his movement planted the seed of black nationalism that would surface again in the form of black power four decades later.

In the meantime, black people did make significant gains in their crusade for human equality. As Washington's philosophy of accommodation declined, it was replaced by the more aggressive, mass-action strategy of the NAACP. Moreover, the liberal trend reflected by Franklin Delano Roosevelt's New Deal created a greater sympathy for the oppressed and poverty-stricken. The insistence of the Congress of Industrial Organizations (CIO) upon the equal treatment of white and black workers also contributed to the realization of black rights.

Finally, in June 1941, President Roosevelt issued an executive order that led to the formation of the Fair Employment Practices Commission. This order prohibited discrimination in government employment and defense industries on the basis of race, creed, color, or national origin, and thereby paved the way to new economic opportunities for blacks and other nonwhites in many of the most important sectors of the economy. President Harry Truman continued Roosevelt's use of the office to further the cause of civil rights, including his leadership in integrating the armed forces in 1949.

"I HAVE A DREAM"

The postwar years proved to be momentous ones for the cause of civil rights. Perhaps the greatest blow to inequality came in 1954, when the United States Supreme Court handed down its desegregation order in the case of *Brown v. the Topeka Board of Education*. The Court ruled that the "separate but equal" clause of the *Plessy* decision of 1896 was contradictory because "separate educational facilities are inherently unequal." The *Brown* decision rendered unconstitutional the elaborate system of segregation that had enjoyed the official approval of the land for more than a half century. This decision was all-important in stirring the national conscience. Now, with the law on their side, blacks began a more active pursuit of their rights.

The symbol of this new mood first appeared in December, 1955 when Mrs. Rosa Parks of Montgomery, Alabama, refused to surrender her seat on a municipal bus to a white man. Her arrest by local authorities led to a massive black protest and boycott of white businesses, catapulting the Reverend Martin Luther King, Jr. into national prominence. Better than any other black leader, the Rev. King articulated the feelings and hopes of his people. Through his philosophy of nonviolence, derived from the tenet of Christian love and the technique used successfully by Mahatma Ghandi in India's struggle for independence, blacks across the nation were inspired to emulate the Montgomery protest.

Direct, nonviolent mass action achieved significant results. Beginning in 1960, an estimated 70,000 blacks and whites participated in more than 800 "sit-ins" followed by economic boycotts by whole black communities that forced the advocates of segregation to capitulate. The "Freedom Rides" in 1961 also confirmed the importance of nonviolent mass action, aided by the coverage of these news events by television and other media. The spectacle of thousands of black people willing to endure beatings, attacks by dogs, police clubs and high-pressure hoses, imprisonment, and even death conveyed a sober impression of black determination to the American nation.

On their television screens, Americans were able to witness these confrontations at Little Rock, Montgomery, Birmingham, and elsewhere, and the national reaction that followed played no small role in civil rights action taken at the highest levels of government. Both John F. Kennedy and Lyndon Johnson gave strong backing to the civil rights movement. The 1963 March on Washington by more than 200,000 persons helped to produce the Civil Rights Act of 1964 in which the federal government insisted that public facilities are for all people. Johnson also played the key role in securing the passage of the Voting Rights Acts of 1964 and 1965. These laws forbade discrimination in public accommodations, education, voter registration, and employment. Blacks could now enter the electoral process throughout the South.

But with the public accommodations and voting rights battles in the Congress over, how complete had the victory been? Certainly some dents in the wall of segregation had been made, yet discrimination persisted and resistance to change was still very strong. The

The willingness of thousands of black Americans to engage in this kind of nonviolent resistance to white supremacy in the South during the early 1960s was important in their quest for human equality.

dream eloquently voiced by the Rev. King before the March-on-Washington crowd was not as easily within the grasp of black people (nor their idealistic white supporters) as had been assumed. Despite their legal gains, blacks were learning that true integration into American life was not as easily attained as they had hoped. Indeed, the belief that the awakening of the American conscience—coupled with the increasing militancy of the civil rights movement after the 1954 decision—would result in equality was beginning to sour.

By the mid-sixties it was apparent to many black people that racism had scarcely lessened. Nor had white resistance disappeared. Nonwhites were not being welcomed into the mainstream of American society. As late as 1967, for example, only 4.3 percent of the South's black children were in desegregated school systems. Increasingly, blacks were beginning to realize that it would be necessary to step up their fight for equality. Rather than rely on the good intentions of their white allies, optimism gave way to mounting pessimism, bitterness, and rage. More than a decade had passed since the shackles of segregation were officially lifted in 1954, and the patience and moderation of the Rev. King gave way to a more strident cry of "Freedom Now!"

"FREEDOM NOW!"

A major shift in the mood of the black civil rights movement occurred during the mid-sixties. For several years the Student Non-violent Coordinating Committee (SNCC) had played a major part in the civil rights struggle. After suffering many insults and risking their lives in their campaign to increase voter registration among Southern blacks, SNCC leaders gradually became convinced that prominent black spokesmen like the Rev. King were willing to compromise with their white allies too much. They concluded that the recently enacted laws were not being enforced vigorously and that the white establishment could not be depended upon to treat the black man fairly. By 1965, SNCC had ceased to operate within the traditional white liberal framework of integration. Since the American political system had not delivered on its promises, SNCC leader Stokely Carmichael stated in 1966 that his people must begin to think in terms of "Black Power" and to seek their strength from within their own ranks rather than to rely upon whites. Symbolically, the assassination of the Rev. King in 1968 ended the liberal, integration phase of the struggle for black human rights.

Perhaps the shift from the civil rights movement to Black Power was inevitable. Despite the seeming progress in "race relations" since 1954, the gap between the earning power of blacks and whites actually increased by the mid-sixties. Although the old system of legal segregation was gone, the more subtle techniques that had been used for so long in the North were adopted across the nation to keep blacks "in their place." Moreover, increasing educational opportunities did not necessarily provide equal employment opportunities. The integration movement had little success in breaking through these barriers because it had to compromise with the white power structure—difficult to do even with the help of white liberals. Agonizingly slow progress frustrated many blacks, particularly those in the ghettos of the North whose quickly rising expectations were not being satisfied. This led to the militant black reaction of the mid-sixties.

These people saw "Black Power" as the answer. The groups that arose during this period claiming to speak for black people had varying definitions of "Black Power." One principle they all agreed on was the rejection of Rev. King's doctrine of nonviolence. Malcolm X, one of the most prominent spokesmen for the Black Muslims (or Nation of Islam) advised his followers that "if someone puts a hand on you, send him to the cemetery." Stokely Carmichael, who had labored in the vineyards of integration earlier, now insisted that integration was merely "a subterfuge for the maintenance of white supremacy." The head of the radicalized SNCC announced that "the days of free head-whippings are over. Black people should and must fight back." Even the representatives of the church came to embrace violence as a just weapon to be used against racism. One clergyman told a worldwide conference of churchmen: "When a society does not permit restructuring power that produces justice through economic and political maneuvers, the church ought not to shy away from aiding and abetting the development of the only other weapon available—the power of violence." Such pronouncements were brazen calls to terror in the eyes of some Americans, but they electrified large sections of the black community and assured the Black Power movement a national audience.

The reaction to this new trend was mixed. Many white Americans felt that the movement was attempting too much and expecting changes too fast. Yet the more heady doctrines of Black Power maintained that greater changes could and must come, and this sparked the anger of blacks—especially those in the Northern ghettos. During the mid-sixties there were more than a dozen large riots in America's

The looting and burning that accompanied the riots in the ghettos during the 1960s was partly the result of the gap between black expectations based on liberal promises and the failure of the government to deliver on those promises. Although the rioters comprised only a tiny fraction of the ghetto population, one commentator stated that the majority of the neighborhood's inhabitants sympathized with those on the streets. As a black girl said after the riot in Watts, "Every time I looked out of my window and saw another fire, I felt new joy."

major cities, including Newark, Detroit, and the Watts section of Los Angeles. Thousands of persons were injured and millions of dollars in property damage occurred as rioters vented their anger and frustrations upon a system that seemed insensitive to their needs.

BLACK NATIONALISM IN THE SEVENTIES: A FAREWELL TO INTEGRATION?

Since the decline of the intoxicating idealism that characterized the March on Washington in 1963, many blacks concluded that if they were not welcome in white society then they should pursue a course of separatism. Numerous factors help explain the rise of black nationalism that occurred in the late sixties. As the white man became identified as the enemy of black interests, doctrines were formulated that stressed self-help, racial pride, and the unity of interests of nonwhite people around the world. One important development in black nationalism was the appearance of the Black Panther Party in 1966, formed by two militants named Huey P. Newton and Bobby Seale in Oakland, California. A year later they were joined by the powerful theoretician and ex-convict Eldridge Cleaver. Deeply influenced by such writers and activists as Malcolm X, Frantz Fanon, Karl Marx, Lenin, Mao Tse-tung, Ho Chi Minh, and Che Guevara, the Panthers declared their intention to liberate the "black colony" from the rule of the "white mother country" (i.e., the black people from white-dominated America). Within three years, Panther membership had grown to an estimated 5000, in 30 chapters across the country.

Another major contribution to the dogma of black nationalism was contained in the writings of Stokely Carmichael. Drawing an analogy between the black communities in the United States and the African colonies under European rule, Carmichael points out that just as the white imperialist powers extracted the wealth of Africa for their own gain, so has the labor of the black ghettos been exploited for the profit of white America. By banding together and exercising their collective economic and political power over their own communities, Carmichael suggests that black people would be following a time-honored principle used by other ethnic groups in American history. The slogan "Black is beautiful" symbolized the hopes of black leaders that self-sufficiency was a realistic goal. Numerous "Black Studies" programs were added to the curricula of many colleges and universities across the nation, aimed at creating an appreciation for a cultural tradition that had suffered from long years of neglect.

Soon after the Nixon administration took office, it indicated its support for the more peaceful processes of change advocated by the black nationalists. The resounding support the nation gave to President Nixon's call for "law and order" made clear that the urban violence associated by many people with the Black Power doctrine would no longer be tolerated. Even the most radical of the blacks realized by 1970 that the temper of America was increasingly hostile to both an aggressive integration movement and the guerrilla militancy associated with groups like the Black Panthers. The Panther organization itself was largely broken up by arrest and imprisonment and in several cases its adherents were killed in shoot-outs with the police. Some of its leaders chose to exile themselves.

Thus with the onset of the seventies the black crusade for human rights and humane treatment entered a new phase in its long struggle. The Nixon administration made clear its opposition to busing and many welfare programs, while condemning permissiveness and praising the work ethic. The President's solution to the black dilemma centered on the notion of black capitalism, a concept put forth by the black nationalists and welcomed by a diverse collection of people who shared some of the President's sentiments. Whereas the integrationists of the sixties demanded confrontation with a seemingly inflexible government and society, the separatists offer Americans social peace. The prospective harmony involves a price—black nationalists are demanding white support for their plans.

Not all blacks have rallied to the banner of separatism, however. Black leaders still associated with the integration movement believe that equality is still possible within white society, and assert that more than 80 percent of the South's black children now attend desegregated schools. Two white writers in *Commentary* magazine early in 1973 argued that:

A remarkable development has taken place in America over the last dozen years: for the first time in the history of the republic, truly large and growing numbers of American blacks have been moving into the middle class, so that by now these numbers can reasonably be said to add up to a majority of black Americans—a slender majority, but a majority nevertheless.

Furthermore, whereas in 1962 there were only three black Congressmen, a decade later there were 16. There were no black city mayors in 1962, now more than 100 occupy city halls. In addition, explaining these advances, the number of black voters in the United States multiplied more than three times in the decade from 1962 to 1972. One writer noted that "hands that picked cotton are now capable of picking Presidents." How realistic this more traditional avenue of power and equality is has been sharply contested by many blacks and their white liberal allies.

Critics of the 1973 Nixon budget pointed out that it included sharp cuts in 70 existing governmental programs, many directly affecting black people in the area of manpower training, welfare, education and housing. The black Congressmen charged that this slash in the budget reflected "repressive and inhumane impulses." This charge was echoed by the report of a blue-ribbon presidential committee appointed to investigate the cause of civil disorder. This commission, headed by former Illinois Governor Otto Kerner, concluded that "our nation is moving toward two societies, one black, one white — separate and unequal."

THE MEXICAN-AMERICANS

Like the blacks, Mexican-Americans have continued to encounter serious obstacles in enjoying the benefits of the "American Dream." Although the Mexican's presence in the United States predates American annexation of Mexican territory in 1848, attaining his constitutional rights has been a painfully slow process. From the Treaty of Guadalupe-Hidalgo through the 1930s, the Mexican-American's role in the United States was almost completely apolitical. Aware of the ever-present forces of prejudice, the early pioneers of Mexican political organization were willing to accept the Anglo definition of the proper role for Mexicans in American politics. They realized that the two decades between the wars were not the time for controversy, especially since the Depression made them vulnerable to the charge of taking jobs away from unemployed whites. Their economic survival depended upon knowing the "place" white Americans had defined for them.

By the time of World War II, however, a policy of accommodation gave way to more aggressive political activity. The war not only created new opportunities in employment, education, and housing (still segregated), but as many as a half-million Mexicans served the United States in the armed forces and returned home determined to be full-fledged citizens of this country. Mexican-Americans began to form organizations designed to advance their interests like the Community Service Organization (CSO). The CSO was based on the premise that American institutions were basically responsive to the needs of Mexican-Americans. One important endeavor of the CSO was a vigorous voter registration campaign. Pressure was also placed on housing agencies, the Federal Employment Practices Commission, and the police to insure more just treatment of Mexican-Americans. By the late 1950s, the CSO seemed to be losing its vitality, and some of its key leaders like Cesar Chavez resigned to pursue the quest for Mexican-American rights in other ways.

The most important phase in the growing political self-consciousness of Mexican-Americans came in the mid-sixties. Profiting from the example set by black militants, Mexican political activity was radicalized and the *Chicanos* (a derivative of the word "Mexicanos") emerged. By the mid-sixties, militant Reies Lopez Tijerina and his followers engaged in unsuccessful guerrilla warfare against the state of New Mexico, protesting the "illegal" seizure of Mexican lands in 1848. For the first time, Mexican-American activists questioned not only the assumptions of their predecessors but some of the more basic premises of American society as well.

The Chicano movement challenged the widespread belief that Mexican-Americans are thriving more than most other nonwhite minorities. Indeed, in income, occupational distribution, and housing, Mexicans are the nation's second-largest disadvantaged group (far outnumbering Indians and Puerto Ricans). Like many blacks, Chicanos see themselves as an oppressed people—evidenced by their loss of communal and private property and the submergence of their culture by the white majority after the 1840s. When they were evicted from their own land, they were often forced to become migrant farm workers. Otherwise, they migrated to the city where their lack of education and unskilled labor made them particularly vulnerable to exploitation.

By the 1960s neither of these choices was acceptable to a large segment of the Mexican-American population. Migratory farm workers responded to Cesar Chavez's efforts to organize them, and then used strikes and boycotts to gain recognition, better pay and working conditions from growers. Adopting Martin Luther King's doctrine of nonviolence, the union's strike and Chavez's promotion of a nationwide boycott of the grape industry in 1967 became the symbol of "la Causa" for all Hispanic-Americans. By the early seventies this movement or "cause" had still not succeeded in convincing the great majority of the growers to sign contracts that would provide recognition of the farm workers' union and increase wages.

Caesar Chavez's efforts in building the N.F.W.A. have succeeded in giving Mexican-Americans in particular and migrant workers in general a rallying point and a voice in their own lives.

The complaint of the Chicano is based on cultural arguments just as much as economic ones. The Mexican community has decried the systemic effort by the Anglo-dominated society to impose its values on the ethnic minority. It is charged that this cultural oppression continues in many school systems attended by Mexican-American children. Thus the Chicano has recognized the urgent need to re-create his concept of self by building his pride in his history and culture. The idea of "La Raza" has played a key role in Chicano ideology, referring not so much to "race" as to a vague sense of ethnic identity. Chicanos believe that the American "melting pot" has been a pressure cooker that has tried to steam off their own culture and mold them into a "standard" American. Many Mexican-Americans are no longer willing to submit to such cultural domination.

The results of the Chicano cultural revival have been mixed. Since textbooks on the secondary and college level have traditionally ignored Mexican-Americans as a minority group, Chicanos have now successfully established "Chicano Studies" in the curricula of many schools. The 1973 Southern California "walkout" conducted by thousands of Chicano pupils to protest the inadequacy of these programs suggests that more progress needs to be made. Some schools still prohibit the speaking of Spanish on school grounds. The cutback in federally aided programs for 1973–1974 required that some of the bilingual programs established in some Southwestern high schools and grammar schools be discontinued for lack of funds. A five-year study made by the U.S. Commission on Civil Rights revealed in 1974 that the public schools continue to systematically discriminate against the Mexican-American child.

By the seventies, despite these continued inequities, the Chicano movement echoed the growing moderation of its black counterpart. The Brown Berets, a quasi-military youth organization with the radical rhetoric and style of the Cuban revolutionaries, entered a period of decline and disbanded officially late in 1972. Relative quiet returned to the "barrios" (ghettos) as Chicano organizations turned away from open demonstrations in favor of working within the system for institutional change. One leader stated that the nature of the struggle had changed by 1973, "shifting to areas that require day-to-day work like the building of a political party. There is less glitter, and less drama, but the indications are that it will be a much more substantial organization." At the same time, however, resorting to more peaceful organizational techniques should not be interpreted as a return to the old policy of submission and accommodation. According to one Chicano spokesman, the quiet of the early seventies was a time of "thoughtful introspection," a "lull before another type of storm, which will not be as visible or vocal, but more prone to producing change."

THE AMERICAN INDIANS:
FROM WOUNDED KNEE TO WOUNDED KNEE

The dying gasp in the Indian quest for autonomy in the land of their forefathers occurred in December 1890. It was on the snow-covered prairie near Wounded Knee Creek in South Dakota that two regiments of United States cavalry opened fire on 350 defenseless men, women, and children, killing nearly 300 of them. After many decades of resistance to the white man's penetration of Indian lands, this massacre represents the final effort in the centuries-long conquest of the original American. From the time that they were subjugated and placed on reservations as wards of the United States government, Indians have endured both the loss of their land and its natural resources to whites and the ravages of cultural destruction.

Out of a growing awareness of the government's historic mal-treatment of the Indian, a campaign began during the 1920s to seek greater justice for Native Americans. Besides providing for more autonomy in tribal cultural matters, the Wheeler-Howard Act of 1934 sought to counter the depletion of Indian lands that occurred during the previous half-century. This bill, which was largely the brainchild of the new, progressive-minded Commissioner of the Bureau of Indian Affairs (BIA), John Collier, stipulated that Indian lands should revert back to the old tribal arrangement of communal ownership. Sales of land to non-Indians were drastically restricted. Provisions were made to restore former Indian lands to their original owners.

Despite the lofty vision of John Collier, repeated violations of agreements between Indians and the federal government persisted. The Department of the Interior continued to lease large sections of reservation lands to giant corporations who tore up the earth, covered it with lumbering wastes, and polluted the waters with mining poisons. As recently as August 1972, Interior officials declared that no environmental impact statements under the terms of the National Environmental Policy Act of 1969 were required for "development" of reservation lands. Despite these years of exploitation, Indians were slower to recognize the need for militancy in pursuit of their rights than were the blacks and Mexican-Americans. By the late 1960s, however, they were no longer willing to accede quietly to the authority of the BIA and had begun to act against these injustices.

The new strident mood of the Indian appeared first in November, 1969 when Indians from various tribes "captured" the abandoned federal prison on Alcatraz Island in San Francisco Bay. They announced that they wished to "liberate" the island from "white rule" and establish an Indian cultural center. They expressed their willingness to pay 24 dollars in glass beads and cloth for the island —the same price the Dutch had paid to Indians for Manhattan Island 300 years earlier.

Of greater significance to the rise of the "Red Power" movement was the "invasion" of the BIA headquarters in Washington, D.C. by young Indian radicals in November, 1972. They raided BIA files and found stacks of documents that, they claimed, support their contention that the federal government has not honestly faced its duty as guardian of the American Indian. These "Broken Treaties Papers" revealed that although the Department of Interior is responsible for protecting Indians, it has been directly involved in the conspiracy to rob them of their land and its natural resources. Despite the numerous treaties made between the Indians and the government, for example, the Broken Treaties Papers demonstrated that they still have not enjoyed justice in the courts. Although individuals and some groups of Indians have been awarded sums totaling millions of dollars in compensation for their losses, there has been a notable lack of success by the Indians in their efforts to correct the violation of their treaties with the United States government. Furthermore, many years of federal aid to the Indians has failed to improve Indian reservation life. The Broken Treaties Papers showed that for many decades the major portion of the funds allocated for the benefit of Indians has been wasted by the vast bureaucracy that administers the government's programs.

At the same time, these documents revealed that the conditions of urban Indians—those who left reservation life—was totally neglected by the government. A secret "Study of Urban Indian Problems" recommenced that the BIA take a more active interest in Indians who have moved to the cities. Although there may be as many as 300,000 urban Indians in the United States suffering from serious economic and social deprivation, this recommendation was rejected by President Nixon with the explanation that the needs of reservation Indians were "sufficiently great that resources available to the BIA should not be dissipated elsewhere."

Perhaps the most dramatic symbol of the Indian's growing impatience with the federal government was the armed takeover of the village of Wounded Knee in January, 1973. The radical, city-based American Indian Movement (AIM) assumed leadership in this act of defiance against the Indian's century-long benefactor. The leaders of the insurrection concluded that the takeover of the 1890 massacre site offered the most effective means of publicizing their plight, and they announced that they would persist in their insurrection until top government officials, including presidential aides, conferred directly with them. During the next four months Wounded Knee was under siege as the talks broke down repeatedly, interrupted by the exchange of thousands of rounds of gunfire, resulting in serious injuries on both sides. A year after the seizure of Wounded Knee, the issues that

The news media's expose of the Broken Treaty Papers in 1972 prompted the radical American Indian Movement to take a dramatic step. AIM members seized the small community of Wounded Knee, South Dakota in March 1973, in order to broadcast their people's plight. The symbol of Indian despair dating back to the Indian massacre by government troops at Wounded Knee in 1890 was now transformed to one of Indian defiance. (Editorial cartoon by Paul Conrad. Copyright, Los Angeles Times. Reprinted with permission.)

sparked the rebellion still had not been resolved by negotiation between the Indians and the government.

Thus, years of neglect had convinced the Indians that the government was incapable of meeting their needs. During the seventies, they began to demand an end to the traditional policy of "white paternalism" and a greater voice in running their own affairs. In an important election early in 1974 voters at the Pine Ridge, South Dakota reservation reelected tribal president Dick Wilson over the more militant AIM challenger Russell Means, who led the insurrection at Wounded Knee. Although there is not complete agreement between AIM and the more conservative tribal leaders on the reservations, the two groups agree that a greater voice in matters affecting Indian life is not negotiable. In addition to more economic and political self-determination, Indians wish to participate in determining the educational needs of their children, and a fairer treatment of their history and culture in the textbooks. By the seventies, Indian studies programs had been added to college curricula across the nation. This has been important not only in building the Indian's sense of worth and ethnic pride, but also because there are important lessons that could benefit whites.

Long before Europeans touched the New World, societies existed there that were supported by sophisticated ideas in government, and dedicated to the concept of living in harmony with their fellow man and with nature. In 1947 former BIA Commissioner Collier wrote eloquently of what non-Indians can learn from the Native Americans: "They had what the world has lost, they have it now; what the world has lost it must have again lest it die. Not many years are left . . . to recapture the lost ingredient—the ancient, lost reverence and passion for the earth and its web of life." Perhaps of greatest concern is that Indians shall finally gain the position of respect and security they have long deserved as the original Americans. The current interest in Indian culture and the ecology "fad" may decline, but the Indians who "liberated" Wounded Knee in 1973 are determined that their people must not become once again America's "forgotten minority."

THE NEW FEMINISM

Another group in American society during the 1960s who joined the crusade for human rights was women. By the early seventies the feminist movement had reached a high-water mark in its strident quest for equality. Although there is much about the modern women's liberation movement that is radical and new, at the same time it bears a strong similarity to its nineteenth-century counterpart. (See Chapter 2, pp. 59 for a discussion of women's reform in pre-Civil War America). Both movements were propelled not by an increase in deprivation and suffering *per se*; they were, instead, revolutions of rising expectations by groups who found themselves deprived of status and frustrated in their hopes of being full participants in American society.

Actually, it was the accelerated pace of industrialization after the Civil War that gave momentum to the movement during the Gilded Age. The factory system provided many new employment opportunities for women during this period, as did new positions in service industries. Before the turn of the century, women outnumbered men in such fields as telephone work, nursing, and teaching. In the business world, the invention of the typewriter opened an additional vocational frontier to women. The vast majority of these working women, however, received lower pay than men in the same jobs. Furthermore, most female wage earners still faced the same domestic chores when they returned home from work. Despite these continuing inequities, it can not be denied that these new economic forces led to profound social changes. As the result of the pioneering efforts of Margaret Sanger, for example, the availability of birth control information by the 1920s led to greater independence for the woman and a new image of her role in society. Not only did the size of the family begin to rapidly diminish, but an increasing number of women found other opportunities more attractive than marriage.

The focal point of the feminist movement during the late nineteenth and early twentieth centuries centered on such urgent

Not all persons in the early suffragette movement chose the moderate approach. Like the lady seated in the cockpit, after the turn of the century there were a growing number of women who rejected their exclusive role as "helpmate" in order to pursue a variety of interests outside the home.

issues as wages and working conditions of women *and* children, the right to birth control information, and living conditions in the urban slums. Spurned by the important trade union groups during the Gilded Age, including the American Federation of Labor, women found the attainment of these goals impossible. The result was the National Women's Trade Union League (NWTUL), founded in 1903, and dedicated to the advancement of the interests of working women within the trade union movement. Absorbed with these immediate economic and social concerns, leaders in the women's movement earlier had regarded the more obvious political issue of voting rights as secondary in importance. It gradually became apparent, however, that it was difficult to correct such inequities without the necessary political power. The NWTUL was instrumental in forging the alliance between upper and working class women that played an important role in gaining the right to vote (or suffrage) in 1919. But the right to vote for women was seen by many of its supporters as a means, rather than as an end, concerned primarily not with women's rights but with a more general reform of American society.

The suffragists decided to adopt the tactic of expediency in gaining the right to vote. During much of its history, the feminist movement had been tainted by the "radical" label, which helps explain its relative lack of success during the nineteenth century. Feminist activists had marched in parades, participated in strikes, been arrested, and even murdered in their militant quest for equal rights. Not until the public was persuaded that the women's movement was "safe," middle-class, and middle-of-the-road could the feminists hope to achieve their goals. Accordingly, they made their appeal to the Progressive reformers: "Give us the vote to double your political power." A 1915 suffrage banner read:

> *For the safety of the nation*
> *To Women give the vote*
> *For the hand that rocks the cradle*
> *Will never rock the boat.*

The leaders who adopted this moderate tactic were confident that although it compromised their objectives to a degree, once suffrage was enacted women would surely support issues that affected them as an oppressed group in American society.

This strategy led to a short-range success, but was a long-range disaster. Although the Nineteenth Amendment was adopted in 1919 giving women the vote, it did not contribute tangibly to the growth of women's rights. The hoped-for bloc vote of female voters failed to materialize. The feminist movement had not been able to convince women of the large middle class that they were an oppressed group. Class, race, and ethnic factors rather than sex proved to be more significant in motivating voting behavior. In a fundamental sense the passage of the Nineteenth Amendment was a hollow victory. As one woman historian has written, "the political and legal gains of feminism amounted to tokenism. Economic advantage proved illusory as well, and consisted for most women in access to low-paid, low-status occupations." The winning of suffrage had failed to emancipate women.

Having gained the right to vote, the feminist movement assumed a low profile for the next 40 years. The morale of the movement received another staggering blow—the loss of any impact as a voting bloc—because during this lengthy period the issues that confronted the electorate were generally oriented along economic lines and determined by class interests. With the possible exception of prohibition, there were no prominent issues that enlisted the special support of women or appeared to arouse their active opposition. In the meantime, statistics reveal that during those interwar years American women lost ground in relation to their counterparts in other industrial nations. Even today, most western European countries and Russia have a higher percentage of women physicians than the United States. There are more women in the English Parliament than in the halls of Congress. Though the number of working women in America is higher than ever before, their occupational segregation is as great as it was in 1900. Moreover, the gap in incomes between working men and women has widened steadily since World War II, evidenced by studies as recent as 1974.

New vigor did not return to the feminist movement until the 1960s when the college-age daughters born of the war generation grew up. Like their suffragette forerunners, they have been generally white, middle class, and well educated. However, unlike their mothers who were raised during the Depression of the 1930s, these girls grew up in a society that was economically secure. Job security seemed an inadequate reward for their college training as they became aware of the pervasive discrimination that persisted on the economic front. It was their generation that had participated in the civil rights revolution of the sixties, although their own ideals and expectations continued to be thwarted by typing and other mundane tasks that they were frequently assigned. Their experiences led them to a closer

Like other dissident political groups, the women's liberation movement has recognized the need for publicizing their grievances. Through such eye-catching tactics as public bra-burning and other forms of protest, they have succeeded in eliminating some forms of sexist discrimination.

examination of their own situation, and increasing numbers of young women in the late 1960s and early 1970s concluded that they too have been the victims of institutional oppression. Mounting impatience with continued second-class citizenship and economic handicaps appeared. This, coupled with an awareness of the psychological damage that women have suffered as a result of their subordinate position in American society, has caused them to act.

The organization of the contemporary movement is comprised of a variety of groups, including the National Organization of Women (NOW) and the National Women's Political Caucus (NWPC), in addition to various radical splinter groups. Generally speaking, the active membership of these groups is made up of the educated, white, and middle class. Leaders prominent in the movement include such diverse personalities as Congresswoman Bella Abzug of New York, journalist and editor of *MS.* magazine Gloria Steinem, and Betty Friedan, whose popular best-seller *The Feminine Mystique* brought so much publicity to the movement. With the notable exception of Shirley Chisholm, black women have been almost totally absent from the women's liberation movement.

The experiences of the racial minorities have impressed upon the women's liberation movement the need for organization and self-determination. Autonomy in their decision-making and organization is a lesson the feminists have borrowed from the Black Power movement. With men labeled as the "oppressor," militant members demand that only females be allowed in women's liberation meetings. They believe that male support should be permitted only in subordinate roles. By putting the "oppressor" in "his place," it is hoped that the woman's sense of human identity will be allowed to develop. These radical tactics are designed to lessen the self-denigration which, women's liberation advocates claim, the male-dominated society has imposed upon them. Once again, the analogy of the plight of women and blacks is noteworthy. A feminist pamphlet explains this parallel: "Women and blacks have been alienated from their own culture; they have no historical sense of themselves because study of their condition has been suppressed . . . . Both women and blacks are expected to perform our economic function as service workers. Thus members of both groups have been taught to be passive and to please white male masters in order to get what we want."

The agitation by "Women's Lib" has resulted in some success. Sex discrimination in employment was finally prohibited by the Civil Rights Act of 1964. In 1972, the Supreme Court declared anti-abortion laws to be unconstitutional and maintained that the decision for abortion within the first three months of pregnancy was entirely up to the woman and her physician. In the same year, an historical first occurred when black Congresswoman Shirley Chisholm from New York was a candidate for the Presidency of the United States. Despite her failure to be nominated, other women took their seats in the Congress. By 1973, the movement had established itself in more than 400 cities where it is accompanied by a spontaneous sprouting of women's groups in churches, businesses, and other organizations. Despite widespread predictions to the contrary, a magazine devoted to the feminist persuasion continued to publish and gain in circulation. In the same year, after a 49-year battle, the Equal Rights Amendment was in the process of state ratification. Its adoption was made more likely by the dramatic gains women made both in Congress and in local courthouses across the country in the 1974 elections. As with other minority movements, women's studies began to appear on college class lists. Fundamental to the current feminist movement is the belief that only after the idea of equality is applied in childraising, education, culture, sex, and family life can legal and economic equality for women be a reality. Only time will tell whether women shall cease being prisoners of their sex.

WHOSE PROBLEM?

Each of the groups prominent in the current human rights struggle—blacks, Orientals, Mexicans, Indians, and women — shares certain characteristics. Each has gradually reached the conclusion that its people have been oppressed. Not only have they been the target of economic and cultural discrimination, but in the past they claim to have been powerless politically. Just as important is the psychological damage they claim has been inflicted upon them by society.

To correct this denial of their human rights, there has been general agreement that no solution is possible without a clearer self-identity—stripped of the masks that social mores have historically expected them to wear. After developing this new image as human beings, the group can then better determine what its needs are, and formulate a means of implementing them. Each group has become increasingly vocal, and by the early seventies demonstrated the willingness to resort to radical steps when necessary to attain its goals. Threats of violence are no longer unexpected.

There is no guarantee, however, that their demands will be met. Father Theodore M. Hesburgh, the President of Notre Dame and former Chairman of the President's Commission on Civil Rights, wrote in early 1973:

As we enter a new era in the civil rights movement, some of us see progress grinding to a halt, even slipping backward. There are few enthusiastic white voices speaking up for minorities in Washington and state capitols today . . . . Impassioned pleas for civil rights, which in the sixties excited millions, now draw a stifled yawn and the politicians, of course, read the signs of the times very well.

There is a growing recognition that the momentum of the human rights movement of the late 1960s and early 1970s has been deflated, replaced by the sobering reminder of an overwhelming majority of American voters who joined forces with President Nixon's "New Majority" in 1972. This middle-income, middle-educated, and middle-aged political coalition demonstrated on numerous issues —busing, women's liberation, fair housing, and employment practices—that it does not hold strong sympathies for the demands of those who see themselves historically as objects of exploitation. The implications of this problem are indeed serious, as the nation prepares for the bicentennial celebration of those Americans who successfully staged a revolution against tyranny and oppression in 1776.

SUGGESTIONS FOR ADDITIONAL READING

Winthrop D. Jordan, *The White Man's Burden*, (1974). An explanation of the historical origins of racism in the United States.

Vine deLoria, *Custer Died for Your Sins*, (1969). An informative and angry catalog of abuses of the Indian in American history.

Wilbur R. Jacobs, *Dispossessing the American Indian*, (1972). A study of the myths about Indians and whites on the colonial frontier.

Robert William Fogel and Stanley L. Engerman, *Time on the Cross*, (1974). A sweeping reexamination of the economic foundations of American Negro slavery.

Leonard Pitt, *The Decline of the Californios*, (1966). A social history of the Spanish-speaking Californians, 1846–1890.

Betty Lee Sung, *Mountain of Gold*, (1967). A history of the Chinese in the United States from the gold rush days to the present.

C. Van Woodward, *The Strange Career of Jim Crow*, (1974 edition). A study of the legal separation of the races at the turn of the twentieth century, tracing its repercussions to the 1970s.

Roger Daniels, *The Politics of Prejudice: The Anti-Japanese Movement in California*, (1962). A brief account of the anti-Japanese movement from its inception in the late nineteenth century to its first major triumph with the Immigration Act of 1924.

Carey McWilliams, *North From Mexico*, (1968). A history of the Spanish-speaking people of the United States.

Stokely Carmichael and Charles V. Hamilton, *Black Power: The Politics of Liberation in America*, (1967). An analysis of the Black Power movement of the 1960s by two noted black activists.

N. Scott Momaday, *House Made of Dawn*, (1969). A Pulitzer Prize-winning novel of the psychological destruction of the Indian in modern America.

Caroline Bird, *Born Female*, (1968). An indictment of the discrimination against women in the United States.

CHAPTER NINE

ECO-CRISIS: THE ENVIRONMENTAL PROBLEM

1864
Man and Nature, written by George P. Marsh, becomes the first book on ecology and conservation in America.

1872
Yellowstone becomes the first national park.

1890
U.S. Census Bureau announces the end of the frontier.

1892
Sierra Club founded to preserve wilderness values.

1908
U.S. Forest Service created: important milestone in conservation movement.

1913
Conservationists and preservationists differ over the fate of Hetch-Hetchy, which is finally dammed several years later.

1924
Teapot Dome scandal appears in the press; Secretary of the Interior is convicted of taking a $500,000 bribe.

1934–36
A long drought and overplanting turns much of the Great Plains into a Dust Bowl.

1964
Congress passes the Wilderness Act.

1973
Arab oil boycott ignites an energy crisis in the United States.

WHAT IS AT STAKE?

World food production is falling so far behind population growth that in 1974 more than 10 million people died of starvation and a half billion more were constantly hungry. Many experts concur in predicting a general global famine in this decade. Smog, now linked by scientists to cancer, lung and heart diseases, threatens human life in nearly every major city of the industrialized world. In Tokyo, Japan, oxygen is available to traffic police and sold in vending machines to the public. Dangerous pesticides are in such widespread use that the DDT intake of infants around the globe is now twice the daily allowable maximum set up by the World Health Organization of the United Nations. Three-fourths of the water treatment plants in the United States do practically nothing to remove pesticides, herbicides, and other dangerous chemicals from drinking water, and in every other nation water standards are even lower. The search for new energy sources and the further development of conventional fuels take on extra urgency in an economy totally dependent on enormous quantities of power.

These are some of the problems that make up the eco-crisis that confronts the human race—problems almost wholly of man's own making. Pollution and the exploitation of the world's natural resources threaten not only mankind's long-range chances for maintaining a comfortable standard of living, but the very balance of earth, water, air, and living organisms necessary to sustain life itself. Within the past few years there has been growing attention paid to this eco-crisis, especially in the United States. Solutions have been proposed and in some cases begun, but they must cope with complex ecological problems that continue to grow in complexity and seriousness. What are the origins of these problems? Why have they been allowed to become so serious?

AMERICANS AGAINST THE WILDERNESS

The answers to these questions lie in American attitudes toward nature and the land. In turn, these attitudes are based partly on the beliefs and prejudices that European colonists brought with them to the New World. Perhaps the strongest element in this Old World attitude was the Judeo-Christian tradition. The Christian church, Catholic or Protestant, played a strong role in molding the European people's attitudes toward life and their relationship to the world around them. One of the primary doctrines placed humanity above the rest of created beings and made nature man's servant. This was based upon the Biblical account of creation where God commands man to "subdue" the earth and "have dominion" over all living things. Mankind could do what it pleased with the earth. A solitary voice of opposition to this doctrine was that of St. Francis of Assisi, who maintained that all in God's creation were equals and deserving of respect and consideration. St. Francis' view, however, was not widely known and its influence was minimal.

Given this doctrine of superiority, the land itself was judged "good" or "bad" depending upon its domination by and usefulness to people. "Good" land was like the garden of Eden—pastoral, productive, and safe. Wilderness was "bad" land, a desolate, dangerously wild place. In the Old Testament, the garden and the wilderness were also spiritual opposites: the Hebrew people's "promised land" was "a land flowing with milk and honey" like "the garden of the Lord," while the wilderness was "accursed" land ruled by the devil. This combination made wilderness something to be avoided. Old World folklore and mythology reinforced the bias by peopling the wild forests and mountains with assorted ogres, werewolves, semihuman wild men (and women), and other fiendish beasts. Many Germans fervently believed that the "Black Forest" hid witches and other evil creatures, while Rumanian Slavs associated the Transylvania country with vampires. It is not hard to understand this supernatural dread. Even today nightfall in wild country plays on the imagination, changing tree limbs into grotesque figures and animal cries into mysterious threats. In the Old World, people shunned the wilderness, keeping to safely cultivated and settled areas where they had "subdued" nature.

Ironically, some persecuted religious sects that righteously hated the wilderness sought it out as a sanctuary from the rest of "sinful" society and as a testing ground to purify one's faith. As justification, they pointed out that the people of Israel escaped from slavery in Egypt and had to journey in the wilderness to become disciplined in faith before they could enter the "promised land." Even more significantly, Jesus Christ "was led up by the Spirit into the wilderness to be tempted by the devil" and emerged ready to speak fearlessly for God. Religious groups like the Puritans and later the Quakers held to the idea of wilderness as a place of refuge and of spiritually purifying trials.

This did not mean that they liked wilderness. When William Bradford stepped off the *Mayflower* in 1620 he referred to the land as "hideous and desolate." In fact, this primeval environment was a direct threat to the colonist's survival. Necessities like food and shelter had to be wrenched from the wilderness by the backbreaking work of clearing the land, planting crops, and erecting cabins. Dreaded Old World myths seemed to come alive in the New World forests—savage Indians, and "rabid and howling wolves" which, according to one colonist, would "make havock among you and not leave the bones until morning." There was also the subtle danger of sliding back into barbarism. A traveler in the backwoods in 1749 noted that "a kind of white people are found here, who live like savages. . . ." A nineteenth-century tale out of the West concerns "Big Phil," a mountain man who made it through the hard Sierra winters by eating his Indian wives when the food supply was exhausted.

Generation after generation, American pioneers struggled with primitive conditions. If wilderness was their sworn enemy, then rural civilization with its productive farms and safe, comfortable villages was their friend and the goal of their labor. A Virginia planter in 1630 could not see "how men should make benefit of (wild land) . . . but by habitation and culture." Wilderness was waste—or, what was worse, a "dark and dismal Devil's den." By "subduing" it and replacing it with rural civilization, the settlers felt they were doing both themselves and God a service. God had commanded humanity to "have dominion," and the pioneers were having it.

CONQUEST EQUALS PROGRESS: THE PIONEER MENTALITY

If this war against wilderness was vigorous it was also careless, and just as frequently as it was waged for survival it was waged out of pure greed. Americans widely assumed that the continent's vast stretches of forest and land were inexhaustible. Coming as they did from Europe, where the land had been occupied for centuries and resources were strictly limited, it is understandable that the abundance they found in the New World seemed infinite by comparison. But people are not likely to take care of land or resources they consider boundless. Virginians eagerly sought new lands west of the Allegheny Mountains because they were destroying their own soil by overplanting it with tobacco, a crop that drew heavily on soil nutrients. George Washington wrote sadly, "Our lands were originally very good, but use and abuse have made them quite otherwise." An Englishman observed in horror while New Jersey farmers, "in order

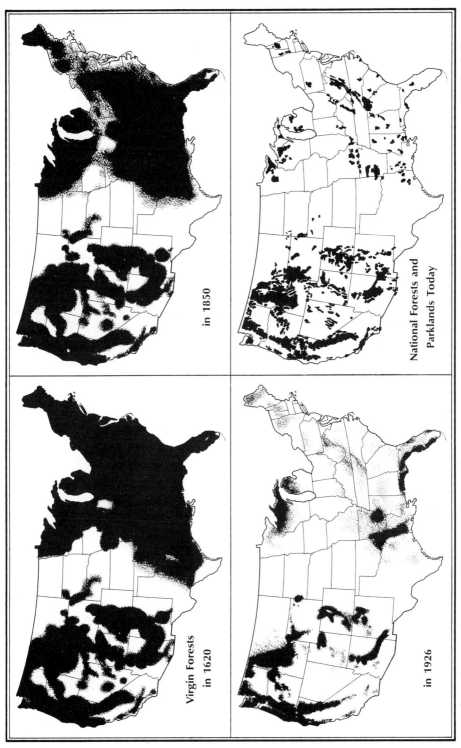

Virgin Forests
in 1620

in 1850

in 1926

National Forests and
Parklands Today

Before the American government imposed effective restrictions on logging activities, private lumber companies had cleared vast areas of virgin forest in the United States. Even today, not all of the remaining stands of timber are adequately protected as wilderness or parklands.

to save themselves the work of shaking or pulling off the nuts . . . find it simpler to cut the tree and gather the nuts from it, as it lies on the ground." Lumbermen of the Great Lakes country, particularly in northern Michigan, stripped the huge forests of white pine within a period of 40 years and left only small stands of hardwoods, tangled jack pines, and aspen. Businessmen and settlers were taking the cheap and easy way, their eyes fixed on immediate gains and blind to the future price.

Although the cost was not yet obvious in the first half of the nineteenth century, the benefits were. Fed by great quantities of natural resources, the United States was experiencing a phenomenal prosperity. Americans rejoiced in their growing development as a nation."What a people we are! What a country is this of ours," exulted one western newsman, "which but as yesterday was a wilderness." Another summarized the advance of the frontier ever further westward as the "tramp, tramp, steady and sure, of the advancing hosts of Civilization and Christianity." There was a rampant enthusiasm for the confidence in the nation's progress as every economic indicator gave proof that young America was growing in wealth and power. That the transformation taking place was right and good no sensible man could doubt. In his 1830 Inaugural Address President Andrew Jackson (a former frontiersman himself) asked, "what good man would prefer a country covered with forests and ranged by a few thousand savages to our extensive Republic, studded with cities, towns, and prosperous farms, embellished with all the improvements art can devise or industry execute?"

A leading minister put it another way—"Progress is God." The continent was in the process of being transformed from "useless" and "ungodly" wilderness into a tamed land of productive farms and villages. Even the Civil War could not halt the momentum. In 1862 Lincoln's government passed the Homestead Act, encouraging settlers to move west and occupy the immense stretches of land that remained open. Nor did the passing of the frontier in 1890 end pioneer attitudes toward the land. Wilderness, wrote one contributor to the Letters to the Editor column of the *Saturday Evening Post*, "is the dark, the formless, the terrible, the old chaos which our fathers held back. . . . when vigilance slackens, it swoops down for a melodramatic revenge." The conquest of nature continued to yield the natural resources necessary for growth and material prosperity. Since Americans judged progress chiefly by these standards, they concluded that conquest equals progress.

THE BEGINNINGS OF APPRECIATION

Not all Americans embraced the pioneer perspective as their own. Some among the well-to-do classes that had leisure enough to read European literature were influenced by a late seventeenth and early eighteenth century philosophical movement called the Enlightenment. This movement was motivated by a strong desire to discover more about the workings of nature through careful observation and rational deductions. Science was reborn in Western society and made great advances. Benjamin Franklin was perhaps the best known American devotee of Enlightenment ideas and principles. Thomas Jefferson was another disciple. His *Notes on the State of Virginia,* published in 1785, record an appreciation for nature beyond its scientific descriptions of the land and its inhabitants. A view of the Potomac River rushing deep in the mountain gorge past Harpers Ferry, Virginia is a sight, Jefferson claimed, "worth a voyage across the Atlantic." Telling of a natural rock arch in western Virginia, the author exulted, "It is impossible for the emotions arising from the sublime to be felt beyond what they are here; so beautiful an arch, so elevated, so light, and springing as it were up to heaven!" Jefferson was also a believer in Deism, a religious movement springing out of the Enlightenment. Deism viewed wilderness more benevolently, as God's creation and part of His beauty and majesty.

Romanticism, the late eighteenth century movement that reacted against the Enlightenment's emphasis upon reason and the power of rational investigation, went a step further. Romanticists preferred the solitude, awesomeness, and mystery of the wilderness over "tame" nature. If wild country was God's creation, they argued, then it was a statement of His nature and the closer one was to wilderness the closer one would be to God. In land uncontaminated by the touch of people, the romanticist could escape "sinful" society and its works. Primitivism, an outgrowth of Romanticism, even maintained that mankind's vigor, strength, and hardiness were the result of direct contact with wild nature. Thus in Europe at least, the American Indian became the "noble savage," imbued with the virtues of innocence and simplicity combined with animal power. Defoe's *The Life and Surprising Adventures of Robinson Crusoe,* an adventure novel about a castaway upon a desert island in the tropics published during this period, became enormously popular. The American author James Fenimore Cooper drew on the "noble savage" and other primitivist ideas to create the Leatherstocking Tales—the first stories casting the frontiersman as a hero.

The ideas of Romanticism and Primitivism reached America in the 1830s. Their New World counterpart was Transcendentalism, born in the villages of New England and raised by Ralph Waldo Emerson and Henry David Thoreau. Emerson was a dissatisfied Unitarian who had left the church to follow his own individualistic path to God. To him wild nature was "a symbol of the spirit," a reflector of "Truth." Behind it lay a higher spiritual world, and the individual having a "spark of the divine" within himself could discover that world and gain insights into its truths. "In the wilderness," Emerson wrote, "I find something more dear than in the streets or villages . . . in the woods we return to reason and faith." Like other Transcendentalists, he was repulsed by the rampant materialism of his day—"things are in the saddle," he protested, "and ride mankind."

Emerson's disciple, Henry David Thoreau, took up this theme and offered his own solution. "I went to the woods," he explained in the preface to *Walden Pond*, a journal of his experiences in living alone, "because I wished to live deliberately. I wanted to live deep and suck out all the marrow of life, to live so sturdily and Spartan-like as to put to rout all that was not life. . . . " Out of this experience came Thoreau's belief that "The forests and wildernesses" furnish "the tonics and barks which brace mankind"—strength, inspiration, self-knowledge, and vigor. Thoreau was not quite a Primitivist, however. His journey into the raw wilderness of northern Maine cured him of those tendencies. There he described the country as "more grim and wild" than he had expected, and he returned convinced that pure wildness was not the answer to mankind's ills. Rather Thoreau conceived of an ideal blend between the influences of wilderness and civilization: people needed "to combine the hardiness of these savages with the intellectualness of the civilized man." The problem, he felt, was that civilization threatened to overwhelm the last vestiges of wilderness and with it the source of the "raw material of life." America needed wild country to offset the spiritual and physical weaknesses that infected civilized society. "In wildness," Thoreau insisted, "is the preservation of the World."

PROTECT WILDERNESS: A PRESERVATIONIST OUTLOOK

But Thoreau's words were not widely read in his day and he was even less well known that his colleague Emerson. Their ideas barely penetrated outside the borders of New England. Transcendentalist and Romantic values would probably have remained intellectual curiosities if the United States had not been experiencing a cultural inferiority complex. American patriots seethed under the taunts of European (particularly British) critics who asked sneeringly if anyone had ever read an American book, viewed an American painting, or seen an American play. What Romantic values did was to provide Americans with a retort—they could point to the unmatched grandeur of the American wilds as a cultural asset and a source of national pride. "Nature has wrought with a bolder hand in America,"

In "Kindred Spirits," one of the artists of the Hudson River school depicts wild country as a source of inspiration for the poet and painter standing on the rock outcropping. A culture-conscious America reacted positively to this stirring of appreciation for wilderness in the 1840s.

proclaimed one pictorial volume, while another declared that America's vast wilderness wonders were "unsurpassed by any of the boasted scenery of other countries." Novelist Washington Irving felt that this asset was more than an esthetic one: "We send our youth abroad to grow luxurious and effeminate in Europe; it appears to me, that a previous tour on the prairies would be more likely to produce that manliness, simplicity, and self-dependence most in unison with our political institutions." James Fenimore Cooper's frontier stories and the Hudson River school's landscape paintings also celebrated the asset of wilderness. The poet William Cullen Bryant urged America to "keep that earlier, wilder image bright."

That image was fast disappearing under the pioneer's onslaught. Strip mines and denuded forests could not qualify as cultural assets, and the "march of civilization" had already trampled many of the eastern natural wonders underfoot. The experience of watching 1400 buffalo massacred just for their tongues moved artist George Catlin to call in 1832 for a "nation's park, containing man and beast, in all the wild freshness of their nature's beauty." The idea was not entirely new. Thoreau had urged that some wild places be set aside, "for modesty and reverence's sake, or if only to suggest that earth has higher uses than we put her to."

But it was among a relatively small group of well-to-do Easterners who lived in the city and escaped to the wilderness for relaxation that the park idea began to take tangible shape. Besides being impressed by the romantic idea that America's scenic resources were her greatest national asset and should be preserved, they had seen many of the endangered areas first hand. One of these areas, Yosemite Valley, was declared a California state park in 1864 largely because of the influence of these traveling easterners. Six years later, responding to the rumor of fantastic "wonders," several others visited the Yellowstone area in Wyoming. They returned determined to preserve the unique geysers, hot springs, and canyons they had seen. A bill was brought before Congress in 1871 proposing the creation of a Yellowstone National Park. Supporters of the measure had to assure skeptical legislators that the country was too high and cold for cultivation and that its preservation would do "no harm to the material interests of the people." Yellowstone was presented as a valuable national scenic resource, but more as a "natural amusement park" than as a wilderness preserve. Congress passed the bill in 1872—the nation had its first national park and preservation had won its first victory.

WISE USE OF RESOURCES: THE CONSERVATIONIST IMPULSE

While these nationalists and romanticists were beginning to act on behalf of wilderness, another group entered the controversy. Pride in the grandeur of the American landscape or romantic love of nature's inspirational qualities were not the primary concern of these people. Instead, they feared that mismanagement and waste were destroying the nation's natural resources at an ominously accelerating rate. One of the first men to warn of the effects of this waste was George Perkins Marsh in his book *Man and Nature* (1864). Marsh pointed out that clear-cutting of the forests of northern New York was resulting in floods and erosion. America, he warned, was repeating the experience of old Mediterranean cultures that had destroyed their land and fallen into decline as a result. "Let us be wise in time," he urged, "and profit by the errors of our older brethren." To safeguard the watershed that regulated stream flow and prevented disastrous runoffs, wilderness forest should be preserved "as far as possible, in its primitive condition." These areas could then be "a garden for the recreation of the lover of nature" as well as serving the practical function of a watershed. During the 1880s the Adirondack country, which Marsh had written about, became a popular recreational area for sportsmen. These people joined with those who agreed with Marsh's economic arguments and pressured the New York State Legislature into preserving 715,000 acres of Adirondack forest.

It was these people who put forth economic arguments that carried the day. Without a constant water supply, these pragmatists feared for their profitable canals and farms and insisted that the cutting of the Adirondack forests "will seriously injure the internal commerce of the State." Nor was this sudden interest in the care of natural resources restricted to the state of New York. The passing of the frontier in 1890 brought the issue before the entire country. America's western frontier had been the symbol of abundance, growth, and progress for nearly 250 years. When it ended it also broke the myth of the land's inexhaustibility and even called into question the creed of perpetual progress. Articles appeared in newspapers and magazines across the country detailing stories of mismanagement and waste. Accustomed to abundance, Americans were afraid of scarcity.

Their response was the conservation movement. It reached a peak during the administrations of President Theodore Roosevelt (1901–1909) and its national spokesman was a European-trained forester named Gifford Pinchot. Conservation proposed, in Pinchot's words, "the use of the natural resources for the greatest good of the greatest number for the longest time" under the careful supervision of the national government. Pinchot and other conservationists conceived of nature as a "farm" whose careful planting and management would yield "crops" like lumber year after year. To do this, areas of the national domain would, from time to time, be set aside and scientifically managed so that a continuous yield might be assured for future generations. In other words, efficiency in the public interest would replace private waste. President Roosevelt hosted a conference of state governors at the White House on the subject of conservation and appointed a commission to inventory national resources in 1908. Congress put the care of newly created national forests into the hands of a professional Forest Service. The Grand Canyon was made a national monument, and other new parks were set aside for the public to visit and enjoy. In almost all of these endeavors conservationists and those preservationists concerned with setting aside wilderness for esthetic reasons worked together. The whole program angered many Westerners who felt that newly created Federal forest reserves and parks and restrictions on water usage "locked up" raw materials, violating the "rights" of private enterprise. Pioneer attitudes were still strong in the West, where there was yet much unoccupied land and a wealth of untapped resources. Conservation was primarily an eastern-led movement.

Roosevelt's conservation efforts were nevertheless widely accepted as necessary and desirable. The doctrine of efficient use of natural resources was practical and utilitarian, matching most Americans' attitudes toward nature. After all, conservationists sought to insure continued growth and progress with less waste and more care. "The first duty of the human race," insisted Pinchot, "is to control the earth it lives upon." Conquest still equaled progress.

CONSERVATION AND PRESERVATION CLASH

Preservationists who fought for the creation of Yellowstone National Park and worked with Pinchot and Roosevelt were nevertheless disappointed in conservation. "It is much to be regretted," wrote the preservationist-minded editor of *Century* magazine, "that the official leaders of the conservation movement have never shown a cordial, much less an aggressive, interest in safeguarding our great scenery."

To this cause the preservationists were dedicated, and they found a champion in John Muir.

Muir grew up in Wisconsin, where he acquired a passion for the out-of-doors. But one could not make a living by camping. He turned to inventing and showed considerable talent for it. An accident in which he nearly lost his sight changed Muir's mind about his life's work—"God has to nearly kill us sometimes, to teach us lessons," he concluded. He lost no time getting back to the wilderness. After a thousand-mile trek to the Gulf of Mexico, he took ship for San Francisco and followed a trail into the Sierra Nevada. It was in the Sierras that he developed a strong love for wilderness that inspired his writings and actions on its behalf. Muir adopted Emerson's and Thoreau's Transcendental views toward nature and wild country. Redwood forests were "temples." "Civilized man chokes his soul," Muir felt, with the cares of the world. He urged Americans to "climb the mountains and get their good tidings. Nature's peace will flow into you as the sunshine into the trees. The winds will blow their

Preservationist John Muir (fourth from right) often guided parties of influential men to his favorite haunts in the Sierras. On these trips Muir hoped that his companions would be imbued with his enthusiasm for wilderness, and would join him in the preservation movement. Here he poses with President Theodore Roosevelt (sixth from right) on an excursion into Kings Canyon.

freshness into you, and the storms their energy, while cares will drop off like autumn leaves." Muir realized that the best way to insure the preservation of wilderness was to build public support for it by getting more people out into wild country where they could appreciate it. He became an avid writer of travel articles, and pieces he wrote for *Century* magazine helped win public support for the creation of Yosemite National Park in 1890—the first park specifically created to protect wilderness. Two years later Muir created the Sierra Club as a source of articles and action for preserving wild country.

Increasingly, Muir's disciples and Pinchot's followers differed with each other over government policy toward the nation's remaining wilderness. Both groups fought private misuse of nature, but the preservationists were mainly interested in preserving wilderness *from* man while the conservationists wanted to use nature to *serve* man. Which "use" was really "wise"?

The two approaches clashed in 1906 when San Francisco, seeking to increase its water supply, asked the federal government for permission to dam the Hetch-Hetchy River in the middle of Yosemite National Park. President Roosevelt, who had vacationed with Muir in the area and appreciated its beauty, hesitated. Government engineers told him that there was no other real alternative to Hetch-Hetchy as the site for construction. Pinchot and the conservationists supported the plan, maintaining that the damage to the valley was "altogether unimportant compared with the benefits to be derived from its use as a reservoir." Reluctantly, Roosevelt agreed and sent the proposal to Congress for approval. A fierce battle developed between the conservationists and the preservationists led by John Muir. As far as the latter were concerned, the measure violated the whole national park concept—wilderness preserves from which the nation could draw enjoyment and inspiration. They were certain that once Yosemite was violated, it would be used as precedent for similar projects in still other parks. So the preservationists marshaled their forces. They appealed to the growing sentiment in America that the remaining wilderness was the nation's last frontier, the last places where people could go and experience what the pioneers had encountered. It was something central to the development of American institutions and the national character. They also made the issue one between God and materialism. Muir wrote angrily that "these temple destroyers, devotees of ravaging commercialism, seem to have a perfect contempt for nature, and instead of lifting their eyes to the God of the Mountains lift them to the almighty dollar."

Muir and the preservationists stirred up such a storm of public protest that the proposal to build the dam was stalled in Congress. But San Francisco was not to be so easily frustrated. Referring to the preservationist's position as "hogwash and mushy esthetics," it renewed lobbying efforts in Washington on behalf of the dam. Conservationists answered the preservation arguments over esthetics by maintaining that the lake behind the dam would be a beautiful area for public recreation. Many Senators agreed with their colleague from Connecticut: "I appreciate the importance of preserving beautiful natural features of landscape as much as anybody else," yet he felt that esthetics could not take precedence over "the urgent needs of great masses of human beings for the necessities of life." Congress finally passed the proposal in 1913. Hetch-Hetchy was dammed, but by their efforts to arouse public support the preservationists had transformed their cause into a national movement.

ENVIRONMENTAL ENGINEERING
AND THE ECOLOGICAL PERSPECTIVE

Encouraged by organizations like the Boy Scouts and fascinated by the exploits of Edgar Rice Burroughs' *Tarzan of the Apes,* Americans retained their interest in wilderness and in camping. The invention of the automobile made primitive areas previously inaccessible more easily reached (and more easily overcrowded) by larger numbers of people. Yet the rising levels of prosperity after World War I and the reassurance that America was not running out of resources so quickly after all dampened public enthusiasm for protecting the environment. In 1924 the Secretary of the Interior leased federal land reserves in Teapot Dome, Wyoming to a private oil company for a $500,000 bribe. Americans were light-headed with the progress and affluence of the 1920s.

The 1929 Crash and the resulting depression brought people back to reality. Ignoring conservationist practices extracted a price; from 1934 to 1936 a drought in the Great Plains caused that area's overplanted, thin soil to blow away in high winds. America's granary was transformed by carelessness and ignorance into a Dust Bowl, making thousands of people homeless and ruining millions of acres of land. When Franklin Roosevelt was appraised of the situation, he decided to revive conservation. Traditional programs of flood control, land reclamation, promoting advanced agricultural practices, and providing for the protection of fish and wildlife were financed. Yet the New Deal proposed to use recent technological and scientific advances to take conservation a step further.

This was the concept of environmental engineering. Developed by planner and engineer Benton MacKaye, it held that the environment could and should be totally controlled and managed in the best interests of society. This meant planning for city green areas, recreation, and parks as well as controlling logging, mining, and water needs. Part of environmental engineering was the concept of multipurpose development, the idea that a single area could be managed to perform several functions. Environmental engineering's greatest achievement was the Tennessee Valley Authority (TVA), which was given wide powers to totally reconstruct and manage the valley's environment for the benefit of its people. Following a master plan and consulting with the valley's residents as the project developed, the TVA totally remodelled the entire valley as an economic and social unit. Roads, dams, power stations, housing, recreation parks, protecting local wildlife, and landscaping were all integrated. The project proved to be one of the most successful ones undertaken by the New Deal, and has yet to be exceeded in size or scope. By creating prosperity in a formerly depressed region, environmental engineering proved that with technology and science Americans now had the power to alter at will the face of their nation.

Like conservation before it, environmental engineering boldly assumed that people could change nature's order without really upsetting her balance. Aldo Leopold was one of the first Americans to see that this assumption was wrong. Leopold began his career in the 1920s as a forester in New Mexico, where he also worked for the preservation of wilderness areas in the state. Like Muir and Thoreau, he believed that wild areas were essential to maintaining the quality of American life. He also agreed with historian Frederick Jackson Turner that the American character and experience had been formed by contact with the frontier. "Is it not a bit beside the point," Leopold wrote during the era of New Deal reform, "for us to be so solicitous about preserving American institutions without giving so much as a thought to preserving the environment which produced them and which may now be one of our effective means of keeping them alive?" Leopold was firmly in the preservationist tradition, and his protests helped to establish an official policy of preservation in the national forests.

But it was not until he began to study the new science of *ecology* (the interrelationship of all living organisms that share an environment) and visited Mexico's Sierra Madre wilderness that Leopold realized that "land is an organism, that all my life I had seen only sick land." Drawing upon the ideas of Muir, Thoreau, and contemporary Albert Schweitzer, Leopold developed a "land ethic." "The land ethic," he explained, "changes the role of *homo sapiens* from conqueror of the land–community to plain member and citizen of it." This was dramatized by the commonly accepted Darwinian theory of evolution, which maintained that mankind, like the rest of life, had evolved from a common origin. People should, therefore, extend their sense of ethics and decide environmental action "in terms of what is ethically and esthetically right, as well as what is economically expedient." "A thing is right," declared Leopold, "when it tends to preserve the integrity, stability, and beauty of the biotic community. It is wrong when it tends otherwise." Leopold now had three reasons for urging the preservation of wilderness: to study scientifically how the community of life operates; to remind people who "fancy that industry supports us, forgetting what supports industry" of the elemental man–land relationship; and simply to demonstrate respect for the biotic community of which people are a part.

AMERICAN ENVIRONMENTAL PROBLEMS

Most Americans have not yet adopted Leopold's "land ethic" as their own. The nation continues to suffer from environmental ills that plague the cities, rural areas, and even extend into national parks and forest preserves that are supposed to be insulated from harm.

DESTRUCTION OF THE LAND

As American cities continue to expand across the countryside, open space is disappearing at the rate of about 3000 acres a day. Much of this land is excellent for farming and would better serve the nation producing agricultural products than as sites for tract homes or parking lots. Clear-cutting has recently been a dangerously widespread practice in the National Forest Reserves. Many square miles of forest are leased to lumber companies who remove all the trees from the area except small, isolated patches that stand out starkly from the

Besides destroying an area's natural beauty, clear-cutting exposes the land to rain and wind that can carry away rich topsoil and permanently scar a forest.

rest of the denuded landscape. The government informed the private companies in 1973 that they were going to have to concentrate on making more of their operations in their own lands, rather than depend on the increasing availability of public lands. Yet the "allowable cut" from public woodlands continues to rise every year. Strip-mining—the bulldozing of the top soil to expose coal near the surface—has left large areas of Kentucky, West Virginia, and Ohio with land on which nothing will grow. Despite laws and environmentalists' protests, little of strip-mined land is adequately restored. A battle is looming between power companies and environmentalists over the Fort Union–Powder River Basin area in Wyoming and Montana (reputed to hold more coal than industry has mined since 1900), where the power interests propose huge strip mine operations.

Areas that are preserved as national parks or wilderness areas (under the Wilderness Act of 1964) are also threatened. Ironically, it is because they are too popular. Nature lovers are smothering nature. More than 400 times as many people visit these parks now as did 20

The process of strip-mining for coal leaves chemicals in the soil that make it extremely difficult to replant a mined area. Loopholes in state reclamation laws have enabled coal companies to avoid responsibility for restoring the face of the land.

years ago, and only two percent of all the land in America remains in a wild and roadless state. Often California campsites must be "booked" months in advance of a major holiday. Backpackers must get permits limiting time of stay and areas to be traveled before they can hike the John Muir trail in the High Sierras and other crowded paths. One solution to the problem of land use and preservation has been adopted by the state of Hawaii—a strict land use law protecting land classified for conservation purposes as opposed to agricultural or urban purposes and imposing heavy penalties upon violators.

WATER POLLUTION

Lake Erie is nearly dead. The Cuyahoga River in Cleveland is so polluted that in 1969 the water burst into flames. By government standards, the water in almost 25 percent of American communities is unsafe to drink. These are a few of the problems created by water pollution. Manufacturing activities, transportation, and agriculture account for about two-thirds of this contamination. Phosphates and

Industry has traditionally regarded America's rivers and lakes as the most convenient receptacle for its wastes. Surrounding the Cuyahoga River, for example, is a huge industrial complex that produces automobiles, rubber, paper, and steel. Only recently has the United States government begun to take significant action against the polluters.

other organic wastes dumped into streams and lakes consume oxygen which various species of marine life need, killing them as well as harming man. Under the Water Quality Act of 1965 and similar legislation, federal and state officials are trying to tighten clean water standards. More efficient water treatment plants like the one now operating near Lake Tahoe are being designed and built. But only a dent has been made in the problem. For example, the effects of thermal pollution—water used by industry as a coolant and then returned to the environment—on stream and marine life have been widely ignored.

Nor has significant attention been paid to the oceans. Thirty-seven million tons of American wastes are poured into the oceans every year. Mercury-contaminated fish, red tide blooms, and closed oyster and clam beds are some of the results. Famous marine biologist Jacques Cousteau claims that compared to 50 years ago undersea life has been reduced 40 percent and more than 1000 species of life have entirely disappeared. The ocean's chain of life is extremely delicate, and the continued pollution of the seas may result in the loss of a major source of food in the near future.

AIR POLLUTION

Wastes are also being blown into the air. Air pollution costs Americans $11 billion a year in property damage. In the United States alone an estimated 110,000 deaths annually have been attributed partly to smog. One expert predicted that by 1985 the United States Weather Bureau will be issuing daily air pollution reports as well as weather forecasts. Eight to ten thousand tons of pollutants are thrown into a large city's air every day. Two-thirds of this come from automobile exhausts. Although both Los Angeles and New York City have tough smog control laws, only 85 communities representing one-third of the country's population have any type of air pollution control agency at all. Yet smog poses serious dangers to human life in the form of cancer and lung disease, and experiments indicate that exposure to "normal" amounts of air pollution can cause birth defects.

The Clean Air Act of 1967 provided some basic federal standards for pollution control and offered aid to local governments to set up control agencies. Due to apathy, ignorance, or fear of costs, however, most cities have done very little. Car manufacturers have been slow to come up with practical alternatives to today's smog-producing internal combustion engine. In fact, the auto industry declared that

Downtown Los Angeles. Despite the toughest laws in the nation regulating emissions, the smog problem in the Los Angeles basin is still very serious.

the requirements contained in the amendments to the Clean Air Act passed in 1970 calling for cars with 90 percent pollution-free exhausts by 1975 were "unrealistic" and the industry in Detroit was able to gain relaxation of some of the provisions of this law.

OVERPOPULATION AND THE REFUSE OF AFFLUENCE

The same affluence that has put so many cars on the roads that they have become a threat to people's health has also produced literally mountains of solid wastes—garbage. More than 48 billion aluminum cans and 28 billion jars and bottles are discarded annually in the United States, all of which contribute to a total of three-quarters of a ton of solid refuse per citizen per year. This is an enormous pile of garbage, and Americans are running out of places to put it. Some novel solutions are being tried—one Virginia community has been piling up layers of trash and layers of soil to create "Mt. Trashmore," which when completed will be planted with trees and become a local park. The U.S. Bureau of Mines has treated garbage with chemicals to produce a good grade of crude oil. But the most commonly proposed solution is increased recycling, turning wastes like old auto hulks into raw materials (in this case, steel) that can be used again. A few companies recycle glass, paper, and aluminum, but this process will continue to be little used, unless prices and costs are adjusted by the government, because it is cheaper to continue to consume new raw materials.

The population problem in the United States is closely connected to this affluent life-style. Americans consume more goods per person than any other people in the world. Thus, even though population growth in this country does not approximate the rate of the underdeveloped areas of the world (Asia, Africa, South America, and most of the Middle East), America's appetite for material resources stretches the environment's ability to support it. Roads, schools, parks, hospitals, and every type of service feel the strain. The present birth rate in the United States is quite low—nearly at the projected zero population growth figure (where births balance deaths). But this trend may be temporary. There may be 60 million more Americans by the year 2000 even if the low birth rate continues. This will add to the burden, and by then the global population problem will have reached crisis proportions.

Part of the overcrowding problem in the United States, where over 90 percent of the people live on nine percent of the land, could be eased by simply redistributing some of the population. Areas away from densely populated places could be made more attractive. But that calls for large funds to be made available for model city programs, funds that do not appear to be forthcoming in the near future. Though abortion within the first three months of pregnancy has been legalized by the Supreme Court, it is even more doubtful that the highly personal and emotional issue of birth control can be made part of a national effort to reduce population growth. The United States can afford to put off dealing with the population problem within its borders for awhile, but overpopulation in the underdeveloped areas is quickly becoming a crisis that must be dealt with soon or famine and its companion diseases will deal with the excess in their own way.

THE ENERGY CRISIS: TARGET 1980?

There can be no doubt that the population boom of the 1950s and '60s and American affluence have contributed to the energy crisis of the mid-70s. Although Americans represent only about six percent of the world's population, they now consume over 35 percent of the planet's total energy and mineral production. The average American uses as much energy in just a few days as half of the world's people on an individual basis consume in one year. At present rates, man's sources of oil and natural gas might be exhausted by the year 2000. Indeed, scientists figure that during the next 25 years the United States will consume more energy than it has in its entire history. In an important sense, therefore, the United States has a special responsibility to develop alternative sources of fuel and, at the same time, use foresight and intelligent planning in meeting tomorrow's needs.

This is one reason why former President Nixon announced "Project Independence 1980" in late 1973. In this speech he described his proposal as "a series of plans and goals set to insure that by the end of this decade Americans will not have to rely on any source of energy beyond our own." However, careful study suggests that this goal of self-sufficiency by 1980 is almost impossible. To accomplish this goal in the short span of five years would require a sharp decrease in our growing demand for oil, accompanied by a large-scale shift from using oil and natural gas to using coal. This would require massive, unrestricted strip-mining, resulting in a serious relaxation of environmental quality standards that are already tottering under constant attack.

Ironically, alternative energy sources have existed for a long time. Some, like coal, geothermal (heat generated by the earth), wind and tides, have been in use for centuries, while the theoretical use of others—like solar and nuclear power—have been known for at least a generation. Yet the United States has scarcely pursued the development of these other energy sources. For 25 years the low cost of fuel for Americans and the vague promise of limitless nuclear energy have prevented any concerted research into fuel sources other than gas and oil. The blame for the nation's failure to plan wisely for the future may go beyond public apathy, however.

A growing chorus of experts are suggesting that the environmental crisis threatening the nation is the result of industry's too-narrow concern with profits. Detergents, for example, are much more profitable than phosphate-free soaps. The same is true of industry's preference for smog-producing, high-compression automobile engines and nonreturnable bottles. But, instead of planning ahead in order to avoid the havoc wreaked by these agents of destruction, one expert charges that by waiting until the situation has become intolerable, American industry is guilty of intentionally planned neglect—"a societal irresponsibility difficult to condone."

The exclusive concern of industry for profits poses another paradox to the "energy crisis." Of all the available alternative sources of energy, none is in more immediate and abundant supply than coal. In terms of our fuel reserves, the United States Geological Survey claims that coal accounts for over 87 percent of all fossil fuels that still remain (oil is 3.5 percent and gas 4.6 percent). There is enough coal within the continental United States to satisfy American fuel needs for at least 400 years. The availability of this fuel, coupled with the appropriate commitment from the federal government, could result in national self-sufficiency by 1985—not too distant from the former President's target date. But despite the abundance of coal and technology's assurance that environmental and safety standards need not be jeopardized by the use of this source of energy, until the mid 1970s there was a marked lack of interest in its development.

The powerful oil companies shared some complicity in this matter. Economists point out that a world without alternatives to conventional oil and gas guarantees to the oil interests more profits than they would get from the research and development of other viable sources of energy, such as hydrogen (which burns to create water, a wonderfully nonpolluting element). One keen observer noted: "You don't refine more gas than you think the country will need, because if you do, the price will go down." Similarly, the oil companies (whose conglomerate interests include coal) had no incentive to expand their coal operations until they could be assured of a good price. Thus the petroleum industry was able to delay the development of alternative fuel sources because the profit potential of petroleum had not been reached. The adverse effects of this policy of neglect was observed by the president of the United Mine Workers: "What is practical for eight or ten companies may be disastrous for 200 million people." What makes this coal issue so thorny is its relationship to other factors. The same UMW official perceived the link between coal and other realities:

You can't talk about coal without talking about energy.
You can't talk about energy without talking about oil.
You can't talk about oil without talking about politics.
You can't talk about politics without talking about corruption.

*You can't talk about corruption without talking about
companies that are so big that they [gave] half a million
dollars to a politician without it even showing up on their
books.** *

*Arnold Mills, "The Energy Crisis as a Coal Miner Sees It", *The Center Magazine*, Vol.
VI, No. 6, November-December, 1973, pp. 35–45.

**Solar power installations like this one in France may soon dot the American
landscape. Using reflector panels to concentrate the sun's rays, it provides
non-polluting energy to heat water and air for home and office use.**

We have only one proven source of energy for now...and the next 400 years

OIL

Known U.S. oil reserves are being depleted. The search is on for new discoveries. Meanwhile, we grow more dependent on imports.

GAS

Our known gas reserves are dwindling fast. Unless new sources are found, demand may soon exceed existing domestic supply.

SOLAR

We would need perpetual sunlight. As yet, there's no full-scale, practical way to store energy from the sun.

COAL

There's enough U.S. coal to last an estimated 400 years. Based on BTU values, coal makes up 88 per cent of the nation's energy reserves. Greater utilization of coal can keep our lights burning and our industry humming both now and for centuries ahead.

WIND

Too primitive. Windmills still work in some areas, but they're unreliable and inefficient.

WATER

Only about 4 per cent of the nation's energy comes from water power. And we've already harnessed our best sources.

NUCLEAR

Promising but slow in developing. Atomic power *may be* our best bet in years to come. Nuclear power today contributes about one per cent of U.S. energy.

Coal is vital to steel

Coal is needed in vast quantities to make steel. And the steel industry is a large consumer of electric power, of which coal is by far the largest source. Bethlehem mined more than 14 million tons of coal last year, and most of this was used in our own blast furnaces.

What about surface mining?

Surface-mined land can be reclaimed responsibly under present state reclamation laws. About 20 per cent of Bethlehem's coal is surface-mined while more than 50 per cent of the nation's coal is surface-mined. If unreasonable restrictions on surface mining are enacted, the nation may be in trouble. That includes all coal users. And steel users. And all who use electric lights and appliances would feel the pinch.

Why restrict our most abundant fuel?

We favor legislation that will make it possible to meet the nation's energy needs and reasonable environmental goals at the same time. More coal is needed now to avert steel shortages. Why cut coal production by unreasonable restrictions on surface mining at a time when all other energy sources—except coal—are in critical supply?

Bethlehem

When the Arab world began applying political pressure on the United States in 1973 by withholding its oil, Americans began to recognize the need to develop alternate sources of energy. About half of the world's known supply of coal, for example, is found in the United States. Similarly, new attention is being focused on solar and nuclear power to meet the nation's future energy needs.

The economic picture is thus complicated by political considerations. The government, which after all is responsible for guarding the public interest, has not acted forthrightly for several reasons. First, the oil lobby is one of the most powerful in Washington. Second, until quite recently the federal government has had to depend on statistics supplied by the oil companies themselves for information on how to conduct energy policy. Most alternative energy sources will require government funding to be developed and marketed, particularly long-range solutions like hydrogen or nuclear fusion. These are crucial to modern industrial society.

"SPACESHIP EARTH"

Aldo Leopold's "land ethic" was a sharp departure from the nearly universal attitude that man was master of the earth, with both the power and the right to do anything he wanted. It challenged that idea by insisting that it is both ethically wrong and scientifically dangerous for man to upset the natural environmental community of which he is a part.

"Spaceship Earth"

The danger is vividly illustrated by R. Buckminster Fuller's concept of "Spaceship Earth." The earth, Fuller explains, is really a spaceship, a globe floating through space with a delicately balanced life support system (ecology) and limited supplies (natural resources) for its astronauts (population) to use. What humanity lacks is an "instruction manual" on how to run the ship. A large "safety factor" was designed into spaceship earth, Fuller points out, that "allowed man to be very ignorant for a long time" until he could discover the fundamental principles governing the ship's operation. That "safety factor" has almost been exhausted. Mankind is rapidly using up his limited amount of natural resources and nothing is being developed fast enough to replace them. Pollution of earth's air, water, and land is threatening the spaceship's life-support system.

We astronauts are therefore in a very precarious position. Garrett Hardin, noted American environmentalist, has even suggested that "lifeboat earth" would be a more appropriate metaphor than "Spaceship Earth." He points out that the rich, industrialized nations now monopolize the "lifeboat" while the poor, underdeveloped nations swim around it trying to get in. "Lifeboat earth" can not hold everyone at the current high standard of living in the rich countries—it would capsize and all would go under. But who will be allowed to come aboard, and what can they say to those who are excluded?

These are some of the serious choices facing this generation that will require international action. The sciences are continually giving us a better understanding of the principles on which our spaceship earth operates. With the convening of the United Nations Conference on the Environment in Stockholm in 1972, nations took the first halting steps toward cooperation and dealing with environmental questions on a worldwide level. If countries follow up this effort with action, life on board may continue—it may even improve.

SUGGESTIONS FOR ADDITIONAL READING

Aldo Leopold, *Sand County Almanac*, (1951). An intimate observation of the land and its inhabitants, with comments on proper man–land relationships.

John Muir, *Gentle Wilderness: The Sierra Nevada*, (1964). A vivid life-portrait by the author of his travels and reflections on the High Sierras.

Roderick Nash, *Wilderness and the American Mind*, (1967). A study of the American conception of wilderness, emphasizing the roots of contemporary wilderness attitudes and how they evolved.

Paul Ehrlich, *The Population Bomb*, (1968). The shocking, controversial study of the dangers of overpopulation to the survival of human civilization.

Raymond Dasmann, *The Destruction of California*, (1965). A case study in California history of the ignorance of sound land management and values.

Barry Commoner, *The Closing Circle*, (1972). A sobering view of how society's refusal to consider ecological principles now endangers not only human welfare but human survival.

Stewart Udall, *1976: Agenda for Tomorrow*, (1968). A sweeping review of current social, political, economic, and environmental problems, with a plea for a holistic solution to them.

Cartoon by Conrad. © Los Angeles Times, 1973. Reprinted with permission.

CHAPTER TEN

THE SPIRIT OF '76

1972
Watergate break-in, which cripples the Nixon Presidency and deepens national pessimism.
1974
President Nixon resigns his office under threat of impeachment.
1976
Bicentennial of the United States of America.

CELEBRATION?

On December 16, 1973, "patriots" once again marched down to a "British" ship moored to a Boston harbor wharf. The occasion was the 200th anniversary of the Boston Tea Party, the opening event of Boston's bicentennial celebrations. Of course, 200 years had brought some changes. The "tea" in the ship's hold was really maple leaves in deference to Sierra Club protests against dumping real tea into tne harbor. Boston "patriots" were not permitted to dress up in Indian disguises as their colonial counterparts had because the Boston Indian Council considered the idea "obnoxious." No sooner had these "sons of liberty" finished dumping the maple leaves into the harbor (to mingled shouts of "down with King George" and "down with King Richard") than the radical People's Bicentennial Commission began dumping oil barrels from the ship to protest high oil company profits. Not to be outdone, another group cruised back and forth in a yacht labeled "taxation is theft." Citizens from nearby Lexington and Concord walked out on the event in disgust, their leader commenting that "we just wanted to re-create history and be non-political."

The likelihood of such a "non-political" happening was remote. Even the American Revolution Bicentennial Commission, which was created to coordinate the multitude of national, state, and local celebrations, posed as its three major themes the nation's past (Heritage '76), present (Festival USA), and future (Horizons '76). It should have been expected that America's 200th birthday would be more than a simple commemoration of the Revolution. Poet and playwright Archibald MacLeish noted the wider possibilities: "What we need precisely at this moment of our history is something which will compel us to face ourselves as we once thought we would be and as we are, and the celebration of our Bicentennial can give us such a time." In the words of the bicentennial motto, Americans have both "a past to remember" *and* "a future to mold."

HISTORY AS IDENTITY

Yet history is more than just stories to remember. A common past is essential to nationhood, especially in a country like the United States, which is so ethnically, culturally, and regionally diverse. It acts as a much-needed bond of unity. Indeed, together with shared ideas and aspirations, a common heritage is what enables a people to call themselves a nation. History then becomes identity, and the word "American" conjures up pictures of Washington at Valley

Forge, Henry Ford at Dearborn, or Martin Luther King at Birmingham.

If most nations are a product of their past, a people emerging out of a shared heritage to become a political state, America has gone about it backwards. The United States was born with scant historical introduction—no glories, heroes, or legends to speak of. When the 13 colonies proclaimed their Declaration of Independence in 1776, George Washington had done little to deserve honorable mention, much less the august title "father of his country." Europeans equated America's lack of a distinguished past with the absence of a distinctive culture and widely scoffed at the new republic's "civilization." Many Americans replied by saying that their nation had no real need of a past because it was so sure of a future. "It is for other nations to boast of what they have been," wrote one novelist. "Ours is the more animating sentiment of hope, looking forward with a prophetic eye." A newspaper editorial similarly declared that "we have no interest in scenes of antiquity, only as lessons of avoidance. . . . The expansive future is our arena." Still other patriots, however, recognized the necessity of a common history to national pride and unity. Thus the nation would create its past.

Novelists, artists, poets, historians, linguists, and people in other walks of life all contributed. Noah Webster chronicled "an American language" in his dictionaries; Gilbert Stuart painted an impressive collection of Founding Fathers for posterity; James Fenimore Cooper preserved the frontier and the frontiersman in his novels; Henry Wadsworth Longfellow immortalized "The Midnight Ride of Paul Revere"; and Francis Scott Key wrote "The Star Spangled Banner." America's historical self-consciousness enshrined symbols like Plymouth Rock and Old Ironsides, men like Daniel Boone and Thomas Jefferson, and places like Mount Vernon and Gettysburg. By the time all of this glory had been tempered by the national tragedy of Civil War and the martyrdom of Abraham Lincoln, the need for a common heritage was filled. Americans had a national identity.

But this image could not be a finished product. Immigrants arrived with their own cultures, and developments like the Industrial Revolution began to alter the American scene. The nation's historical identity had to be continually revised because parts of its self-image were symbols (Washington at Valley Forge, the Pilgrims at Thanksgiving) or ideas (Democracy). Not all of America's diverse peoples could relate their experiences to these symbols very easily— for example, the blacks and Valley Forge—and the recent effort to include these peoples' contributions in America's heritage has created some anxiety. Those Americans who have identified strongly with the traditional set of symbols have felt threatened by this constant need to widen the meaning of the national experience.

Regardless of how they define them, all Americans put great emphasis on loyalty to these national symbols and ideas and on the celebration of their history. These are sensitive points because they involve our very character as a nation. Periodically, groups like the Oriental Exclusion League during the 1880s or the Ku Klux Klan have taken it upon themselves to zealously defend their version of "Americanism" against "corruption by foreign elements." Yet the most serious threats to our national character and the viability of our traditions have come not by widening our definition of the national experience, but from larger, more complex upheavals like the Civil War, the Industrial Revolution, and its later counterpart the technetronic revolution.

THE TECHNETRONIC REVOLUTION

Those "forces of change" appear to be working a fundamental and far-reaching revolution in the lives of Americans and in the very nature of society in the United States. Just as the Industrial Revolution altered the whole culture by changing its orientation from agriculture to industry, so the current advances in technology are rapidly shifting the emphasis away from industrial employment toward a service economy dominated by automation and computer science. Together, these twin developments of technology are affecting a new revolution in American society—the technetronic revolution.

The effects of this revolution are already being seen. Though businesses have only partially tapped the possibilities of automation, most of the labor force now holds white-collar jobs in administration, retail markets, research, or education and other service categories rather than blue-collar (factory or manual labor) positions. By loading and unloading cargo in the shipyards of Seattle, milking cows at dairy farms in Wisconsin, turning out telephones in a New Jersey factory, offering food and drink from vending machines across the country, or manufacturing microcircuit transistors in Houston, machine systems are proving that they can replace human labor at a variety of tasks and do some things that people cannot do. Automation can also do it faster and cheaper. Computers are not only sending spaceships to the moon and Mars, but are also overseeing purchasing and selling at the larger department stores, controlling traffic in large metropolitan transit systems, and conducting research into cancer and heart disease in Los Angeles. Able to analyze a problem faster and drawing upon more data than a human can, computers are finding their way into offices, homes, and even children's toys. In addition, they are responsible for the sweeping advances in communications and transportation that have shrunk the world and rendered events in one corner of the globe of immediate consequence to the rest (e.g., President Nixon's visits to China and the Soviet Union). Whether Americans are in front of the television or fighting against an inaccurately billed computer invoice, they encounter the effects of the technetronic revolution.

But these are still small compared to what is coming. Many scientists are convinced that when the full possibilities of the revolution begin to be felt, Americans (and the rest of the technologically advanced world) will be faced with the "greatest changes in the whole history of mankind." Indeed, some feel that this era is the "second great divide in human history, comparable in magnitude only with that first great break in historical continuity, the shift from bar-

By the 1960s the computer industry was eager to convince the public that its products can help society without dehumanizing man. In this advertisement, a major effort is made to counter the popular image of the impersonal computer by echoing an aphorism that was common in the 1960s: "Do not bend, fold or mutilate; I am a frog."

barism to civilization." The reason that some scientists are so certain of this is perhaps best summed up by former United Nations Secretary-General U Thant: "The central stupendous truth about developed economies today is that they can have—in anything but the shortest run—the kind and scale of resources they decide to have . . . . It is no longer the resources that limit the decisions. It is the decision that makes the resources." Even the energy crisis is an issue that can be solved through the development of several available alternate fuel sources, though many ecologists would differ from Thant's "no limits" statement. Nevertheless, the technetronic revolution offers a promise to produce more than people can consume, to free them from manual labor, and to stimulate the advance of medicine, education, and nearly every level of scientific and social activity. But it also conjures up the problems of mass unemployment, what to do with now-increased leisure time, and how to "control and humanize" the whole process so that the changes it generates do not overwhelm society.

A NEW ECONOMIC ROLE?

There is no doubt that the United States is at the forefront of the technological revolution, although nations like Japan and Germany are close behind. Among the few areas where America still maintains a strong balance of payments surplus are in nuclear power plants, computers, and sophisticated electronics equipment. The whole space effort has been a showcase of technological expertise and innovation that, besides increasing mankind's knowledge of the universe, has been supporting further developments in weather prediction and control, mineral detection, communications, and environmental planning.

Yet at the same time America's traditional role as the leading industrial, manufacturing, and producing economy in the world is no longer assured. In fact, many economists are convinced that the United States' role as industrial leader is already over. They point to statistics that show a continuing drop in the industrial work force and a rise (topping 70 percent of the labor force) in service employment. Teachers, programmers, consultants, secretaries, salespeople, and professionals now outnumber factory workers. What one economist has called the "knowledge sector"—that area of the economy devoted to developing and distributing new ideas—is producing more than one-third of the gross national product.

Why the drop in manufacturing and heavy industry? One reason may be traced to the burden of obsolete plants and equipment that cripple competition with more modern facilities overseas. Another factor is the rising costs of labor in the United States as compared with other nations having a lower standard of living. "The general rule is that if it can be made abroad," affirms one expert, "it can be made cheaper," even without loss of quality. Both of these developments are brought out by the actions of large, multinational corporations based in America. These huge companies build most of their new production facilities abroad because they find fewer governmental restrictions, lower construction costs, an abundance of workers willing to labor for lower wages, and a generally more positive attitude toward industrial growth.

Significantly, most of the skilled personnel needed to operate these facilities are brought over from the United States. It is American professional and managerial talent along with American technical skill that continues to be in high demand. The nation's most vital resource may very well be trained, creative individuals. Drawing upon inherited national wealth and individual and technological innovation, the United States may well find that its most profitable export is ideas—concepts in economics, science, social development, and life-style that are the products of concentrated research and development. America could realize a new role as an "arsenal of experimentation."

One area where American expertise in experimentation and development is already evident is in agriculture. The "green revolution" (hybrid food grains that produce harvests many times as large as those of standard grains on equal plots of land) is one example. The United States produces and exports more agricultural products than any other country despite the steady decrease in the farm labor force. Soybeans, not industrial products, are the highest earner of foreign exchange for America. Since the demand for food is expected to keep pace with energy demands, and the United States still has an enormous capacity to increase its agricultural output, this country may return to its pre-1900 role as primarily an exporter of foodstuffs. Such a change would, of course, take place gradually.

SOCIAL TRANSITION

If the United States appears to be undergoing a profound change economically, an even more significant transformation is taking place on the social scene. The very nature of American society is being altered. This can best be seen when comparing current statistical trends with earlier periods in the nation's history.

When George Washington was inaugurated as the first President of the United States in 1789, the American population stood at four million. A vast majority lived in rural areas (95 percent), and the largest city in the country (New York) boasted 33,000 residents. An average American would have been about 16 years old—a young population indeed. Living in small, relatively isolated communities, popular concerns were limited to local issues.

Just over a century later in 1900, the population had grown to 75 million. Although the urban character of the nation was beginning to emerge, nearly 60 percent of the people still lived in rural areas. Industrialization had arrived, but the largest part of the work force (11 million) was still engaged in agricultural pursuits. There were no automobiles, no radios, no movies. Despite an increasing emphasis on education, only six percent of the nation's youth had completed high school.

By 1970 the United States had reached 205 million persons. More than seventy percent of the population now lived in urban areas. Only three million people were farmers while twenty million worked in manufacturing and another 12.5 million were employed in a greatly enlarged government. Automobiles (owned by 82 percent of all families) had transformed the pattern of transportation, and television (possessed by 95 percent of American households) had revolutionized communications. Since society required more trained personnel, education assumed unprecedented importance. Better than 78 percent of the nation's young people graduated from high school and more than eight million enrolled in colleges and universities.

These statistics reveal massive changes in the nature of American society that have taken place in a relatively short period of time. One of the most obvious is the population explosion. From 1960 to 1970 alone more than 30 million people were added to the nation, each requiring expensive services such as roads, sewers, and schools, all of which are financed by the taxpayer. Nearly all of this increase has been absorbed by urban areas, putting a great strain on city resources. The developments in transportation have widened people's horizons by giving individuals great mobility, while advances in communication have allowed social, political, and economic shocks to register from coast to coast simultaneously. Local events that used to have only local impact now generate nationwide consequences, like the consumer meat boycotts in late 1973. As the society becomes more complex, areas and individuals become more interdependent, so that an oil pipeline proposed for the remote reaches of Alaska arouses a storm of controversy and becomes a national issue.

America is only just beginning to come to terms with these new developments. Since most of the issues are complex and wide in scope, attention is naturally centered on what the national government is doing—wage and price controls, environmental regulations, mass rapid transit aid, national health plans. Meanwhile, the pace of change continues.

THE PRICE OF AFFLUENCE

In the course of these developments, the United States has transcended its simple agrarian origins and become the most affluent nation in world history. By world standards, all but a tiny minority of Americans are rich and living materially far beyond the wildest fantasies of three-fourths of the earth's people. Yet affluence does not seem to have satisfied most Americans. Foreign visitors to the United States ever since colonial times have noted a certain amount of discontent among the people—a discontent that has increased rather than diminished with the growth of an affluent society. Certainly one reason for this puzzling phenomenon lies in the fact that progress never seems to keep pace with people's expectations. No matter how high the level of luxury is, as long as there is a gap between the material condition of an affluent society and its expectations, there will be dissatisfaction.

Still, the problem goes deeper than that. Prosperity levies a price even beyond the raw materials and energy needed to produce it. By changing the very fabric and conditions of American society, affluence also threatens to undermine certain values and characteristics that have been deeply embedded in the nation's culture.

The idea that hard work was good for human character, that it should be pleasurable, that a person should take pride in his labor, and that a good worker would eventually be rewarded by success has been one of these values. Early American craftsmen always engraved their work with their name or initials and the date. "Idle hands," the Puritans insisted, "are the Devil's tools." "See only that thou work hard," moralized a needlework sampler from the early 1800s, "and thou canst not escape the reward." Now industry is complaining that workers are more interested in the "reward," in the form of more pay for less work and greater fringe and retirement benefits, than they are in their labor. Consumers echo that cry, wondering why the items they purchase for increasingly higher prices last for a shorter period of time. Automobile recalls due to potentially dangerous production defects have steadily increased over the past five years. Many factory workers retort that mechanization and depersonalization have destroyed any sense of satisfaction or pride of accomplishment in their labor. Beyond the factory, a controversial federal study completed in 1973 revealed that a large minority of Americans (nearly 40 percent) do not like their jobs and are in them "only for the money."

Traditionally, pride in one's work has been accompanied by frugality, another aspect of the work ethic. Before the Industrial Revolution most families fertilized their own gardens with cow manure and old plaster, made scented soap from meat-fat scraps and sewed "rag rugs" from old pieces of fabric. Today, Americans are producing so many tons of refuse—cans, newspapers, plastics, and other "garbage," much of which could be recycled—that city sanitation departments are running out of places to dump it.

Another major concern has been the erosion of commonly held moral values. Alexis de Tocqueville, the perceptive French visitor to the United States during the 1830s, noted that American society was able to enjoy wide personal liberties because it was bound together by a common moral code and a deep regard for the rule of law. The churches, though of many different and often abrasive denominations, promoted similar brands of Judeo-Christian ethics. By their vital social role in early America they contributed to a widely accepted moral standard. Within the last decade, however, the "new morality" has caused sweeping changes. By making values relative—that is, leaving moral decisions up to the individual—the "new morality" has eliminated the old consensus. The churches find their social role diminishing and seem themselves divided and confused. Sociologists warn that breaking of the law has gone beyond the soaring crime rates and spectacular outbreaks of civil violence during the late 1960s. They claim that "beating the law" on income tax returns or business deals and in other countless little ways has become a national pastime.

Perhaps the most disturbing development in the United States today is the apparently deepening pessimism of Americans regarding their own and their country's future. This is all the more troubling because Americans have traditionally been an optimistic people with an almost stubborn confidence that the present is better than the past, and the future would be better still. When Benjamin Franklin signed the Constitution he remarked that he now knew that the sun painted on the back of chairman George Washington's seat was, for America, a rising sun. A similar buoyancy was expressed by Lyndon Johnson as he announced his and the nation's determination to win "the war on poverty." Are the 1970s signaling a turning point in America's tradition of optimism? In the wake of Watergate, pollsters indicated that over half of the American people feel there is something deeply wrong in the United States, and that current difficulties are not merely like others the nation has overcome in the past.

The same poll recorded that many citizens have perceived a *decline* in the quality of life since 1963. This represented a significant break

In the years following World War II, Americans flocked to the subdivision tracts being built as a result of the mass production technique pioneered by William Levitt. Never before had the American dream of owning one's own home been realized by so many people. The conveniences of suburban living continue to attract millions of people despite the tendency toward sameness and depersonalization that have been identified with suburbia.

from earlier trends, where persons were slightly pessimistic about the future of the country but relatively satisfied and optimistic about the rising quality of their own lives. One reason for the change was the increasing encroachment of national problems (like the energy crisis and inflation) into people's personal lives. Another factor appeared to be the loss of a sense of community with other people, attributed in part to technology. Labor-saving innovations seem to be mixed blessings: computer diagnoses in hospitals, teaching machines, and computerization in business offices tend to transfer people's dependence from other people to machines, lessening a sense of personal interdependence and human experience. One alarmed observer contended that in pursuing technological "timesavers," we are creating "elegant instruments for our mutual estrangement."

Judging by contemporary trends, increasing numbers of Americans are rejecting affluence as an end in itself and, instead, are seeking satisfaction in a less complex, more tranquil life-style. These people value a balance between material comfort and a more simple, soul-enriching life. One trend reflecting this desire is the "back-to-nature" movement. Another is the exodus from large urban areas into small rural villages. Between 1970 and 1973 more people moved away from city areas (including suburbs) than moved into them, reversing a trend nearly 100 years old. Most of these urban exiles cared "less about a glossy standard of living than about tranquility, friendliness, a sense of community and human proportion." Indeed, many social critics appear to be questioning whether the "good life,"

a more settled way of living, less frenzy, more margin, a sense of space and ease, an environment of natural beauty and architectural dignity, a rehabilitation of norms of propriety and taste, can ever be realized by rich consumer societies. . . .

The price of affluence in modern society has occasioned an introspective look at the present to judge if the product is worth it, or if the cost cannot at least be reduced. It has also sparked an increasing interest in America's past, an attempt to recapture the bedrock values and characteristics of the American culture. In a way, Americans are repeating the question poet Walt Whitman asked more than a century ago: "Where is what I started for so long ago? And why is it yet unfound?"

*E. J. Mishan, "America and the Future of Man: Cost of Abundance," *Santa Barbara News-Press*, November 4, 1973, Section D, p. 11.

RETREAT TO THE PAST?

A strong tendency to look back to the "good old days" is everywhere in evidence: fashion styles from the 1920s, rock music from the 1950s and early 1960s, movies from Hollywood, and even a revival of interest in American history. That this interest coincides with the coming bicentennial is, of course, no coincidence. But the urge to return to the past goes deeper. As one inhabitant of Connecticut's living museum at Mystic Seaport theorized, "When the country is in turmoil, history is our only stabilizing factor.

Places like the boyhood home of Mark Twain at Hannibal, Missouri and the still-colonial village of Williamsburg, Virginia seem to provide a touchstone of reassuring familiarity to the tens of thousands of visitors they attract each year. The past, appropriately cleaned-up and tinged with romanticism, provides a sense of common identity—a noncontroversial (except among historians) set of values and symbols that are an unchanging part of the heritage of many

"Wagons West"—reliving America's past.

Americans. Regaining a sense of "who we are" appears to be a major reason why so many are attracted to historic sites and reenactments. A Wyoming entrepreneur operating "Wagons West," a tour through the Teton Mountains by Conestoga "covered wagons" complete with cowboys and meals served on the trail, reports that "We've had a lot of them psychiatrists here, and we get a lot of riders from New York, Chicago and Los Angeles."

People from large urban areas looking for America's past seem particularly attracted because they view it as a simpler time. Visiting a restored village in Georgia "where it is always 1850," one traveler declared, "When you see these hand-hewn pieces of lumber, you know people were happier then." The passion for antiques and hand-crafted items that has spurred a run on everything from grandfather clocks to Navajo silverwork is significant because they embody a quieter, more down-to-earth life-style. This is related to the back-to-nature movement. Western ghost towns like Tombstone, Arizona are making a stronger bid for the tourist trade by stressing "authenticity" and incorporating craft artisans into their operation. The National Park Service has created its own synthesis of nature and history at Turkey Run, near Washington, D.C., where semipermanent residents will live and work just as farmers did during colonial times. In part, this reflects a positive attempt to move modern culture toward a balanced life-style that allows the comforts of modern life and recognizes man's need for contact with nature and his fellow man. But there is also a definite aspect of retreat in all of this—retreat from the complexity, controversy, and turmoil of the modern world. Touching the American past at Gettysburg, Pennsylvania or Salem, Massachusetts seems to instill a sense of identity, community, and security. As one bicentennial organizer put it, the pilgrimage reassures people by emphasizing the positive achievements and values of the nation. It gives them a reason to say "We're Americans—that's not so bad."

A POLITICAL SLUMP?

Even deeper questioning and reevaluation is taking place concerning government and politics in America. Increasing numbers of Americans appear disillusioned with the men and institutions that shape political policy and feel disconnected with the process through which they might be able to change things. This came out most clearly in a poll commissioned by the Senate subcommittee on intergovernmental relations, released in late 1973. Over 60 percent of these people surveyed agreed that "what you think doesn't count much anymore" and 55 percent felt that "the people running the country don't really care what happens to you"—figures nearly double those of 1966. A solid majority of those polled (60 percent) believed that "most elective officials are in politics for all they personally can get out of it for themselves," and nearly three-fourths responded positively to the statement that "special interests get more from the government than the people do."

Yet the public had not despaired of government entirely. Though political ignorance and a lack of involvement were apparently widespread, the poll also showed an encouraging interest in political affairs and a desire to participate more in the democratic process. Hefty majorities said that they would either pitch in through local groups to which they already belonged or join one of the citizen-action groups. Nearly half agreed that these groups were "having more effect in getting government to get things done than they did five years ago." Ninety percent said that they were convinced that government can work effectively, an opinion shared by a similar percentage of state and local political officials. There was also an expressed faith in the ability of government to "help the country" and "care about the people," given first-rate personnel.

In fact, disillusionment seemed to focus directly on politicians. By the 1970s a sizable gap had developed between the general public and their political leaders. Although 70 percent of the citizens polled cited "corrupt politicians" as a real problem, only 48 percent of local and state officials shared their opinion. Most political leaders claimed that they really "care about the people," but only a third of the people polled felt that this was really true. Just how broad this gap of perception was became obvious when over 60 percent of the public officials polled insisted that "the quality of life has improved" while 45 percent of the public maintained that it had "grown worse." "America," the study concluded, "looks to the top of the governmental structure for inspiration and finds it missing."

Watergate was the spark that ignited these smoldering doubts and discontents into a political firestorm. The eye of the storm was over the "White House," that arm of the national government that had steadily grown in size and power since the administration of Franklin Roosevelt. Interestingly, the architects of the American Revolution directed their protests not only against the "injuries and usurpations" done to them by the King of England, but against "a kind of

fourth power that the Constitution knows nothing of, or has not provided against." This threat was seen as an "overruling arbitrary
power" exercised by the "ministers and favorites" of the King who
"extend their usurped authority infinitely too far." Many observers
began to feel that the powers of the executive branch, particularly
those wielded by special appointees of the President outside of the
traditional cabinet offices, had grown to the point of disrupting the
balance of powers provided for in the Constitution. The Presidency
itself, enveloped by the morass of Watergate, came under increasing
attack. Though the powerful executive had been praised in liberal
circles since the New Deal, liberals of both parties began the process
of limiting presidential powers. This attack climaxed with the unprecedented resignation of a President. Some political analysts claimed
that the country was gripped by a plebiscite system, where every four
years the people voted for a President who then felt that he had been
given a mandate to do as he chose during his term in office and was
therefore above criticism. This "imperial presidency," as one historian labeled the practice, threatened the very basis of constitutional
democracy by challenging the concept of "legitimate opposition"
that has been central to American politics since 1800. Congress itself,
though free of the taint of Watergate, became the target of reformers.
They pointed to its narrow vision, its tendency to delegate key powers and decisions to the executive (Congress once had the important
"purse strings" power of drawing up the budget, which now belongs
to the Office of Management and Budget), its members' preoccupation with doing favors for each other ("to get along," counseled one
congressman, "go along"), and its susceptibility to the influence of
powerful "special interest" lobbies.

In fact, the whole issue of the power of vested interests in Washington gained new exposure from the Watergate scandals. The high
expense of political campaigning has required candidates (unless
they are independently wealthy) to seek large contributions from
special interests, and American history has shown that "strings" are
often attached to such donations. Several corporation executives
were fined by federal courts for yielding to demands by officials in the
Nixon reelection campaign for "donations," and the dairy industry
gave several thousand dollars to Mr. Nixon's campaign shortly after
being allowed to raise prices in 1972. The tax structure itself continues to favor the rich: the tax rate on property is only 65 percent of
that on wages, and the rate on capital gains (e.g., profits from selling
stocks) is only half that on wages. Tax loopholes permit serious in-

equities: an unmarried stenographer earning $150 a week paid about $1060 in federal income taxes, while former President Nixon, with a taxable income of $250,000 paid only $878 in one year of his annual tax returns. Indeed, although the IRS concluded early in 1974 that the President must pay an additional $467,000 in back taxes for the first four years of his Presidential term, his deductions for the donation of his Vice-Presidential papers would have been legal had he observed certain legal requirements. Is it any wonder that by the 1970s Americans' confidence in their government had seriously declined?

CAPITALISM—THE ROOT OF ALL EVIL?

This crisis of confidence has been attributed by New Left historians to the failure of the "Establishment" and the American capitalist system. They feel that the country faces a massive breakdown "in every section, class, and stratum" because of a loss of faith in the country's ideals, institutions, and future prospects. But, although the roots of this "loss of faith" are related to the political system itself, it is important to recognize its basic economic implications. New Left historians believe that the current crisis "can only be resolved through the creation of a political movement capable of realizing our national ideals by the restructuring of our economy." The crux of the problem is the nature of the American capitalist system.

Many of these historians trace the beginning of today's problems to the Depression of the 1930s. They agree that the New Deal failed to take advantage of this period of economic crisis to effect a significant redistribution of power in American society. Instead, corporate capitalism, which had brought on the economic collapse, was "conserved and protected." The result, they observe, was a "permanent army of unemployed" and 20 million poverty-stricken Americans all masked by a large and avidly consuming middle class. Another observer notes that the nation was still stuck with "a tremendously efficient yet wasteful productive apparatus that was efficient because it could produce limitless supplies of what it decided to produce, and wasteful because what it decided to produce was not based on what was most needed by society but on what was most profitable to business."*

It was only with the coming of World War II that the problem of unemployment was solved—at the cost of depending upon massive

*Howard Zinn. Quotation taken from an article by Staughton Lynd in *Newsweek*, July 6, 1970, p. 30.

public defense spending. New Left historians point out that instead of returning to a peace-oriented economy after the conflict ended, defense spending continued to be the backbone of the system and a "permanent war economy" resulted. This resulted partly from the international political situation, but was also aided by businesses seeking to avoid another depression and wishing to expand into the world market. War, or at least "a condition of permanent war-readiness," had become "most profitable for business," and was somehow fused with the mystique of patriotism. These historians believe that the interests of business and the armed forces have coincided and created a "military-industrial complex" that dominates American society. Another critic adds that the "overseas imperialism of Coca-Cola and napalm is accompanied by a 'domestic imperialism' which tries to make people buy things which they don't really need." This mass indoctrination by television has produced a "plastic" culture.

The New Left historians firmly maintain that the only alternative to this rule by an elite is to reassert democratic principles and extend them to apply to economic management. This would benefit all people instead of just big private interests. In short, they believe America should adopt democratic socialism. Only by destroying the hold of corporate capitalism on the nation's political priorities can Americans restore their commitment to social justice, democracy, and individual freedom, and end their sense of alienation from their own government. Particular problems could then be attacked with certainty of success.

THE SPIRIT OF '76

But could they? Does the source of America's problems really lie in corporate capitalism, or does it lie deeper? The radical historians make their case from history as well as from contemporary observations and, indeed, if history is anything more than the collection of interesting stories about the past, people ought to be able to draw conclusions from the experiences of their ancestors. A truly "radical" solution must go all the way back to the roots (for that is the definition of "radical") of the American Republic—back to the Revolutionary generation. That generation met and conquered its formidable challenges. It won independence in war from the most powerful country in the world, forged a nation out of 13 jealously separate states, and built the most stable and most frequently copied constitutional democracy in history. Seeing how they met their challenges may help us to see how we may meet ours.

Of course, the times are different, and the Founding Fathers enjoyed some particularly beneficial conditions of their time. After the ties to England were severed, the young United States was relatively free to develop because the Atlantic Ocean protected America from the constant and complex power struggles of Europe. While problems in foreign affairs did lead to two conflicts in the new nation's first quarter century, neither affected the personal lives of most Americans as vitally as the Vietnam war or the Arab oil embargo after the 1973 Arab-Israeli military contest. Another blessing for the Revolutionary generation, and for many generations to follow, was the immense stretch of land that comprised the American frontier. The western territories provided a seemingly endless bounty of natural resources to feed progress, an arena for political and social experimentation and expansion, and a possible "safety valve" for the restless, frustrated, and discontented. Abundant land (then the basis of wealth and position) permitted great social mobility and narrowed the gap between the upper and the middle or even lower classes. There is the picture of patrician George Washington borrowing $500 to attend his own inaugural, or Thomas Jefferson returning from his first Presidential address to wait his turn at a boarding house for dinner. Now the frontier is gone, "shortages" are a national concern, and the gap between rich and poor is greater than it was in Imperial Rome.

Perhaps the most important difference between early and modern America was time itself—the slower pace of a rural, agrarian society. Transportation and communication were based on the horse and the sailing ship. It took nine days for news to travel from Boston to New York and close to three months for European events to become known in America. The Founding Fathers had ample opportunity to recognize, analyze, and address issues without the need for frantic haste. For instance, despite strong initial Republican opposition to the Alien and Sedition Acts passed by the Federalist-dominated Congress in June and July of 1798, the Republican response (the Kentucky and Virginia Resolutions) did not materialize until November and December. Contrast the accelerating and hectic pace of time in twentieth-century America that Alvin Toffler analyzed in his book *Future Shock*. The media permitted President Nixon to be seen live, half a world away, walking on the Great Wall of China, and jet transportation makes no place on earth more than 24 hours away from any other place. Events seem to require quick reactions, and there is little time for thought and reflection.

Yet the differences between the generations of 1776 and 1976 go beyond the differences of the times—they also involve people. The Founding Fathers were well equipped to meet the challenges of their day, and those who met in Philadelphia in 1787 to draw up the Constitution have been called "the most able group of statesmen ever gathered together under one roof." Though most of them were very well versed in the principles of political theory and the history of governmental institutions (which is expected of "founding fathers," anyway), they were also "hard-nosed and practical merchants, planters, lawyers, and men of affairs." A few, like Benjamin Franklin, were of a now-extinct breed—talented generalists whose expertise spanned a whole range of human activities. Franklin founded the Philosophical Society of Philadelphia, schemed with the best in Pennsylvania's legislature, did research in the theoretical sciences while working on a more efficient stove, and played in his lifetime the roles of lawyer, foreign diplomat, printer, and postmaster.

Above all, the Revolutionary generation was a "child of the Enlightenment." These men believed that human affairs were governed by "natural laws" like those that governed the physical universe. They were convinced that these laws could be uncovered by human reason, and that once uncovered, social and governmental rules based on the laws would lead to greater human happiness and the progress of mankind. In short, problems had solutions and dedicated, skilled people could find those solutions. The Founding Fathers were committed to finding and instituting the laws that would make the American Republic "the most blessed of states." What one historian has said of Franklin might be said of Jefferson, Washington, Adams, and their peers as well: They had a "steady belief that in helping create the American Republic [they were] founding a truer order of society." In pursuit of this aim the Revolutionary generation was not adverse to radical measures (such as a revolution, or scrapping an entire system of government in the Articles of Confederation for a new system in the Constitution) when such measures seemed necessary. At times this devotion to the commonwealth was costly. But, as another historian commented on Washington's character at Valley Forge, "when the chips were down all the agreeable things of life — parties, good food, comfort, professional dignity — were baubles." Not that the architects of America were entirely selfless. Their reward was the excitement and fame involved in creating something new.

This is the Spirit of '76. These qualities of leadership, these attitudes and character together with the conditions of the times enabled the Revolutionary generation to overcome the challenges they faced in creating the United States. Modern times are certainly different and so are the problems facing America as it marks its bicentennial. But who is to say that the process of revitalizing and reforming the American political system is more formidable than the struggle to build that system's structure in the first place? Why do political leaders spend most of their time "managing" one problem after another just in an effort to "keep the lid on?" Why do they attempt "patchwork" solution of the nation's ills instead of seeking more comprehensive solutions? Is it necessarily more complicated and difficult for resource-rich modern America to deal with the grip of vested interests than it was for resource-poor Revolutionary America to overthrow the most powerful nation in the world and maintain its independence? Is the reward of creative involvement, excitement, and fame for the people who move toward solutions to contemporary problems any less than the reward that secured the devotion of Washington or Jefferson? Some observers feel they see in the United States the same pattern of rise and decline that has been the fate of many great nations in history, and conclude that there is something inevitable about America's own "decline." Will and Ariel Durant, who have written a monumental study of the history of western civilization, feel otherwise: "When the group or a civilization declines, it is through no mystic limitation of a corporate life, but through the failure of its political or intellectual leaders to meet the challenge of change." Is America ready to learn from its founders —and from the Spirit of '76?

SUGGESTIONS FOR ADDITIONAL READING

Alvin Toffler, *Future Shock*, (1970). An impactful study of rapid change in nearly all aspects of modern life.

Arthur S. Schlesinger, Jr., *The Imperial Presidency*, (1973). A careful examination of how the presidency has gradually accumulated power throughout American history.

Alstair Cooke, *America*, (1973). A perceptive, personal view of American history by a former British citizen—expanded from the dramatic TV series of the same name.

John Kenneth Galbraith, *Economics and the Public Purpose*, (1973). An extensive study of the myths and realities of American capitalism, with bold proposals for making the system serve public needs and goals.

THE DECLARATION OF INDEPENDENCE

When, in the course of human events, it becomes necessary for one people to dissolve the political bonds which have connected them with another, and to assume, among the powers of the earth, the separate and equal station to which the laws of nature and of nature's God entitle them, a decent respect to the opinions of mankind requires that they should declare the causes which impel them to the separation.

We hold these truths to be self-evident, that all men are created equal; that they are endowed by their Creator with certain unalianable rights; that among these, are life, liberty, and the pursuit of happiness. That, to secure these rights, governments are instituted among men, deriving their just powers from the consent of the governed; that, whenever any form of government becomes destructive of these ends, it is the right of the people to alter or to abolish it, and to institute a new government, laying its foundation on such principles, and organizing its powers in such form, as to them shall seem most likely to effect their safety and happiness. Prudence, indeed, will dictate that governments long established, should not be changed for light and transient causes; and, accordingly, all experience hath shown, that mankind are more disposed to suffer, while evils are sufferable, than to right themselves by abolishing the forms to which they are accustomed. But, when a long train of abuses and usurpations, pursuing invariably the same object, evinces a design to reduce them under absolute despotism, it is their right, it is their duty, to throw off such government and to provide new guards for their future security. Such has been the patient sufferance of these colonies, and such is now the necessity which constrains them to alter their former systems of government. The history of the present King of Great Britain is a history of repeated injuries and usurpations, all having, in direct object, the establishment of an absolute tyranny over these States. To prove this, let facts be submitted to a candid world:—

He has refused his assent to laws the most wholesome and necessary for the public good.

He has forbidden his governors to pass laws of immediate and pressing importance, unless suspended in their operation till his assent should be obtained; and, when so suspended, he has utterly neglected to attend to them.

He has refused to pass other laws for the accommodation of large districts of people, unless those people would relinquish the right of representation in the legislature; a right inestimable to them, and formidable to tyrants only.

He has called together legislative bodies at places unusual, uncomfortable, and distant from the depository of their public records, for the sole purpose of fatiguing them into compliance with his measures.

He has dissolved representative houses repeatedly for opposing, with manly firmness, his invasions on the rights of the people.

He has refused, for a long time after such dissolutions, to cause others to be elected, whereby the legislative powers, incapable of annihilation, have returned to the people at large for their exercise; the state remaining, in the meantime, exposed to all the danger of invasion from without, and convulsions within.

He has endeavored to prevent the population of these States; for that purpose, obstructing the laws for naturalization of foreigners; refusing to pass others to encourage their migration hither, and raising the conditions of new appropriations of lands.

He has obstructed the administration of justice, by refusing his assent to laws for establishing judiciary powers.

He has made judges dependent on his will alone, for the tenure of their offices, and the amount and payment of their salaries.

He has erected a multitude of new offices, and sent hither swarms of officers to harass out people, and eat out their substance.

He has kept among us, in time of peace, standing armies, without the consent of our legislatures.

He has affected to render the military independent of, and superior to, the civil power.

He has combined, with others, to subject us to a jurisdiction foreign to our Constitution, and unacknowledged by our laws; giving his assent to their acts of pretended legislation:

For quartering large bodies of armed troops among us:

For protecting them by a mock trial, from punishment, for any murders which they should commit on the inhabitants of these States:

For cutting off our trade with all parts of the world:

For imposing taxes on us without our consent:

For depriving us, in many cases, of the benefit of trial by jury:

For transporting us beyond seas to be tried for pretended offences:

For abolishing the free system of English laws in a neighboring province, establishing therein an arbitrary government, and enlarging its boundaries, so as to render it at once an example and fit instrument for introducing the same absolute rule into these colonies:

For taking away our charters, abolishing our most valuable laws, and altering, fundamentally, the powers of our governments:

For suspending our own legislatures, and declaring themselves invested with power to legislate for us in all cases whatsoever.

He has abdicated government here, by declaring us out of his protection, and waging war against us.

He has plundered our seas, ravaged our coasts, burnt our towns, and destroyed the lives of our people.

He is, at this time, transporting large armies of foreign mercenaries to complete the works of death, desolation, and tyranny, already begun, with circumstances of cruelty and perfidy scarcely paralleled in the most barbarous ages, and totally unworthy the head of a civilized nation.

He has constrained our fellow citizens, taken captive on the high seas, to bear arms against their country, to become the executioners of their friends, and brethren, or to fall themselves by their hands.

He has excited domestic insurrections amongst us, and has endeavored to bring on the inhabitants of our frontiers, the merciless Indian savages, whose known rule of warfare is an undistinguished destruction of all ages, sexes, and conditions.

In every stage of these oppressions, we have petitioned for redress, in the most humble terms; our repeated petitions have been answered only by repeated injury. A prince, whose character is thus marked by every act which may define a tyrant, is unfit to be the ruler of a free people.

Nor have we been wanting in attention to our British brethren. We have warned them, from time to time, of attempts made by their legislature to extend an unwarrantable jurisdiction over us. We have reminded them of the circumstances of our emigration and settlement here. We have appealed to their native justice and magnanimity, and we have conjured them, by the ties of our common kindred, to disavow these usurpations, which would inevitably interrupt our connections and correspondence. They, too, have been deaf to the voice of justice and consanguinity. We must, therefore, acquiesce in the necessity which denounces our separation, and hold them, as we hold the rest of mankind, enemies in war, in peace, friends.

We, therefore, the representatives of the United States of America, in general Congress assembled, appealing to the Supreme Judge of the world for the rectitude of out intentions, do, in the name, and by the authority of the good people of these colonies, solemnly publish and declare, that these united colonies are, and of right ought to be, free and independent states: that they are absolved from all allegiance to the British Crown, and that all political connection between them and the state of Great Britain is, and ought to be, totally dissolved; and that, as free and independent states, they have full power to levy war, conclude peace, contract alliances, establish commerce, and to do all other acts and things which independent states may of right do. And, for the support of this declaration, with a firm reliance on the protection of Divine Providence, we mutually pledge to each other our lives, our fortunes, and our sacred honor.

THE CONSTITUTION OF THE UNITED STATES OF AMERICA

We the people of the United States, in order to form a more perfect union, establish justice, insure domestic tranquillity, provide 'for the common defense, promote the general welfare, and secure the blessings of liberty to ourselves and our posterity, do ordain and establish this Constitution for the United States of America.

ARTICLE I

SECTION 1

All legislative powers herein granted shall be vested in a Congress of the United States, which shall consist of a Senate and House of Representatives.

SECTION 2

1. The House of Representatives shall be composed of members chosen every second year by the people of the several States, and the electors in each State shall have the qualifications requisite for electors of the most numerous branch of the State legislature.

2. No person shall be a representative who shall not have attained to the age of twenty-five years, and been seven years a citizen of the United States, and who shall not, when elected, be an inhabitant of that State in which he shall be chosen.

3. Representatives and direct taxes* shall be apportioned among the several States which may be included within this Union, according to their respective numbers, which shall be determined by adding to the whole number of free persons, including those bound to service for a term of years, and excluding Indians not taxed, three fifths of all other persons.† The actual enumeration shall be made within three years after the first meeting of the Congress of the United States, and within every subsequent term of ten years, in such manner as they shall by law direct. The number of representatives shall not exceed one for every thirty thousand, but each State shall have at least one representative; and until such enumeration shall be made, the State of New Hampshire shall be entitled to choose three, Massachusetts eight,

*Revised by the Sixteenth Amendment.
†"Other persons" refers to Negro slaves. Revised by the Fourteenth Amendment, Section 2.

Rhode Island and Providence Plantations one, Connecticut five, New York six, New Jersey four, Pennsylvania eight, Delaware one, Maryland six, Virginia ten, North Carolina five, South Carolina five, and Georgia three.

4. When vacancies happen in the representation from any State, the executive authority thereof shall issue writs of election to fill such vacancies.

5. The House of Representatives shall choose their speaker and other officers; and shall have the sole power of impeachment.

SECTION 3

1. The Senate of the United States shall be composed of two senators from each State, chosen by the legislature thereof,* for six years; and each senator shall have one vote.

2. Immediately after they shall be assembled in consequence of the first election, they shall be divided as equally as may be into three classes. The seats of the senators of the first class shall be vacated at the expiration of the second year, of the second class at the expiration of the fourth year, and of the third class at the expiration of the sixth year, so that one third may be chosen every second year; and if vacancies happen by resignation, or otherwise, during the recess of the legislature of any State, the executive thereof may make temporary appointments until the next meeting of the legislature, which shall then fill such vacancies.*

3. No person shall be a senator who shall not have attained to the age of thirty years, and been nine years a citizen of the United States, and who shall not, when elected, be an inhabitant of that State for which he shall be chosen.

4. The Vice President of the United States shall be President of the Senate, but shall have no vote, unless they be equally divided.

5. The Senate shall choose their other officers and also a president pro tempore, in the absence of the Vice President, or when he shall exercise the office of the President of the United States.

6. The Senate shall have the sole power to try all impeachments. When sitting for that purpose, they shall be on oath or affirmation. When the President of the United States is tried, the chief justice shall preside: and no person shall be convicted without the concurrence of two thirds of the members present.

7. Judgment in cases of impeachment shall not extend further than to removal from office, and disqualification to hold and enjoy any office of honor, trust or profit under the United States: but the party convicted shall nevertheless be liable and subject to indictment, trial, judgment and punishment, according to law.

SECTION 4

1. The times, places, and manner of holding elections for senators and representatives, shall be prescribed in each State by the legislature thereof;

*Revised by the Seventeenth Amendment.

but the Congress may at any time by law make or alter such regulations, except as to the places of choosing senators.

2. The Congress shall assemble at least once in every year, and such meeting shall be on the first Monday in December, unless they shall by law appoint a different day.*

SECTION 5

1. Each House shall be the judge of the elections, returns and qualifications of its own members, and a majority of each shall constitute a quorum to do business; but a smaller number may adjourn from day to day, and may be authorized to compel the attendance of absent members, in such manner, and under such penalties as each House may provide.

2. Each House may determine the rules of its proceedings, punish its members for disorderly behavior, and, with the concurrence of two thirds, expel a member.

3. Each House shall keep a journal of its proceedings, and from time to time publish the same, excepting such parts as may in their judgment require secrecy; and the yeas and nays of the members of either House on any question shall, at the desire of one fifth of those present, be entered on the journal.

4. Neither House, during the session of Congress, shall, without the consent of the other, adjourn for more than three days, nor to any other place than that in which the two Houses shall be sitting.

SECTION 6

1. The senators and representatives shall receive a compensation for their services, to be ascertained by law, and paid out of the Treasury of the United States. They shall in all cases, except treason, felony, and breach of the peace, be privileged from arrest during their attendance at the session of their respective Houses, and in going to and returning from the same; and for any speech or debate in either House, they shall not be questioned in any other place.

2. No senator or representative shall, during the time for which he was elected, be appointed to any civil office under the authority of the United States, which shall have been created, or the emoluments whereof shall have been increased during such time; and no person holding any office under the United States shall be a member of either House during his continuance in office.

SECTION 7

1. All bills for raising revenue shall originate in the House of Representatives; but the Senate may propose or concur with amendments as on other bills.

*Revised by the Twentieth Amendment, Section 2.

2. Every bill which shall have passed the House of Representatives and the Senate, shall, before it becomes a law, be presented to the President of the United States; if he approves he shall sign it, but if not he shall return it, with his objections to that House in which it shall have originated, who shall enter the objections at large on their journal, and proceed to reconsider it. If after such reconsideration two thirds of that House shall agree to pass the bill, it shall be sent, together with the objections, to the other House, by which it shall likewise be reconsidered, and if approved by two thirds of that House, it shall become a law. But in all such cases the votes of both Houses shall be determined by yeas and nays, and the names of the persons voting for and against the bill shall be entered on the journal of each House respectively. If any bill shall not be returned by the President within ten days (Sundays excepted) after it shall have been presented to him, the same shall be a law, in like manner as if he had signed it, unless the Congress by their adjournment prevent its return, in which case it shall not be a law.

3. Every order, resolution, or vote to which the concurrence of the Senate and the House of Representatives may be necessary (except on a question of adjournment) shall be presented to the President of the United States; and before the same shall take effect, shall be approved by him, or being disapproved by him, shall be passed by two thirds of the Senate and House of Representatives, according to the rules and limitations prescribed in the case of a bill.

SECTION 8

The Congress shall have the power

1. To lay and collect taxes, duties, imposts and excises, to pay the debts and provide for the common defense and general welfare of the United States; but all duties, imposts, and excises shall be uniform throughout the United States;

2. To borrow money on the credit of the United States;

3. To regulate commerce with foreign nations, and among the several States, and with the Indian tribes;

4. To establish a uniform rule of naturalization, and uniform laws on the subject of bankruptcies throughout the United States;

5. To coin money, regulate the value thereof, and of foreign coin, and fix the standard of weights and measures;

6. To provide for the punishment of counterfeiting the securities and current coin of the United States;

7. To establish post offices and post roads;

8. To promote the progress of science and useful arts, by securing for limited times to authors and inventors the exclusive right to their respective writings and discoveries;

9. To constitute tribunals inferior to the Supreme Court;

10. To define and punish piracies and felonies committed on the high seas, and offenses against the law of nations;

11. To declare war, grant letters of marque and reprisal, and make rules concerning captures on land and water;

12. To raise and support armies, but no appropriation of money to that use shall be for a longer term than two years;

13. To provide and maintain a navy;

14. To make rules for the government and regulation of the land and naval forces;

15. To provide for calling forth the militia to execute the laws of the Union, suppress insurrections and repel invasions;

16. To provide for organizing, arming, and disciplining the militia, and for governing such part of them as may be employed in the service of the United States, reserving to the States respectively, the appointment of the officers, and the authority of training the militia according to the discipline prescribed by Congress;

17. To exercise exclusive legislation in all cases whatsoever, over such district (not exceeding ten miles square) as may, by cession of particular States, and the acceptance of Congress, become the seat of the government of the United States, and to exercise like authority over all places purchased by the consent of the legislature of the State in which the same shall be, for the erection of forts, magazines, arsenals, dockyards, and other needful buildings; and

18. To make all laws which shall be necessary and proper for carrying into execution the foregoing powers, and all other powers vested by this Constitution in the government of the United States, or in any department or officer thereof.

SECTION 9

1. The migration or importation of such persons as any of the States now existing shall think proper to admit, shall not be prohibited by the Congress prior to the year one thousand eight hundred and eight, but a tax or duty may be imposed on such importation, not exceeding ten dollars for each person.

2. The privilege of the writ of habeas corpus shall not be suspended, unless when in cases of rebellion or invasion the public safety may require it.

3. No bill of attainder or ex post facto law shall be passed.

4. No capitation, or other direct, tax shall be laid, unless in proportion to the census or enumeration hereinbefore directed to be taken.*

5. No tax or duty shall be laid on articles exported from any State.

6. No preference shall be given by any regulation of commerce or revenue to the ports of one State over those of another: nor shall vessels bound to, or from, one State be obliged to enter, clear, or pay duties in another.

*Revised by the Sixteenth Amendment.

7. No money shall be drawn from the treasury, but in consequence of appropriations made by law; and a regular statement and account of the receipts and expenditures of all public money shall be published from time to time.

8. No title of nobility shall be granted by the United States: and no person holding any office of profit or trust under them, shall, without the consent of the Congress, accept of any present, emolument, office, or title, of any kind whatever, from any king, prince, or foreign State.

SECTION 10

1. No State shall enter into any treaty, alliance, or confederation; grant letters of marque and reprisal; coin money; emit bills of credit; make anything but gold and silver coin a tender in payment of debts; pass any bill of attainder, ex post facto law, or law impairing the obligation of contracts, or grant any title of nobility.

2. No State shall, without the consent of the Congress, lay any imposts or duties on imports or exports, except what may be absolutely necessary for executing its inspection laws: and the net produce of all duties and imposts laid by any State on imports or exports, shall be for the use of the treasury of the United States; and all such laws shall be subject to the revision and control of the Congress.

3. No State shall, without the consent of the Congress, lay any duty of tonnage, keep troops, or ships of war in time of peace, enter into any agreement or compact with another State, or with a foreign power, or engage in war, unless actually invaded, or in such imminent danger as will not admit of delay.

ARTICLE II

SECTION 1

1. The executive power shall be vested in a President of the United States of America. He shall hold his office during the term of four years,* and together with the Vice President, chosen for the same term, be elected as follows:

2. Each State shall appoint, in such manner as the legislature thereof may direct, a number of electors, equal to the whole number of senators and representatives to which the State may be entitled in the Congress: but no senator or representative, or person holding an office of trust or profit under the United States, shall be appointed an elector.

The electors shall meet in their respective States, and vote by ballot for two persons, of whom one at least shall not be an inhabitant of the same State with themselves. And they shall make a list of all the persons voted for, and of

*The Twenty-second Amendment limits a President to two terms.

the number of votes for each; which list they shall sign and certify, and transmit sealed to the seat of the government of the United States, directed to the president of the Senate. The president of the Senate shall, in the presence of the Senate and House of Representatives, open all the certificates, and the votes shall then be counted. The person having the greatest number of votes shall be the President, if such number be a majority of the whole number of electors appointed; and if there be more than one who have such majority, and have an equal number of votes, then the House of Representatives shall immediately choose by ballot one of them for President; and if no person have a majority, then from the five highest on the list the said House shall in like manner choose the President. But in choosing the President, the votes shall be taken by States, the representation from each State having one vote; a quorum for this purpose shall consist of a member or members from two thirds of the States, and a majority of all the States shall be necessary to a choice. In every case, after the choice of the President, the person having the greatest number of votes of the electors shall be the Vice President. But if there should remain two or more who have equal votes, the Senate shall choose from them by ballot the Vice President.*

3. The Congress may determine the time of choosing the electors, and the day on which they shall give their votes; which day shall be the same throughout the United States.

4. No person except a natural born citizen, or a citizen of the United States, at the time of the adoption of this Constitution, shall be eligible to the office of President; neither shall any person be eligible to that office who shall not have attained to the age of thirty-five years, and been fourteen years a resident within the United States.

5. In case of the removal of the President from office, or of his death, resignation, or inability to discharge the powers and duties of the said office, the same shall devolve on the Vice President, and the Congress may by law provide for the case of removal, death, resignation, or inability, both of the President and Vice President, declaring what officer shall then act as President, and such officer shall act accordingly, until the disability be removed, or a President shall be elected.*

6. The President shall, at stated times, receive for his services a compensation, which shall neither be increased nor diminished during the period for which he shall have been elected, and he shall not receive within that period any other emolument from the United States, or any of them.

7. Before he enter on the execution of his office, he shall take the following oath or affirmation:—"I do solemnly swear (or affirm) that I will faithfully execute the office of President of the United States, and will to the best of my ability, preserve, protect and defend the Constitution of the United States."

*This paragraph has been superseded by the Twelfth Amendment.
ˮAffected by the Twenty-fifth Amendment.

SECTION 2

1. The President shall be the commander in chief of the army and navy of the United States, and of the militia of the several States, when called into the actual service of the United States; he may require the opinion, in writing, of the principal officer in each of the executive departments, upon any subject relating to the duties of their respective offices, and he shall have power to grant reprieves and pardons for offenses against the United States, except in cases of impeachment.

2. He shall have power, by and with the advice and consent of the Senate, to make treaties, provided two thirds of the senators present concur; and he shall nominate, and by and with the advice and consent of the Senate, shall appoint ambassadors, other public ministers and consuls, judges of the Supreme Court, and all other officers of the United States, whose appointments are not herein otherwise provided for, and which shall be established by law: but the Congress may by law vest the appointment of such inferior officers, as they think proper, in the President alone, in the courts of law, or in the heads of departments.

3. The President shall have power to fill up all vacancies that may happen during the recess of the Senate, by granting commissions which shall expire at the end of their next session.

SECTION 3

He shall from time to time give to the Congress information of the state of the Union, and recommend to their consideration such measures as he shall judge necessary and expedient; he may, on extraordinary occasions, convene both Houses, or either of them, and in case of disagreement between them with respect to the time of adjournment, he may adjourn them to such time as he shall think proper; he shall receive ambassadors and other public ministers; he shall take care that the laws be faithfully executed, and shall commission all the officers of the United States.

SECTION 4

The President, Vice President, and all civil officers of the United States, shall be removed from office on impeachment for, and conviction of, treason, bribery, or other high crimes and misdemeanors.

ARTICLE III

SECTION 1

The judicial power of the United States shall be vested in one Supreme Court, and in such inferior courts as the Congress may from time to time ordain and establish. The judges, both of the Supreme and inferior courts, shall hold their offices during good behavior, and shall, at stated times, receive for their services, a compensation, which shall not be diminished during their continuance in office.

SECTION 2

1. The judicial power shall extend to all cases, in law and equity, arising under this Constitution, the laws of the United States, and treaties made, or which shall be made, under their authority;—to all cases affecting ambassadors, other public ministers and consuls;—to all cases of admiralty and maritime jurisdiction;—to controversies to which the United States shall be a party;*—to controversies between two or more States;—between citizens of different States;—between citizens of the same State claiming lands under grants of different States, and between a State, or the citizens thereof, and foreign States, citizens or subjects.

2. In all cases affecting ambassadors, other public ministers and consuls, and those in which a State shall be party, the Supreme Court shall have original jurisdiction. In all the other cases before mentioned, the Supreme Court shall have appellate jurisdiction, both as to law and to fact, with such exceptions, and under such regulations as the Congress shall make.

3. The trial of all crimes, except in cases of impeachment, shall be by jury; and such trial shall be held in the State where the said crimes shall have been committed; but when not committed within any State, the trial shall be at such place or places as the Congress may by law have directed.

SECTION 3

1. Treason against the United States shall consist only in levying war against them, or in adhering to their enemies, giving them aid and comfort. No person shall be convicted of treason unless on the testimony of two witnesses to the same overt act, or in confession in open court.

2. The Congress shall have power to declare the punishment of treason, but no attainder of treason shall work corruption of blood, or forfeiture except during the life of the person attainted.

ARTICLE IV

SECTION 1

Full faith and credit shall be given in each State to the public acts, records, and judicial proceedings of every other State. And the Congress may by general laws prescribe the manner in which such acts, records and proceedings shall be proved, and the effect thereof.

*Revised by the Eleventh Amendment.

SECTION 2

1. The citizens of each State shall be entitled to all privileges and immunities of citizens in the several States.*

2. A person charged in any State with treason, felony, or other crime, who shall flee from justice, and be found in another State, shall on demand of the executive authority of the State from which he fled, be delivered up to be removed to the State having jurisdiction of the crime.

3. No person held to service or labor in one State under the laws thereof, escaping into another, shall, in consequence of any law or regulation therein, be discharged from such service or labor, but shall be delivered up on claim of the party to whom such service or labor may de due.*

SECTION 3

1. New States may be admitted by the Congress into this Union; but no new State shall be formed or erected within the jurisdiction of any other State; nor any State be formed by the junction of two or more States, or parts of States, without the consent of the legislatures of the States concerned as well as of the Congress.

2. The Congress shall have power to dispose of and make all needful rules and regulations respecting the territory or other property belonging to the United States; and nothing in this Constitution shall be so construed as to prejudice any claims of the United States, or of any particular State.

SECTION 4

The United States shall guarantee to every State in this Union a republican form of government, and shall protect each of them against invasion; and on application of the legislature, or of the executive (when the legislature cannot be convened) against domestic violence.

ARTICLE V

The Congress, whenever two thirds of both Houses shall deem it necessary, shall propose amendments to this Constitution, or, on the application of the legislatures of two thirds of the several States, shall call a convention for proposing amendments, which in either case, shall be valid to all intents and purposes, as part of this Constitution when ratified by the legislatures of three fourths of the several States, or by conventions in three fourths thereof, as the one or the other mode of ratification may be proposed by the Congress; Provided that no amendment which may be made prior to the year one thousand eight hundred and eight shall in any manner affect the first and fourth clauses in the ninth section of the first article; and that no State, without its consent, shall be deprived of its equal suffrage in the Senate.

*Elaborated by the Fourteenth Amendment, Section 1.
*See the Thirteenth Amendment abolishing slavery.

ARTICLE VI

1. All debts contracted and engagements entered into, before the adoption of this Constitution, shall be as valid against the United States under this Constitution, as under the Confederation.*

2. This Constitution, and the laws of the United States which shall be made in pursuance thereof; and all treaties made, or which shall be made, under the authority of the United States, shall be the supreme law of the land; and the Judges in every State shall be bound thereby, anything in the Constitution or laws of any State to the contrary notwithstanding.

3. The senators and representatives before mentioned, and the members of the several State legislatures, and all executive and judicial officers, both of the United States and of the several States, shall be bound by oath or affirmation to support this Constitution; but no religious test shall ever be required as a qualification to any office or public trust under the United States.

ARTICLE VII

The ratification of the conventions of nine States shall be sufficient for the establishment of this Constitution between the States so ratifying the same. Done in Convention by the unanimous consent of the States present the seventeenth day of September in the year of our Lord one thousand seven hundred and eighty-seven, and of the independence of the United States of America the twelfth. In witness whereof we have hereunto subscribed our names.

AMENDMENTS

First ten amendments submitted by Congress September 25, 1789. Ratified by three-fourths of the states December 15, 1791

AMENDMENT I

Congress shall make no law respecting an establishment of religion, or prohibiting the free exercise thereof; or abridging the freedom of speech, or of the press; or the right of the people peaceably to assemble, and to petition the government for a redress of grievances.

AMENDMENT II

A well regulated militia, being necessary to the security of a free State, the right of the people to keep and bear arms, shall not be infringed.

*See the Fourteenth Amendment, Section 4, for additional provisions.

AMENDMENT III

No soldier shall, in time of peace be quartered in any house, without the consent of the owner, nor in time of war, but in a manner to be prescribed by law.

AMENDMENT IV

The right of the people to be secure in their persons, houses, papers, and effects, against unreasonable searches and seizures, shall not be violated, and no warrants shall issue, but upon probable cause, supported by oath or affirmation, and particularly describing the place to be searched, and the persons or things to be seized.

AMENDMENT V

No person shall be held to answer for a capital, or otherwise infamous crime, unless on a presentment or indictment of a grand jury, except in cases arising in the land or naval forces, or in the militia, when in actual service in time of war or public danger; nor shall any person be subject for the same offense to be twice put in jeopardy of life or limb; nor shall be compelled in any criminal case to be a witness against himself, nor be deprived of life, liberty, or property, without due process of law; nor shall private property be taken for public use without just compensation.

AMENDMENT VI

In all criminal prosecutions, the accused shall enjoy the right to a speedy and public trial, by an impartial jury of the State and district wherein the crime shall have been committed, which district shall have been previously ascertained by law, and to be informed of the nature and cause of the accusation; to be confronted with the witnesses against him; to have compulsory process for obtaining witnesses in his favor, and to have the assistance of counsel for his defense.

AMENDMENT VII

In suits at common law, where the value in controversy shall exceed twenty dollars, the right of trial by jury shall be preserved, and no fact tried by a jury shall be otherwise reëxamined in any court of the United States, than according to the rules of the common law.

AMENDMENT VIII

Excessive bail shall not be required, nor excessive fines imposed, nor cruel and unusual punishments inflicted.

AMENDMENT IX

The enumeration in the Constitution of certain rights shall not be construed to deny or disparage others retained by the people.

AMENDMENT X

The powers not delegated to the United States by the Constitution, nor prohibited by it to the States, are reserved to the States respectively, or to the people.

AMENDMENT XI

Submitted by Congress March 5, 1794, declared ratified January 8, 1798.

The judicial power of the United States shall not be construed to extend to any suit in law or equity, commenced or prosecuted against one of the United States by citizens of another state, or by citizens or subjects of any foreign state.

AMENDMENT XII

Submitted by Congress December 12, 1803, declared ratified September 25, 1804.

The electors shall meet in their respective States, and vote by ballot for President and Vice President, one of whom, at least, shall not be an inhabitant of the same State with themselves; they shall name in their ballots the person voted for as President, and in distinct ballots, the person voted for as Vice President, and they shall make distinct lists of all persons voted for as President and of all persons voted for as Vice President, and of the number of votes for each, which lists they shall sign and certify, and transmit sealed to the seat of the government of the United States, directed to the President of the Senate;—The President of the Senate shall, in the presence of the Senate and House of Representatives, open all the certificates and the votes shall then be counted;—The person having the greatest number of votes for President, shall be the President, if such number be a majority of the whole number of electors appointed; and if no person have such majority, then from the persons having the highest numbers not exceeding three on the list of those voted for as President, the House of Representatives shall choose immediately, by ballot the President. But in choosing the President, the votes shall be taken by States, the representation from each State having one vote; a quorum for this purpose shall consist of a member or members from two thirds of the States, and a majority of all the States shall be necessary to a choice. And if the House of Representatives shall not choose a President whenever the right of choice shall devolve upon them, before the fourth day of March next following, then the Vice President shall act as President, as in the case of the death or other constitutional disability of the President.* The person having the greatest number of votes as Vice President shall be the Vice President, if such number be a majority of the whole number of electors appointed, and if no person have a majority, then from the two highest numbers on the list, the Senate shall choose the Vice President; a quorum for the purpose shall consist of two thirds of the whole number of Senators, and a majority of the whole number shall be necessary to a choice. But no person constitutionally ineligible to the office of President shall be eligible to that of Vice President of the United States.

AMENDMENT XIII
Submitted by Congress February 1, 1865, declared ratified December 18, 1865.

SECTION I
Neither slavery nor involuntary servitude, except as punishment for crime whereof the party shall have been duly convicted, shall exist within the United States, or any place subject to their jurisdiction.

SECTION 2
Congress shall have power to enforce this article by appropriate legislation.

AMENDMENT XIV
Submitted by Congress June 16, 1866, declared ratified July 28, 1868.

SECTION 1
All persons born or naturalized in the United States, and subject to the jurisdiction thereof, are citizens of the United States and of the State wherein they reside. No State shall make or enforce any law which shall abridge the privileges or immunities of citizens of the United States; nor shall any State deprive any person of life, liberty, or property, without due process of law; nor deny to any person within its jurisdiction the equal protection of the laws.

SECTION 2
Representatives shall be apportioned among the several States according to their respective numbers, counting the whole number of persons in each State, excluding Indians not taxed. But when the right to vote at any election for the choice of electors for President and Vice President of the United

*Superseded by the Twentieth Amendment, Section 3.

States, representatives in Congress, the executive and judicial officers of a State, or the members of the legislature thereof, is denied to any of the male inhabitants of such State, being twenty-one years of age, and citizens of the United States, or in any way abridged, except for participation in rebellion, or other crime, the basis of representation therein shall be reduced in the proportion which the number of such male citizens shall bear to the whole number of male citizens twenty-one years of age in such State.

SECTION 3

No person shall be a senator or representative in Congress, or elector of President and Vice President, or hold any office, civil or military, under the United States, or under any State, who having previously taken an oath, as a member of Congress, or as an officer of the United States, or as a member of any State legislature, or as an executive or judicial officer of any State, to support the Constitution of the United States, shall have engaged in insurrection or rebellion against the same, or given aid or comfort to the enemies thereof. But Congress may by a vote of two thirds of each House, remove such disability.

SECTION 4

The validity of the public debt of the United States, authorized by law, including debts incurred for payment of pensions and bounties for services in suppressing insurrection or rebellion, shall not be questioned. But neither the United States nor any State shall assume or pay any debt or obligation incurred in aid of insurrection or rebellion against the United States, or any claim for the loss of emancipation of any slave; but all such debts, obligations, and claims shall be held illegal and void.

SECTION 5

The Congress shall have power to enforce by appropriate legislation, the provisions of this article.

AMENDMENT XV

Submitted by Congress February 27, 1869, declared ratified March 30, 1870.

SECTION 1

The right of citizens of the United States to vote shall not be denied or abridged by the United States or by any State on account of race, color, or previous condition of servitude.

SECTION 2

The Congress shall have power to enforce this article by appropriate legislation.

AMENDMENT XVI

Submitted by Congress July 12, 1909, declared ratified February 25, 1913.

The Congress shall have power to lay and collect taxes on incomes, from whatever source derived, without apportionment among the several States, and without regard to any census or enumeration.

AMENDMENT XVII

Submitted by Congress May 16, 1912, declared ratified May 31, 1913.

The Senate of the United States shall be composed of two senators from each state elected by the people thereof, for six years; and each senator shall have one vote. The electors in each State shall have the qualifications requisite for electors of the most numerous branch of the State legislature.

When vacancies happen in the representation of any State in the Senate, the executive authority of such State shall issue writs of election to fill such vacancies: *Provided,* That the legislature of any State may empower the executive thereof to make temporary appointments until the people fill the vacancies by election as the legislature may direct.

This amendment shall not be so construed as to affect the election or term of any senator chosen before it becomes valid as part of the Constitution.

AMENDMENT XVIII*

Submitted by Congress December 18, 1917, declared ratified January 29, 1919.

After one year from the ratification of this article, the manufacture, sale, or transportation of intoxicating liquors within, the importation thereof into, or the exportation thereof from the United States and all territory subject to the jurisdiction thereof for beverage purposes is hereby prohibited.

The Congress and the several States shall have concurrent power to enforce this article by appropriate legislation.

This article shall be inoperative unless it shall have been ratified as an amendment to the Constitution by the legislatures of the several States, as provided in the Constitution, within seven years from the date of the submission hereof to the states by Congress.

AMENDMENT XIX

Submitted by Congress June 5, 1919, declared ratified August 26, 1920.

The right of citizens of the United States to vote shall not be denied or abridged by the United States or by any State on account of sex.

*Repealed by the Twenty-first Amendment.

The Congress shall have power by appropriate legislation to enforce the provisions of this article.

AMENDMENT XX

Submitted by Congress March 3, 1932, declared ratified February 6, 1933.

SECTION 1

The terms of the President and Vice President shall end at noon on the 20th day of January, and the terms of Senators and Representatives at noon on the 3d day of January, of the years in which such terms would have ended if this article had not been ratified; and the terms of their successors shall then begin.

SECTION 2

The Congress shall assemble at least once in every year, and such meeting shall begin at noon on the 3d day of January, unless they shall by law appoint a different day.

SECTION 3

If, at the time fixed for the beginning of the term of the President, the President-elect shall have died, the Vice President-elect shall become President. If a President shall not have been chosen before the time fixed for the beginning of his term, or if the President-elect shall have failed to qualify, then the Vice President-elect shall act as President until a President shall have qualified; and the Congress may by law provide for the case wherein neither a President-elect nor a Vice President-elect shall have qualified, declaring who shall then act as President, or the manner in which one who is to act shall be selected, and such person shall act accordingly until a President or Vice President shall have qualified.

SECTION 4

The Congress may by law provide for the case of the death of any of the persons from whom the House of Representatives may choose a President whenever the right of choice shall have devolved upon them, and for the case of the death of any of the persons from whom the Senate may choose a Vice President whenever the right of choice shall have devolved upon them.

SECTION 5

Sections 1 and 2 shall take effect on the 15th day of October following the ratification of this article.

SECTION 6

This article shall be inoperative unless it shall have been ratified as an amendment to the Constitution by the legislatures of three-fourths of the several States within seven years from the date of its submission.

AMENDMENT XXI

Submitted by Congress February 20, 1933, declared ratified December 5, 1933.

SECTION 1

The Eighteenth Article of amendment to the Constitution of the United States is hereby repealed.

SECTION 2

The transportation or importation into any State, Territory, or possession of the United States for delivery or use therein of intoxicating liquors in violation of the laws thereof, is hereby prohibited.

SECTION 3

This article shall be inoperative unless it shall have been ratified as an amendment to the Constitution by conventions in the several States, as provided in the Constitution, within seven years from the date of the submission thereof to the States by the Congress.

AMENDMENT XXII

Submitted by Congress March 24, 1947, declared ratified March 1, 1951.

No person shall be elected to the office of the President more than twice, and no person who has held the office of President, or acted as President, for more than two years of a term to which some other person was elected President shall be elected to the office of the President more than once.

But this article shall not apply to any person holding the office of President when this article was proposed by the Congress, and shall not prevent any person who may be holding the office of President, or acting as President, during the term within which this article becomes operative from holding the office of President or acting as President during the remainder of such term.

This article shall be inoperative unless it shall have been ratified as an amendment to the Constitution by the legislatures of three-fourths of the several states within seven years from the date of its submission to the states by the Congress.

AMENDMENT XXIII

Submitted by Congress June 16, 1960, declared ratified April 3, 1961.

SECTION 1

The District constituting the seat of Government of the United States shall appoint in such manner as the Congress may direct:

A number of electors of President and Vice President equal to the whole number of Senators and Representatives in Congress to which the District would be entitled if it were a State, but in no event more than the least populous State; they shall be in addition to those appointed by the States, but they shall be considered, for the purpose of the election of President and Vice President, to be electors appointed by a State; and they shall meet in the District and perform such duties as provided by the twelfth article of amendment.

SECTION 2

The Congress shall have power to enforce this article by appropriate legislation.

AMENDMENT XXIV

Submitted by Congress August 27, 1962, declared ratified February 4, 1964.

SECTION 1

The right of citizens of the United States to vote in any primary or other election for President or Vice President, for electors for President or Vice President, or for Senator or Representative in Congress, shall not be denied or abridged by the United States or any State by reason of failure to pay any poll tax or other tax.

SECTION 2

The Congress shall have the power to enforce this article by appropriate legislation.

AMENDMENT XXV

Submitted by Congress July 6, 1965, declared ratified February 23, 1967.

SECTION 1

In case of the removal of the President from office or of his death or resignation, the Vice President shall become President.

SECTION 2

Whenever there is a vacancy in the office of the Vice President, the President shall nominate a Vice President who shall take office upon confirmation by a majority vote of both houses of Congress.

SECTION 3

Whenever the President transmits to the President pro tempore of the Senate and the Speaker of the House of Representatives his written declaration that he is unable to discharge the powers and duties of his office, and until he transmits to them a written declaration to the contrary, such powers and duties shall be discharged by the Vice President as Acting President.

SECTION 4

Whenever the Vice President and a majority of either the principal officers of the executive departments, or of such other body as Congress may by law provide, transmit to the President pro tempore of the Senate and the Speaker of the House of Representatives their written declaration that the President is unable to discharge the powers and duties of his office, the Vice President shall immediately assume the powers and duties of the office as Acting President.

Thereafter, when the President transmits to the President pro tempore of the Senate and Speaker of the House of Representatives his written declaration that no inability exists, he shall resume the powers and duties of his office unless the Vice President and a majority of either the principal officers of the executive departments, or of such other body as Congress may by law provide, transmit within four days to the President pro tempore of the Senate and the Speaker of the House of Representatives their written declaration that the President is unable to discharge the powers and duties of his office. Thereupon Congress shall decide the issue, assembling within forty-eight hours for that purpose if not in session. If the Congress, within twenty-one days after receipt of the latter written declaration, or, if Congress is not in session, within twenty-one days after Congress is required to assemble, determines by two-thirds vote of both houses that the President is unable to discharge the powers and duties of his office, the Vice President shall continue to discharge the same as Acting President; otherwise, the President shall resume the powers and duties of his office.

ILLUSTRATION CREDITS

Maps by John V. Morris.

CHAPTER ONE: Opener: "The Residence of David Twining 1787" by Edward Hicks. Courtesy Abby Aldrich Rockefeller Folk Art Collection. Page 4 & 5: From *The Viking* by Bertil Almgren. Copyright © 1966, Tre Tryckare ab, Gothenburg, Sweden. Page 9: From T. de Bry, *America* Part X, 1618, Plate XI. Courtesy Rare Book Division, The New York Public Library, Astor, Lenox and Tilden Foundations. Page 11: From *Pioneers in America*. Courtesy The National Historical Society, Harrisburg, Pennsylvania. Page 13: Harper's Magazine, April 1883. Page 26: Historical Society of Pennsylvania.

CHAPTER TWO Opener: "The County Election" by George Caleb Bingham, Collection of the Boatmen's National Bank of St. Louis. Page 39: The Granger Collection. Page 43: Brown Brothers. Page 53: Painting by John Woodside. Courtesy of Davenport West, Jr. Page 55: The New York Public Library Picture Collection. Page 57: Library of Congress. Page 59: The New York Public Library Picture Collection. Page 64: The New York Public Library Picture Collection. Page 65: Copyright © 1960, American Heritage Publishing Company, Inc. Reprinted by permission from *The American Heritage Picture History of the Civil War* by Bruce Catton.

CHAPTER THREE Opener: Denver Public Library, Western History Department. Page 78: "Trail of Tears" by Robert Lindneux. Courtesy Woolaroc Museum, Bartlesville, Oklahoma. Page 79: Collection of Harry T. Peters, Jr. Page 84: Los Angeles County Museum of Natural History. Page 90: Courtesy of Kennedy Galleries, Inc. Page 92: Western History Collections, University of Oklahoma Library. Page 93: Library of Congress. Page 94: NASA.

CHAPTER FOUR Opener: "The Gun Foundry, Cold Spring, N.Y." by John Ferguson Weir. Courtesy Putnam County Historical Society, Cold Spring, N.Y. Page 99: "The Lackawanna Valley" by George Inness. Courtesy National Gallery of Art, Washington, D.C. Gift of Mrs. Huttleston Rogers. Page 108: (Top) The Jacob A. Riis Collection, Museum of the City of New York; (bottom) The Vanderbilt Mansion, 1908. Courtesy The Byron Collection, Museum of the City of New York. Page 110: Courtesy of the Solberg Family. Page 116: (Top) Courtesy of the I.L.G.W.U.; (bottom) Culver Pictures. Page 120: The Granger Collection.

CHAPTER FIVE Page 127: The Kansas State Historical Society, Topeka. Page 133: The Granger Collection. Page 139: (Top) United Press International; (bottom) Brown Brothers. Page 140: Brown Brothers. Page 146: Ken Heyman.

CHAPTER SIX Opener: The National Archives. Page 170: U.S. Signal Corps./National Archives. Page 174: Brown Brothers.

CHAPTER SEVEN Opener: Leonard Freed/Magnum. Page 188: The original painting hangs in the Selectmen's Room, Marble head, Massachusetts. Page 194: (Top) "First Virginia Regiment" by Richard Grays Courtesy Valentine Museum, Richmond, Virginia; (bottom) Library of Congress. Page 195: Courtesy of the New York Historical Society, New York City. Page 199: Culver Pictures. Page 202: United States Air Force. Page 208: Donald McCullin/Magnum. Page 209: Newsweek.

CHAPTER EIGHT Opener: Bruce Davidson/Magnum. Page 218: Thomas Gilcrease Institute of American History and Art, Tulsa, Oklahoma. Page 220: Library of Congress. Page 227: Library of Congress. Page 230: The National Archives. Page 234: Bob Adelman/ Magnum. Page 237: Burt Glinn/ Magnum. Page 242: George Ballis/Black Star. Page 248: Library of Congress. Page 251: John Messina/ Black Star.

CHAPTER NINE Opener: Ernest Haas/Magnum. Page 265: Painting by Asher B. Durand, Courtesy of the New York Public Library. Page 269: Courtesy The Bancroft Library, University of California, Berkeley. Page 274: David Van de Mark. Page 275: Grant Heilman. Page 276: Laurence Lowry/National Audubon Society. Page 278: Fred Lyon/ Rapho Guillumette. Page 282: Bethlehem Steel Corporation. Page 283: Mady Victor/Rapho Guillumette. Page 284: NASA.

CHAPTER TEN Page 293: Courtesy Honeywell Information Systems. Page 299: Cornell Capa/Magnum. Page 301: Lawrence Fried/Magnum.

Index

INDEX

Abolitionism, 62, 63
Abzug, Bella, 252
Adams, John, on commerce, 157
  foreign policy of, 158
  on neutrality, 155
  as President, 50-51, 190
Adams, John Quincy, and Monroe Doctrine,
    162
  as President, 54, 76
  and Transcontinental Treaty, 162
Adams, Sam, 43
Agricultural Adjustment Act (AAA), 141
Alcatraz Island occupation, 244
Alger, Horatio, 104
Alien and Sedition Acts, 51, 53, 190, 307
American character, and equality, 23
  formation of, 2
  and mobility, 23
  and optimism, 23
  and practicality, 24
American Federation of Labor (AFL), and
    women, 249
American Indian Movement (AIM), 245
American Peace Society, 58, 196
American Revolution Bicentennial Commission,
    290
Annapolis Naval Academy, 192
Anti-Federalists, 48-49
Articles of Confederation, 45, 46, 308
Asians, and Progressivism, 132
Atlanta Compromise address, 232
Atomic bomb, 202, 203

Barbary War, 190, 192
Bellamy, Edward, 105
Berlin blockade, 175
Berlin Wall, 177
Bill of Rights, 48
Black capitalism, 239
Black Muslims, 236
Black Panthers, 238-239
Black Power, 235-239
Blacks, and civil rights movement, 232-235
  and Civil War, 196

and Colored Farmers National Alliance, 126
and Constitution, 221
and Declaration of Independence, 221
and Eisenhower administration, 144-145
as freemen in North, 62
in government, 239-240
and Johnson administration, 147, 234
and John F. Kennedy, 145, 234
and Ku Klux Klan, 137
and Knights of Labor, 115
as middle-class, 239
and Nashoba experiment, 60
nationalism of, 238-239
Nat Turner uprising, 63
and Nixon administration, 239, 240
and "Personal Liberty Laws", 63
and Progressivism, 131, 136
and Franklin D. Roosevelt, 233
and segregation, 222-223
and slavery, 62, 64, 219-222
and slave trade, 219-220
stereotypes of, 223
and William H. Taft, 223
and 3/5 Compromise, 61
and Truman administration, 144-145
and Harry S. Truman, 233
and urban riots, 236-238
in West, 83, 92
and World War II, 202-203
"Bloody shirt", 196
Boston massacre, 42
Boston Tea Party, 42, 43, 290
Bracero program, 225
Brown Berets, 243
Brown vs. Topeka Board of Education case,
    222, 233
Bryan, William Jennings, and election of 1896,
    129
  as progressive, 130
Bunker Hill, battle of, 188
Bureau of Indian Affairs (BIA), 86-87
Burr, Aaron, 51

Cabot, 6, 8

Calhoun, John C., 61
"Californios", 88, 89
Capone, Al, 134
Carmichael, Stokely, 235, 236, 238
Carnegie, Andrew, 102, 104, 105, 110, 196
Central Intelligence Agency (CIA), 205
Chavez, Cesar, 241-242
Child labor, 120, 131, 143
  and Jane Addams, 135
Chinese, and nativism, 226
  and Oriental Exclusion League, 292
  segregation of, 228
  as workforce, 226-227
Chisholm, Shirley, 252
Cities, attractions of, 105
  growth of, 106
  and immigrants, 118
  life in, 107
  and political bosses, 118
Civil Rights Act, 252
Civil War, 193-197, 291, 292
  and business, 101
  economic effects of, 196
  John Brown's Raid, 64
  modern nature of, 195
  results of, 66, 83, 196-197
Clay, Henry, 54, 76, 191
Clean Air Act, 277-278
Clearcutting, 267, 273-274
Cleaver, Eldridge, 238
Cleveland, Grover, 196
  and election of 1892, 129
  and election of 1896, 129
Cold War, 203-206
  and Containment, 175-177
  and detente, 177-182
  and dissent, 205
  in election of 1964, 147
  origins of, 173-174
Columbus, Christopher, 6, 19
Commercial Revolution, 4
Common Law, English, 35
Common Sense, 44, 155
Communes, in 19th century, 60
Community Service Organization (CSO),
  240-241
Compromise of 1850, 63
Computers, 292, 293, 300
Confederacy, 66, 193, 195, 196
Congress, First Continental, 43
Congress, Second Continental, 44, 45
Congress of Industrial Organizations (CIO),
  143, 232

Conservation, and Civilian Conservation Corps
  (CCC), 141
  and Depression, 271
  and Dust Bowl, 143, 271
  and Franklin D. Roosevelt, 271
  and conquest-progress mentality, 260-262
  and Indians, 244
  and timber resources, 261
  and Truman administration, 267-268
Constitution, 47-49
  and Balance of powers, 304
  on foreign policy, 157-158
  implied powers of, 49
  as a model, 34
  ratification of, 48
  on slavery, 61, 221
Constitutional Convention, 46
Containment, 175-177, 204
"Contingent necessity," 7
Coolidge, Calvin, 137
Cooper, James Fenimore, 263, 266, 291
Coxey, Jacob, 129
Crash of 1929, 138
Crevecoeur, Jean de, 29

Da Gama, 6
Davis, Jefferson, 195, 196
Debs, Eugene, 130, 135, 199
Declaration of Independence, 44, 291
  and blacks, 221
  and equal rights, 62
Deism, 263
Democrats, and election of 1912, 135
  and election of 1964, 147
Depression of 1930's, 138-139
Detente, 177, 182
Dewey, John, 130
Dix, Dorothea, 58, 59
"Domino" theory, 206
Douglas, Stephen, 63
Draft law, peacetime, 201
Draft Riots, 195
Drake, 6
Dred Scott case, 222
Du Bois, W. E. B., 232
Durant, Will and Ariel, on civilization's
  decline, 309
Dutch, see Netherlands

Ecology, 273
Education, and blacks, 235, 238
  and campus war protest, 207-209
  in 19th century, 58

Federal aid to, 204
and Free Speech Movement, 207
growth of, 296
and Mexicans, 242, 243
Eisenhower, Dwight D., and civil rights, 144-145
on military-industrial complex, 204
as President, 144-145
and Vietnam, 206
Embargo, 160, 190
Emerson, Ralph Waldo, 57-58, 269
on nature, 264
Enclosure acts, 8
Energy, 258, 279-284
alternative sources of, 280-284
and coal, 281
crisis, 154
and oil companies, 281-282
and self-sufficiency, 280
England, explorations by, 6
imperial power of, 7
English imperial policy, Hat Act, 28
Intolerable Acts, 42
Iron Act, 28
Molasses Act, 27
Navigation Act, 27
Proclamation Line of 1763, 73
Quartering Act, 187
Stamp Act, 29, 42
Sugar Act, 29
Tea Act, 42
Enlightment, 19, 44, 263, 308
Environmental engineering, 271-272
Tennessee Valley Authority, 272
Equal Rights Amendment, 253
"Era of Good Feelings," 53

Fair Deal, 144
Farmers Alliances, 126-127
Federal Bureau of Investigation (FBI), 205
Federal Employment Practices Commission (FEPC), 241
Federal Trade Commission (FTC), 135
Federalist Papers, 48
Federalists, 48-52, 190
decline of, 52-53
and Hartford Convention, 191
Fitzgerald, F. Scott, 137
Ford, Gerald, as President, 149, 182
Forest Service, United States, 268
France, empire of, 8, 29
exploration by, 6
undeclared war with, 51, 158, 190

Franklin, Benjamin, 18, 21, 25, 26
on American future, 78, 299
on Constitution, 47
and Enlightment, 263, 308
on Europe, 154-155
as Founding Father, 308
and Indian federation, 70
on war and peace, 186
"Freedom Rides," 233
Free Speech Movement, 207
Fremont, John C., 192
French and Indian War, 40, 187
Friedan, Betty, 252
"Frontier hypothesis," 93-95
"safety valve" theory, 94-95
Fugitive Slave Act, 221
Fuller, R. Buckminster, 285
Future Shock, 307

Galbraith, John Kenneth, 147
Garrison, William Lloyd, 62
Garvey, Marcus, 232
Gentleman's Agreement, 229
George, Henry, 105
Georgia, colony of, 16
Ghent, Treaty of, 160, 191
"Gilded Age," 119
Glorious Revolution, 44
Gold Rush, 88, 101
Gompers, Samuel, 115
Gospel of Wealth, 103
Graduated Income Tax, 135
Grange, 113, 126
Great Awakening, 26
Great Society, and Economic Opportunity Act, 146
and Head Start, 147
and Job Corps, 146
and Nixon administration, 148-149
and Vietnam, 147-148
and Vista, 146, 147
Greenback movement, 113
"Green Revolution," 295
Guadalupe-Hidalgo, Treaty of, 88, 89, 164, 193, 240

Hamilton, Alexander, and economic program, 48-49
as Federalist, 49, 50, 51
and Federalist Papers, 48
Hardin, Garrett, and "lifeboat earth," 285
Harding, Warren, and election of 1920, 136
and "Normalcy," 136

as President, 136-137
Hartford Convention, 191
Hat Act, 28
Haymarket strike, 115
Headright system, 12
Hemingway, Earnest, 137
Henry, Patrick, 39, 41
Hetch-Hetchy, 270-271
Hill, J. J., 102
History, as identity, 290-292
    as security, 301-302
Homestead Act, 91, 262
Homestead strike, 116
Hoover, Herbert H., and Bonus Expeditionary
        Force, 140
    and Depression, 138
    and election of 1932, 140
    and Food Administration, 200
    as President, 137
House of Burgesses, 12, 36, 38
    on taxation, 41
Hudson, Henry, 13
Hudson River school, 265, 266
Hutchinson, Anne, 15

Immigration, 2
    and American letters, 109
    18th century non-English, 22
    in 19th century, 98, 101, 108
    Chinese, 226, 227
    and cultural diversity, 111
    Japanese, 228
    and Homestead Act, 91
    and living conditions, 111
    and *melting pot*, 111
    Mexicans, 88, 90
    and motives of colonists, 71, 109-110
    and nativism, 131
    new, 109
    old, 109
    and social pressures, 111
    as work force, 109-111, 197
Impressment, 160
Indentured servitude, 20, 219
Indians, British policy toward, 73
    and "Broken Treaties Papers," 245, 246
    and Bureau of Indian Affairs, 86-87
    and Chief Joseph, 87
    and clash with white values, 215-216
    colonial battles with, 186
    conquest of, 70, 72-73, 86, 197
    and Custer, 217
    and European "gifts," 72

and first colonists, 215
    and Ghost Dance, 86
    and influence on government, 70
    and Jackson administration, 56, 60
    and land ownership, 216-218, 219
    and Little Big Horn, 86
    and "Manifest destiny," 163
    and Mexican experience, 224
    North American population of, 72
    Plains, 71, 80, 85
    and Pontiac's Rebellion, 73
    Pueblo, 71
    and "Red Power" movement, 244-247
    reservation policy toward, 244-245
    stereotypes of, 217-218, 263
    and Supreme Court, 217
    and Tecumseh, 74
    and Theodore Roosevelt, 216-217
    and Thomas Jefferson, 217
    and "Trail of Tears," 76-78
    and tribal disunity, 85
    urban, 245
    and U.S. Army, 192
    U.S. policy toward, 74
    woodland tribes, 70, 77, 215, 217
    and Wounded Knee, 243-244, 245, 246, 247
International Workers of the World (IWW), 117
Interstate Commerce Commission (ICC), 133
Intolerable Acts, 42
Iron Act, 28
"Iron Curtain," 174, 205

Jackson, Andrew, on conquest of wilderness,
        262
    and election of 1828, 54-55, 61
    as General in Florida, 162
    as hero of New Orleans, 54, 76, 160, 191
    on Indians, 262
    as President, 56, 76
    and states rights, 60, 61
Jackson, Helen Hunt, 87
Japanese, and economy, 229
    and Gentleman's Agreement, 229
    immigration of, 228
    and internment, 203, 229-231
    stereotypes of, 228
    and World War II, 203
Jay, John, and *Federalist Papers*, 48
Jay's Treaty, 50-51, 158
Jefferson, Thomas, and anti-slavery, 221
    and Declaration of Independence, 44
    on Deism, 263
    and election of 1800, 51

342 Index

and embargo, 160, 190
on force, 157
foreign policy of, 158
inaugural of, 307
and Indian rights, 217
and Kentucky and Virginia Resolutions, 51
and Louisiana Purchase, 75, 159
on nature, 263
and parties, 49
on power politics, 157
as President, 52, 190-191
on slavery, 61
as symbol, 291
on U.S. future, 78
view of America, 2
on war and peace, 186
western policy of, 75
Jim Crow, 222, 231
John Birch Society, 205
Johnson, Lyndon B., on America's future, 299
and civil rights, 146-147, 234
and Congress, 146
and election of 1964, 147
and election of 1968, 148, 209
and Great Society, 147-148
and New Deal, 146
as President, 145-148
and War on Poverty, 146-147

Kansas-Nebraska Act, 63
Kellogg-Briand Pact, 171
Kennedy, John F., 94, 203
assassination of, 145
and civil rights, 234
and election of 1960, 145
and missile crisis, 177
and "New Frontier", 145
and Peace Corps, 145
as President, 145
Kent State University, 209
Kentucky and Virginia Resolutions, 51, 61, 307
King, Martin Luther Jr., 233, 235, 241, 291
Kissinger, Henry, 180-182
Knights of Labor, 114-115
Korean War, 175
Ku Klux Klan, 292
and nativism, 137

Labor, American Federation of, 115, 117
LaFollette, Robert M., 132
as pacifist, 198
as progressive, 130

"La Raza," 242
League of Nations, 136, 169, 171
Lease, Mary Elizabeth, 127
Leopold, Aldo, 272-273
and "land ethic," 284
Lewis and Clark expedition, 52, 75
Lexington, battle of, 34, 43, 187
Lincoln, Abraham, on amnesty, 209
on Civil War, 34
and election of 1864, 195
as martyr, 291
on Mexican War, 193
as President, 66, 196
Locke, John, 44
Long, Senator Huey, 142
Louisiana Purchase, 52, 159
Loyalists, 44, 189
Lusitania, 169

MacArthur, General Douglas, 205-206
MacKaye, Benton, 272
Madison, James, and *Federalist Papers*, 48
and Kentucky and Virginia Resolutions, 51
on parties, 49
as President, 191
Magellan, 6
Mahan, Alfred Thayer, 164-165, 197
Maine, 165, 197
Malcolm X, 236
Man Nature, 267
"Manifest destiny," 62, 79-81, 161-164, 192
and Indian removal, 163
and Oregon, 81, 163
Marshall, John, 77
Marsh, George Perkins, 267
Mayflower Compact, 36
McCarthy, Senator Joe, 205
McGovern, George, 148
McKinley, William, assassination of, 132
and election of 1896, 129
foreign policy of, 165-166
Means, Russell, 247
"Melting pot," 111
and Mexicans, 242-243
Mercantilism, 7, 28, 157
Mexicans, and Chicano movement, 241-243
and civil rights movement, 240-241
conquest of, 70
and Depression, 225
discrimination against, 88-91
government policy toward, 225-226
and Indian experience, 224
and "Manifest destiny", 79-81

and migration to U.S., 88, 90
and roles in West, 88, 90
stereotypes of, 224
as workforce, 224-225
and World War II, 240
Mexico, and California, 81
and Texas, 80
War with, 62, 81, 88, 164, 192-193
Military-industrial complex, 200-202, 204, 207
and New Left, 306
"Minutemen," 43, 188, 191
Minutemen, post-World War II, 205
Molasses Act, 28
Monroe Doctrine, 162-163, 165, 177
Monroe, James, foreign policy of, 162-163
as President, 53
Morgan, J. P., 102-103
Mott, Lucretia, 59
"Mountain men," 80, 85
"Muckrakers," 134
Muir, John, 269-271
and Hetch-Hetchy, 270-271

National Aeronautics and Space Administration
(NASA), 204
National Association for the Advancement of
Colored People (NAACP), 232
National Farm Workers Alliance, 242
National Industrial Recovery Act (NRA), 141
National Labor Union, 114
National Organization of Women (NOW), 251
National Parks, origins of, 266, 268, 270
National Temperance Union, 58
National Women's Political Caucus (NWPC),
251
National Women's Trade Union League
(NWTUL), 249
Nation-state system characteristics of, 6
Nativism, 131
and Ku Klux Klan, 137
Navigation Act, 27
Netherlands, empire of, 7, 13
Neutrality Acts (1930's), 200
New Deal, Agricultural Adjustment Act (AAA),
141, 143
and blacks, 232-233
and child labor, 143
and Civilian Conservation Corps (CCC), 141
and labor, 143
and National Industrial Recovery Act (NRA),
141, 143
and New Left, 305
and 100 Days, 141

results of, 143-144
and Second 100 Days, 142
Social Security Act, 142, 144
and Tennessee Valley Authority (TVA), 142,
144
and Works Progress Administration (WPA),
142
and World War II, 143, 203
"New Federalism," 149
"New Frontier," 94, 145
New Left, 148, 209, 305-306
and democratic socialism, 306
on military-industrial complex, 306
on New Deal, 305
New Orleans, battle of, 191
Newton, Huey, 238
Niagara Movement, 237
Nixon, Richard M., and blacks, 239, 240
economic program of, 148-149
and election of 1960, 145
and election of 1972, 148
and reelection campaign, 304
on energy, 280
and "New Federalism," 149
as President, 148-149
taxes of, 304-305
visits USSR and China, 177-178, 293, 307
and wage and price controls, 206-207
and Watergate, 149
Noblesse oblige, 114
Norsemen, 5, 6
and Vinland settlement, 3
North Atlantic Treaty Organization (NATO),
175
Northwest ordinances, 74
Nuclear Test Ban Treaty, 177
Nullification, 61
Nye Committee, 200

Oglethorpe, James, 16
"Open Door" policy, 166, 168

Paine, Thomas, 44   )
on independence, 155
Parliament, relations with colonies, 38
workings of, 34-35
Patroon system, 14
Peace Corps, 145, 207
Pearl Harbor, 172, 201, 229
People's Bicentennial Commission, 290
Philadelphia, reflection of Enlightenment, 21
Pike, Zebulon, 52, 75
Pilgrims, 36

Plymouth Bay Colony founded by, 14
Pinchot, Gifford, 134, 267-268
  and Hetch-Hetchy, 270-271
Plessy vs. Ferguson case, 222, 233
Polk, James, as President, 163-164
Pollution, air, 258, 277-278
  DDT, 258
  Jacques Cousteau on, 277
  water, 276-277
Pontiac's Rebellion, 73
Population, 258
  and affluence, 278-279
  and birth control, 279
  growth in U.S., 296
Populism, 93, 127, 128-230
  and American Federation of Labor (AFL),
    129
  and election of 1892, 129
  failure in 1896, 129
  and James Weaver, 129
  and Knights of Labor, 128
  nativism of, 131-132
  reform program of, 128
  results of, 129-130
Portugal, empire of, 6, 7
Pragmatism, philosophy of, 130
Progressive Party, collapse of, 135
  and election of 1912, 134-135
Progressivism, 130
  and Asians, 132
  and blacks, 131
  its diversity, 130
  nativism of, 131-132
  in New Deal, 144
  and the 1920's, 200
  principles of, 130-131
  and Prohibition, 132
  results of, 136
Prohibition, 132, 137
"Project Independence, 1980," 280
Protestant work ethic, 16, 216, 297-298
Primitivism, 263-264
Pullman strike, 116
Puritans, on civil disobedience, 16
  challenged by Baptists and Quakers, 15
  and Congregational form of government, 14,
    36
  Massachusetts Bay Colony founded by, 14
  mission of, 2, 16, 36
  persecution in England, 9
  stress on learning, 16
  and town meeting, 16
  and witch trials, 15

on work, 297

Red Scare of 1920's, 136, 199
  post-World War II, 205
Reconstruction Finance Corporation (RFC),
  138
Religion, in 19th century, 57
  and Ralph Waldo Emerson, 57-58
  role in colonies, 26, 298
  and Salvation Army, 107
  and *social gospel*, 107, 130
"Relocation camps," 203, 229-231
Report from Iron Mountain, 207
Republicans, Jeffersonian, 49, 51
Reserve Officers Training Corps (ROTC), 202,
  207
Revolution, American, and American identity,
  30
  as a model, 34
Revolutionary War, 188-189
Rhode Island, founding of, 15
Rockefeller, John D., 102-103, 105, 196
Romanticism, 263-264, 265
Roosevelt, Franklin D., and blacks, 232-233
  and conservation, 271
  death of, 144
  and election of 1932, 138-140
  and election of 1936, 143
  and growth of presidency, 303, 304
  and neutrality, 171-172
  and New Deal, 140-143
  as President, 140-144
  and Supreme Court, 143
  and World War II, 144, 201-203
Roosevelt, Theodore, and conservation, 134,
  267-268
  and election of 1912, 135
  and Gentleman's Agreement, 229
  and Hetch-Hetchy, 270-271
  and Indians, 216, 217
  and Moroccan crisis, 168
  and New Nationalism, 135
  and Progressive Party, 133
  as progressive president, 132-134
  and Rough Riders, 197
  on rural life, 113
  and Russo-Japanese War, 168
  and World War I, 135

"Salutary neglect," 28, 29, 40
Sanger, Margaret, 248
Seale, Bobby, 238
Secession, 66, 196

"Seward's folly," 164
Sharecropping, 113
Shays' Rebellion, 46
Sherman Anti-Trust Act, 118
Sierra Club, 270
"Silent generation," 204-205, 207
Sinclair, Upton, 134
Social Darwinism, 104
Social gospel, 107, 130
Socialism, party in election of 1912, 135
  reasons for failure, 117
Social Security Act, 142
"Spaceship Earth," 285
Spain, empire of, 6, 7, 71, 87
  in North America, 162
Spanish-American War, and Philippines, 165-
  166, 197-198
Spencer, Herbert, 104
Stamp Act, 29, 42
Stanton, Elizabeth, 59
States rights, 61, 196
Steffens, Lincoln, 134
Steinem, Gloria, 252
Stowe, Harriet Beecher, 63
Stripmining, 274-275, 280
Student Non-violent Coordinating Committee
  (SNCC), 235-236
Sugar Act, 29
Sumner, William Graham, 104
Supreme Court, and abortion, 252, 279
  Brown vs. Topeka Board of Education case,
    222, 233
  Dred Scott case, 222
  and Franklin D. Roosevelt, 143
  and Indian rights, 217
  and National Industrial Recovery Act, 141,
    143
  Plessy vs. Ferguson case, 222, 233
  and segregation, 145
Sweden, empire of, 7

Taft, William Howard, on blacks, 223
  as President, 134
  as progressive, 130
Tarbell, Ida, 134
Tea Act, 42
Teapot Dome, 136, 271
Technetronic Revolution, 292-294
Tecumseh, 74
Tennessee Valley Authority (TVA), 142, 272
Texas rebellion, 80, 163, 224
"Third World," 177
Thoreau, Henry David, 58, 264, 269

  and "civil disobedience," 193
  on nature, 266
Tijerina, Reies Lopez, 241
Tocqueville, Alexis de, 298
Tories, 44, 189
Townsend, Dr. Francis, 142
Transcendentalism, 58, 264
Transcontinental Treaty, 162
Transportation, in 18th century, 307
  in 19th century, 100-101, 102
  and economic growth, 100-101, 102
  jet travel, 307-308
  railroads, 83, 89, 99, 197
  urban, 106
Treaty of 1778, 156, 158
Treath of Paris, 156, 189
Truman Doctrine, 175
Truman, Harry S., and atom bomb, 172-173
  and civil rights, 233
  and election of 1948, 144
  and Fair Deal, 144
  and General MacArthur, 206
  as President, 144
Trust, 103
Turner, Frederick Jackson, 93, 272
Turner, Nat, 163

Uncle Tom's Cabin, 63
United Nations, 173, 175, 176, 203
  Conference on the Environment, 285
usofruct, 216-217

Vietnam, 307
  and Barry Goldwater, 147
  and Cambodian invasion, 148
  and dissent, 148, 180, 207-209
  and Eisenhower administration, 176, 206
  and election of 1964, 147
  and F. Roosevelt's administration, 176
  and Kennedy administration, 180
  and Johnson administration, 180, 206, 209
  and Nixon administration, 180
  and strain on Great Society, 147
  and U. S. economy, 206-207
Vikings, *see Norsemen*
Virginia, and indentured servitude, 11
  settlement of, 10, 36
  tobacco industry, 12
Voting Rights Acts (1964 and 1965), 234

Walden Pond, 264
Washington, Booker T., 222-223, 232
Washington, George, 296

character of, 307, 308
Farewell Address of, 158, 166
as General, 48, 188-189
on independence, 43
on land misuse, 260
and officers' rebellion, 189
on parties, 49
as President, 48, 50, 189-190
as symbol, 290, 291
War Hawks, 76, 160, 191
War of 1812, 53, 76, 160, 162, 191
War on Poverty, and Vietnam, 206
Watergate, 149, 299, 303, 304
Water Quality Act, 277
West Point Military Academy, 192
Whigs, 56
Wilderness Act, 274
Wilderness, appreciation of, 263-264
    and colonial attitudes, 259-260
    and conquest-progress mentality, 260-262
    and European attitudes, 258-259
    preservation of, 266
Williams, Roger, 15
Wilson, Woodrow, and election of 1912, 135
    and New Freedom, 135
    as progressive president, 135-136
    and World War I, 168-170, 198
Women, abortion and birth control, 248-249,
    279
    and black power, 252
    colonial education of, 25
    and feminist movement, 250-253

and industrialization, 248-249
and Knights of Labor, 115
and 19th century reform, 59
and right to vote, 135, 249-250
and role in colonization, 8
in Virginia, 12, 13
as work force, 110
Women's Rights Convention, 59
Women's Trade Union League (WTUL), 119
Works Progress Administration (WPA),
    142
World War I, 198-200
    and economic effects, 199-200
    and government propaganda, 198-199
    and League of Nations, 169-170
    origins of, 168
    and postwar disillusionment, 200
    and submarine warfare, 169
    U.S. neutrality, 168-169
    U.S. war aims, 169
    and Versailles Treaty, 169
    and Woodrow Wilson, 168-170
World War II, 172-173, 200-203
    and Bracero program, 225
    economic effects of, 143, 201-202
    and end of New Deal, 203
    and Mexicans, 240
Wounded Knee, 243-244, 245-246, 247

"Yellow Peril," 226-231
Yalta, 173-174
Yorktown, battle of, 156